WOW! RÉSUMÉS 2011 – 2012 EDITION:

GET GREAT JOBS, EXTRA INCOME AND HAPPINESS!

100 + *W*ONDROUS *O*UTSTANDING *W*INNING RÉSUMÉS: *W O W!*

(OVER 375 JOB TITLES!)

By

Nelson Abaya

M.S., LEED AP

wowresumes.net

WOW! RÉSUMÉS 2011 – 2012 EDITION:

GET GREAT JOBS, EXTRA INCOME AND HAPPINESS!

Suggested Authorized Library of Congress Subject Headings:
1. Résumés (Employment) Handbooks, Manuals, etc.
2. Résumés (Employment) United States – Handbooks, Manuals, etc.
3. Career Advantage. Section 1, Self-knowledge and exploration
4. Career Aids
5. Career Guidance
6. Résumé Services
7. Résumés Online
8. Job Searching

I. Title: *WOW!* RÉSUMÉS 2011 – 2012 Edition: Get Great Jobs, Extra Income and Happiness!

Dedication,

To job-seekers, opportunity-pursuers and career-changers, whether you are unemployed, underemployed or even employed but unhappily…

To the youthful masses around the planet who are the brand-new or recently minted graduates from national, state and private universities and training schools…

To the disenfranchised but hopeful millions whether you be the countless Shabab Youth of Egypt, the "irregulars" and "fretters" of Japan, or the "ant tribes" of Beijing, Shanghai and other large world cities…

MAY YOUR PERSEVERANCE, ENTHUSIASM AND ENERGY PROPEL YOU TO FINANCIAL, SOCIAL AND PERSONAL SUCCESSES IN A WORLD THAT NEEDS YOUR TALENT, IDEALISM AND WORK ETHIC. YOU RUN THE OFFICES, FACTORIES, FARMS, GOVERNMENTS, BUSINESSES, HOSPITALS AND SCHOOLS. YOU HAVE DIGNITY, POWER, AND THE RIGHT TO GAINFUL EMPLOYMENT THAT IS SATISFYING, FULFILLING AND MEANINGFUL FOR YOURSELF, YOUR COMMUNITY AND YOUR PLANET!

AUTHOR'S NOTE, 2011:

The 105 Model *WOW!* Résumés featured in this Book are the composite backgrounds of real people (names fictionalized and contact data generalized but with accurate street names, zip codes, area codes, companies, organizations and schools for reference) gathered by the Author for the last 20 years with a focus on current material with the latest industry information and jargon. The Résumés were created using Microsoft Word 2010, powerful state-of-the-art word-processing software from the most popular Office software suite in the world. The Résumé files can be accessed as Word or PDF files, available to purchasers of this Book for their own use in creating, editing or updating their own prospective *WOW!* Résumés! Please see the back of this book for more detailed information.

Author's Profile and own mini-Résumé (with thumbnail photo) appear on Page 197.

WOW! RÉSUMÉS 2011-2012: Great Jobs...Extra Income...Happiness...

TABLE OF CONTENTS

THE *WOW!* RÉSUMÉS

WOW! RÉSUMÉS 2011-2012: Great Jobs...Extra Income...Happiness...

INTRODUCTION

PRACTICAL NEW TOOLS, WINNING APPROACHES & NOVEL STRATEGIES

Practical, Convenient, Cost-Effective and *WOW!* in Results!

This Book is meant to be interesting to read (people's backgrounds and histories), and be very practical, useful and valuable. The *WOW!* Résumé Service, available to the public at wowresumes.net uses this Book as its base material to model a Résumé and create a *WOW!* Résumé with a full consultation based on the Customer's input, source/original documents and the Fill-In Guides found in the Appendices.

All 105 Model Résumés (each with multiple related Jobs and Career Occupations) have a 2011 Retail Price listed that is the regular price for the *WOW!* Résumé Service to do a customized Résumé with consultation. (More on discounts below!)

A typical Résumé customer-oriented scenario is for an individual to go to a retail outlet such as a bookstore or retail outlet (ideally a print shop) where this Book is available: the Customer reviews the Model *WOW!* Résumés and chooses the Model *WOW!* Résumé to base their own creation or to have a *WOW!* Résumé Consultant/Writer to create and perfect!

The customer can call toll free (in the U.S.) 888-503-3133 or go to wowresumes.net to set up an appointment or get a preliminary consultation on the phone, Skype or Internet Chat (as available). Retail outlets affiliated with *WOW!* Résumés (registration online for the Retail Outlet) can also offer face-to-face appointments as available and are the local outlets to pick up completed hard-copy *WOW!* Résumés, and final Free Résumé copies on special Résumé paper.

Buying this book entitles the purchaser to a free one-year membership in wowresumes.net with various benefits and discounts offered by *WOW!* Résumé Service for all services and *WOW!* products (such as *WOW!*-Card® Résumés, Social Network Profiles, etc.). There are exciting Free Offers and Opportunities for Members of wowresumes.net, in addition to any discounts that may be available at affiliated retail outlets. Please go to wowresumes.net or review the Back Cover of this Book for more information.

The *WOW!* Résumés and Structure of Book

WOW! Résumés offer new winning approaches in the marketing and presentation of the qualifications and competitive advantages of job-seekers, career-changers, new graduates, and entrepreneurs. The Book's first 5 Chapters feature Résumés in the major Career/Job Categories of 1) Office and Administration; 2) Sales and Marketing; 3) Accounting and Finance; 4) Technology and Engineering; and 5) Healthcare/Education/Miscellaneous.

WOW! RÉSUMÉS 2011-2012: Great Jobs...Extra Income...Happiness...

The last 5 Chapters present more powerful tools to find great jobs, earn extra income and achieve happiness (satisfaction) in outstanding Careers and through entrepreneurial opportunities. The major category of Government Jobs is covered in Chapter 6. The U.S. Federal Government is one of the largest and most diversified employers in the world covering all levels from minimum wage to very high-paying positions in the U.S. and abroad. In Chapter 7, Green (Environmental) Jobs are covered. Green Jobs are truly proliferating globally in the millions and is a new large Category defined explicitly for the first time in 2010 by the Bureau of Labor Statistics of the United States Department of Labor.

Chapters 8, 9 and 10 are the innovative novel strategies in Résumés, personal marketing and entrepreneurship that reflect the dynamism of the global economy and the need for extra income for people in the "rich" countries (the U.S., Canada, Western Europe, Japan, Australia and Singapore) as well as the newly developing countries that include China, India, Brazil, Indonesia, Egypt and Mexico, in addition to Russia, Nigeria, South Africa, Pakistan, Bangladesh, the Philippines and the rest of Southeast Asia. There are indeed multiple strategies to market a person's qualifications, skills and abilities in order to land a job or two or three! (or start a new venture) to earn a living and gain personal and social freedoms.

Network Marketing (Chapter 8) is a huge unappreciated "occupation" and career. There are at least 50 million "Independent Representatives" in over 3,000 Network Marketing Companies worldwide. National economies go through crises and volatility, yet opportunities abound for starting legitimate home-based businesses made possible by the global internet and international markets. In many countries, network marketing is often one of the very few real prospects for those outside the commercial mainstream, especially women, to become viable economic participants. Even in the West, one may even have a "day job" but there is still a need or desire to try a career in a part-time business or venture.

A novel strategy is presented in Chapter 9 in the form of a "Unique Story Résumé" which can be a powerful substitute to the customary and expected "cover letter". In a narrative style, a new graduate or long-time unemployed or minority or "older" job-seeker may present what is unique and valuable about himself or herself. Beyond and in addition to talent, skills and abilities, the "Unique Story Résumé" can portray the "real" person that can make the applicant stand out from the competition in a format that includes both a person's work or business/technical skills as well as human factors.

The final Chapter (10) on *WOW!*-Card® Résumés are inventive novel strategies of *WOW!* Marketing: creative, efficient and cost-effective! Added to brochures, business cards, letters, Curriculum Vitae and Résumés, now perhaps *WOW!*-Card® Résumés as new tools to market, present and "advertise".

With a full array of tools, approaches and strategies, job-applicants, opportunity-seekers and entrepreneurs can maximize their possibilities for landing a job or a new career and ultimately represent themselves as valuable "products" and worthwhile people! In the pathway to financial and personal success (happiness), a person's story must be bold, told and sold!

NOTE:

The reader can choose to do their own Résumé by modeling any of the *WOW!* Résumés found in this Book or become a Customer of the *WOW!* Résumé Service that will use the *WOW!* Résumé Models and the principles of *WOW!* (Wondrous, Outstanding, Winning) Résumés. Either way, by using the principles of *WOW!* and by following the Guides in the Appendices, a customized *WOW!* Résumé will result!

WOW! RÉSUMÉS 2011-2012: Great Jobs...Extra Income...Happiness...

CHAPTER 1:

<u>OFFICE and ADMINISTRATION RÉSUMÉS</u>

10 Model *WOW!* Résumés
(53 Job Titles)

<u>CREATE YOUR OWN RÉSUMÉ</u>:

If you are doing your own Résumé in the Occupational Category of <u>Office and Administration</u>, you can choose from among the *WOW!* Résumés in this Chapter modeling the wording, styles, formatting, bullets, borders, etc. You can also model any of the elements in the other *WOW!* Résumés in this Book.

Complete the Guides in the Appendices including the *WOW!* Action Verbs and specific targeted Keywords (that must be researched) to fully customize and create a unique and powerful *WOW!* Résumé!

If you have purchased this Book (and thus become an automatic 1-year Member of wowresumes.net) you can get Free unrestricted downloads (Word or PDF Files) of up to 5 *WOW!* Résumés in addition to a Free download of the Guides in the Appendices for you to print out or edit on your computer.

<u>DISCOUNTED RÉSUMÉ SERVICE</u>:

If you need help to create a *WOW!* Résumé call 888-503-3133 or go to wowresumes.net to work with professional Résumé Writers who practice *WOW!* Résumé principles. Book purchasers have up to one year to avail of a 30% Instant Discount on any *WOW!* Résumé or other *WOW!* Résumé products such as *WOW!*-Card® Résumés, as well as other benefits including <u>Free Résumé Posting</u> on the ever-growing wowresumes.net Website and <u>Updating from Twitter, Facebook, LinkedIn & Google Profiles</u>. Members get <u>Free Updates for 1 year</u> on their Main Résumé and <u>up to 90% Discounts</u> on additional (2nd, 3rd, 4th, etc.) Customized Résumés to target Specific Jobs, Careers, Industries or Special Urgent Applications.

*See the Back Cover for *WOW!* Résumé Service & Free Membership Information*

WOW! RÉSUMÉS 2011-2012: Great Jobs...Extra Income...Happiness...

<u>CHAPTER 1: OFFICE and ADMINISTRATION RÉSUMÉS</u>

Changing Office Technologies and Economic Conditions

As defined by the Bureau of Labor Statistics (BLS, United States Department of Labor), Office and Administrative (Support) Workers "perform the day-to-day activities of the office, such as preparing and filing documents, dealing with the public, and distributing information...Office and Administrative Support *Supervisors* and *Managers* plan or supervise support staff to ensure that they can work efficiently...allocating work assignments and issuing deadlines...overseeing the work to ensure that it is proceeding on schedule and meeting established quality standards."

In 2008, employment for Office and Administrative Support *Supervisors* and *Managers* in the U.S. numbered 1,457,200 (the latest figures from the U.S. Department of Labor in its Occupational Outlook Handbook, 2010-2111 Edition as of this book's first printing in early 2011). The recession years of 2007 - 2009 made competition intense as the number of applicants greatly exceeded the number of job openings. However, there is a projected growth rate of 11% (about as fast as the average for all occupations) so that as the U.S. economy recovers in 2011 and 2012 and with the normal increase in U.S. population, by 2018 there will be about 1,617,500 Office and Administrative Support *Supervisors* and *Managers* in the United States.

Prospects and Earnings

Counting all Office and Administrative support occupations, 5 of the 15 largest occupations in the U.S. are in this Office and Administration Category, with a combined employment of 10.4 million (as of 2008). The growth rate for all Office and Administrative support occupations will be 8% through 2018, weaker than the 11% growth rate of Office and Administrative Support *Supervisors* and *Managers*.

The global economy has been growing faster than the U.S. so by extrapolation (statistics are not as accurate or publicized in other countries), Office and Administrative (Management) positions will be in the tens of millions in India, China, Brazil, Canada, Australia, South America and Europe combined.

As recessions end and job growth resumes as is happening in the U.S. in 2011, the hiring of temporary Office and Administrative workers increases (up 26% in U.S. companies in 2010 according to Manpower, Inc.), as a precursor of the hiring of more permanent workers to meet greater business demand.

According to BLS (Bureau of Labor Statistics) the median annual wages for Office and Administrative Support *Supervisors* and *Managers* were $45,790 in May 2008 in the U.S. The recession of 2007 - 2009 put downward pressure on wages. Those who have fared better are those job-holders and job-seekers with post-secondary education/training, especially holders of bachelor's degrees.

Who will be the winning applicants in this large but competitive Occupational and Career category? Obviously education and training will be competitive advantages, both continuing and formal education. During tougher economic times and likely corporate restructurings, more are expected of Office Workers and Managers. Managers are performing more clerical tasks while Administrative Assistants and Secretaries are taking up more professional work. As technology improves productivity, everyone in the office is expected to do more tasks and execute higher functions. Those who are flexible, trainable and adaptable will have better job prospects, while those who are employed and satisfied with their careers can find management opportunities.

WOW! RÉSUMÉS 2011-2012: Great Jobs...Extra Income...Happiness...

<u>CHAPTER 1: OFFICE and ADMINISTRATION RÉSUMÉS</u>

Surveys conducted by the International Association of Administrative Professionals (IAAP) indicate that Administrative Professionals want to remain in their field and advance into higher support positions or become Office Managers.

The *WOW!* Résumés in this first chapter include Office Manager; Administrative Assistant to Senior Management; Corporate Recruiter; Employee Benefits Administrator; as well as Secretary/Receptionist and Temporary/Freelance Office Worker. Related Occupations that require similar aptitudes, skill sets and education/training are: Administrative Services Managers; Education Administrators; General Office Clerks and Customer Service Representatives.

Also included are *WOW!* Résumés for positions that overlap with the job/career category covered in Chapter 2 (Sales and Marketing Résumés): Public Relations Specialist and Management Analyst.

Source of above wage, employment numbers and projections: Bureau of Labor Statistics, U.S. Department of Labor, *Career Guide to Industries, 2010-11 Edition*, Office and Administration Support Worker Supervisors and Managers, on the Internet at http://www.bls.gov/oco/cg/cgs034.htm (visited *March 1, 2011*).

WOW! RÉSUMÉS 2011-2012: Great Jobs...Extra Income...Happiness...

BLANK PAGE

-FOR NOTES-

WOW! RÉSUMÉS 2011-2012: Great Jobs...Extra Income...Happiness...

VICTORIA C. PRATNEY-BLUM

123 Groove Avenue Day; Nashville, TN 38128
vickycpratneyblum@wowresumes.net

Cell: 901.123.4567
Home and Fax: 901.345.6879

OBJECTIVE: Office Manager/Specialist/Supervisor in a High-Tech Environment

CAREER HIGHLIGHTS

☐ Extremely well-organized and efficient
☐ Quickly learn procedures and methods
☐ Able to develop and implement new Systems when necessary
☐ Strong bookkeeping and managerial experience
☐ Capable of handling multiple projects concurrently
☐ Excellent public relations and customer contact ability
☐ Computer Skills include Web Development and Databases

EXPERIENCE

Diversified Workforce

In-Service Training

Technology Overhauls

Cross-Departmental Planning

Organizational Mission/Actions

TENNESSEE CENTER FOR THE ARTS, Nashville, TN
Assistant Office Manager, General IT Intern/Trainer-Supervisor
2009 to Present
• Assisted with web development tasks in the marketing department, including help desk
• Promoted to Assistant Office Manager after training other Interns

GOLDSTEIN'S DEPARTMENT STORES, INC., Nashville, TN
Administrative Assistant / Office Manager
2002 to 2008
• Managed all accounts payable and receivable for this multi-million dollar department store
• Performed standard bookkeeping, ledger maintenance & monthly statements, using Excel
• Processed all account executives' sales reports and maturities
• Developed timetables, utilizing GANTT charts, to manage workflow efficiently
• Supervised three secretaries in clerical pool
• Assisted in development of new employee training manuals
• Trained new employees in computer software programs, including MS Office Programs

TRUST FIRST BANK, Cordova, TN
Customer Service Representative and Senior Teller
1999 to 2002
• Opened new customer accounts, explaining all program details and options
• Assisted customers in balancing checking accounts and investment statements
• Operated safety vaults, safe deposit boxes and performed reconciliations
• Received note payments on loans
• Processed payroll checks for employees

EDUCATION

SHELBY STATE COMMUNITY COLLEGE, Nashville, TN
Bachelor of Science, Business Administration, 2006
LEARN IT COMPUTER SCHOOL, Franklin, TN 2007, 2009

TECHNICAL SKILLS

Dreamweaver CS3-CS5, Photoshop CS5, HTML5, css3, Joomla 1.5, Windows XP, Mac OSX
Databases: Oracle 11i, Oracle R12, Remedy 5.0, SAP, Peoplesoft, MS Access, MS Project

COMMUNITY

First Harvest Food Banks, 2008 to Present
Activities: Big Sisters of Nashville, 2005 to 2008

Related Jobs/Careers:
(IT Office Manager, Administrative Assistant, Office Supervisor)

RÉSUMÉ #1: Office Manager with Technical Skills (2011 U.S. Retail: $299)

WOW! RÉSUMÉS 2011-2012: Great Jobs...Extra Income...Happiness...

<u>CHAPTER 1: OFFICE and ADMINISTRATION RÉSUMÉS</u>

Timothy S. Atters

TSAtters@wowresumes.net

755 Atlantic Court • Trenton, NJ 07079
(201) 123-4567

OBJECTIVE: Administrative Assistant to Senior-Level Management

---

EXPERIENCE

BRF, Inc.
Office Manager

Trenton, NJ
2003 to 2010

→ Supervised and managed a 35-person office for a multi-million dollar environmental sciences firm
→ Automated payroll and bookkeeping procedures
→ Served as Network Coordinator for all office equipment, including off-site computers and telecom equipment
→ Reorganized filing system, speeding up access time and increasing productivity
→ Developed voice-mail system and Skype communications
→ Prepared training manuals for office personnel on all aspects of office procedures

Trenton Community College
Administrative Assistant to Financial Aid Director

Trenton, NJ
2000 to 2003

→ Developed computerized procedures for student financial aid check disbursement, which earned an award given by the college president for "Office Innovations"
→ Supervised three work-study students
→ Prepared payroll statements for office personnel
→ Typed approximately 60 error-free words/minute and implemented Financial Aid software

Food Way
Customer Service Representative

Orange, NJ
1997 to 2000

→ Greeted customers in person and on the telephone
→ Offered accurate directions to store items for customers
→ Communicated well with customers and co-workers, even in the face of corporate and management changes

"Tim is an indispensable asset for our company..."; "Outstanding work ethic..."; "Ability to adapt and thrive..."
-From Most Recent Work Evaluations-

EDUCATION

New Jersey College
Bachelor of Science in Management
Maintained a 3.2 grade point average while working 25-30 hours per week
Served as President of Computer/Internet Club

Orange, NJ
1998

COMMUNITY

President of Trenton PTA, 2005
Publicity Chairman for Beautify Orange County Committee, 2004-2006
Fundraising Committee Member of Toys for Girls and Boys, 2009 to present

---

SPECIFIC SOURCES OF ABOVE EVALUATIONS: Available upon request

---

Related Jobs/Careers:
(Administrative Supervisor, Customer Service Representative)

WOW! RÉSUMÉS 2011-2012: Great Jobs...Extra Income...Happiness...

ELTON PACINSKI

1234 Lebanon Road # 123
Charlotte, North Carolina 25601
(919) 123-4567
epacinski@wowresumes.net

CORPORATE / HIGH TECHNOLOGY RECRUITER

15 Years of Experience in Full Life Cycle Recruiting Corporate Management
Exceptionally skilled and disciplined in sourcing and producing qualified candidates for Hiring Managers
Highly organized, proactive and resourceful with excellent communications, follow-up and telemarketing skills
Excellent time management, able to multitask in a fast pace and changing global environment
Superlative closing abilities: Know when and how to overcome objections and concerns
Proven organizational and inter-personal abilities in working with a diverse management and work force
Computer savvy in recruitment and office software including social media and internet recruitment

TECHNICAL RECRUITMENT SKILLS

Successful recruitment of professionals for High Tech Companies and Internet Start-ups
Manage all phases of the recruitment process including job requirements, postings & interviews
Coordinate agency relationships, technical job fairs & employ user groups, blogs & other online sources
Interact and collaborate with hiring managers and executive management to streamline hiring process
Project competitive edge for candidates and companies: ultimate customer service while meeting goals/quotas

EDUCATION & TRAINING

Georgetown University, Washington D.C.
Post-graduate Work in International Business, 2001 to 2002

Duke University, Durham North Carolina
Bachelor of Arts Degree, Political Science, 1998

Myers & Briggs, Durham, North Carolina, Advanced Internet Recruiting Class, 2010
XMetrics Technologies, Palo Alto, CA, Advanced Internet Recruiting Class, 2006

COMMUNITY & MEMBERSHIPS

Habitat for Humanity, Raleigh-Durham, North Carolina, Yearly Volunteer, 2008 to Present
Coats for Kids, Charlotte, North Carolina, Sponsor & Coordinator, 2008 to Present
High Technology Human Resources Society of America (HTHRSA), Member 2003 to Present
North Carolina Chamber of Commerce, Member, 2010 to Present

WOW! RÉSUMÉS 2011-2012: Great Jobs...Extra Income...Happiness...

ELTON PACINSKI
Page Two

1234 Lebanon Road # 123
Charlotte, North Carolina 25601
(919) 123-4567
epacinski@wowresumes.net

EMPLOYMENT HISTORY

MYERS & BRIGGS, Durham, North Carolina
Technical Recruiters and Staffing Consultants Company
Senior Recruiting Consultant, 2009 to Present
Hired: Sales Operations and Strategy Manager, Sales Managers, Sales Quality Supervisor, Sales Training Specialist, Sales Media Manager, Account Manager, Sales Reps (Inbound and Outbound), Business Analysts)

GETIN!, Durham, North, Carolina
A mobile Ad Network, enabled by a Platform for Broadcasters and Advertisers
Senior Recruiting Manager, 2008
Hired: Web Developers, Programmers employing Java Script, SQL, Linux and Ruby on Rails

MONTGOMERY SERVICES (BANK OF AMERICA AFFILIATE), Raleigh, North Carolina
Investment Advisory and Financial Services Company
Recruitment Consultant and Manager, 2007 to 2008
Hired: Financial Advisors, Web Designers and Technical Support Personnel

XMETRICS TECHNOLOGIES, Palo Alto, CA
A Web Automated Testing Service Company for mid to large organizations
Recruitment Manager / Corporate Placement, 2005 to 2006
Hired: HR Manager, Enterprise Business Sales Manager/Associate, Channel Sales Manager/Associate, Inside Sales Reps, Product Manager, Project Manager, Tech Support Executives

WINFIRE, Sunnyvale, CA
Software Developer for indexing, searching, and automatically categorizing data
Hiring Manager, 2004 to 2005
Hired: Software Engineers, Marketing, Sales, Administration

ONZBOARD, San Jose, CA
Provider of Free Hosted Message Board for use by Webmasters and Message Board Administrators
Career Consultant, 2004
Hired: VP of Operations, Software Engineer, Accountant, Technical Writer

WISEDIRECT, San Francisco, CA
Online Direct Marketing Services Provider Company
Recruitment Manager, 2002 to 2004
Hired: Business Development Manager, Business Development Associate, Product Manager, Account Executives, Inside Sales Reps, Staff Accountant, Senior Programmers, Web Programmers, System Administrators, Client Service Engineer, Customer Support Engineers

Related Jobs/Careers:
(Corporate Recruiter, Corporate Placement, Career Consultant, Headhunter, Executive Recruiter)

WOW! RÉSUMÉS 2011-2012: Great Jobs...Extra Income...Happiness...

SARA H. DELANEY

1234 Ascuaga St. #123
Los Angeles, CA 91234

(213) 123-4567
shdelaney@wowresumes.net

Customer Service / Administration / Marketing / Management in Spa and Salon Industry

HIGHLIGHTS OF QUALIFICATIONS

- ➢ Excellent verbal and written communication skills
- ➢ Works well in busy office handling wide variety of tasks
- ➢ Takes pride in doing a good job; eager to learn and adept at training
- ➢ Responsible, reliable, diligent and thorough in procedures and regulations
- ➢ Over 8 Years in the Upscale Spa and Salon Industry with bottom-line results
- ➢ Experienced in Marketing and Telemarketing Campaigns including Product Introductions
- ➢ Skilled in MS Office Software, POS (Point of Sale) Systems, Siemens PBX Systems, Typing 60 wpm

WORK HISTORY

Salon de Barge, Los Angeles, CA
General Manager, 2006 to Present
- o Profitably manage and operate the salon in downtown Los Angeles
- o Carry out necessary measures for recruiting, training and coordinating salon personnel
- o Perform market research surveys on customer needs and requirements including new markets
- o Execute merchandising, ordering and maintenance with necessary cash and inventory/payroll control
- o Grow new clientele and corporate accounts with expanded marketing of new products and services
- o Coordinate events and promotions including local market enhancement programs and advertising planning

Xpres Day Spa, Santa Barbara, CA
Operations Manager, 2004 to 2006
- o Opened and closed spa upon quick promotion from Assistant Manager
- o Ordered spa products, office supplies and managed inventories of spa products
- o Oriented and trained staff on corporate policies and guidelines ensuring compliance and cooperation
- o Directly accountable for increasing daily spa revenue by successful sales of retail products and services

The Body Shop, Beverly Hills, CA
Receptionist / Sales Specialist / Part-time Stylist, 2002 to 2004
- o Worked with customers upon request, sold products and assisted General Manager
- o Greeted customers, scheduled and coordinated appointments for 21 professional Stylists

Debonair Beauty Salon, Fullerton, CA
Hair Stylist and Esthetician, 2000 to 2001
- o Excelled as a new Hair Stylist and Beauty Consultant with immediate increase in loyal customers

EDUCATION

UNIVERSITY OF CALIFORNIA AT LOS ANGELES, Bachelor's Program in Liberal Arts, 2009 - Present
CITY COLLEGE OF SANTA BARBARA, Management and Computer Courses
FULLERTON SCHOOL OF COSMETOLOGY, 2000

Related Jobs/Careers:
(Personal Services, Hair Stylist, Esthetician)
RÉSUMÉ #4: Secretary – Receptionist – Customer Service (2011 U.S. Retail: $249)

WOW! RÉSUMÉS 2011-2012: Great Jobs...Extra Income...Happiness...

Stephanie Lynn Heaney

1234 Clark Rd.
Chicago, IL 60601

(517) 123-4567
slheaney@wowresumes.net

Marketing / Communications / Administration

10 Years of Diversified Experience and Documented Performance and Contributions

in Office Administration, Marketing and Communications Support

for Design Firms, Non-Profits, High Technology and Telecommunications

PROFESSIONAL EXPERIENCE

Administrative Coordinator / Marketing Specialist, **Genesis Networks Inc.**, Chicago, IL   2009 to Present
- Support Supply Chain, Social and Environmental Sustainability Department at progressive high technology company. Created newsletter, updated department website, reconciled expense reports and executed press releases

Events Coordinator, **Top of the Mark Productions**, Kalamazoo, MI   2007 to 2008
- Executed and administered event and rental requests for Kalamazoo hospitality and conference venues, including planning events, invoicing and coordination. Conceived and produced email marketing campaign, print materials and brochures

Marketing Coordinator, **Lakeside Architects**, Chicago, IL   2005 to 2007
- Designed and co-managed marketing projects, running office including administrative tasks, reception and bookkeeping. Developed marketing and PR plans; Provided design and copy editing support for submission of RFQs (Request for Quotes)

Marketing Coordinator, **Tanturi and Jacobs Architecture**, Oak Park, IL   2003 to 2005
- As part of busy Marketing Department of large architecture firm, provided design and editing for marketing and promotional material including brochures, electronic ads and media placements

Communications Coordinator, **Eyecare MidAmerica**, Chicago, IL   2002 to 2003
- Crafted and edited press releases for non-profit's monthly campaigns using VOCUS PR, created content for radio & TV PSAs, supported Director of Communications and helped design brochures and posters

Program Coordinator, **The Michigan Conservancy**, Ann Arbor, Battle Creek, MI   2000 to 2002
- Excelled in supporting Science Department of nationally known non-profit; Assisted in conference planning for 100 region- wide participants; Arranged travel itineraries for management and performed general administrative duties

EDUCATION

University of Michigan, Ann Arbor, Michigan, B.A. Degree in English, 1999
Kalamazoo College, Kalamazoo, Michigan, Post-graduate studies in Journalism, , Summers 2002, 2003

CORE COMPETENCIES & SKILLS			
Writing/Editing	Graphic Design	Desktop Publishing	Marketing/Public Relations
Office Management	Event Planning	Blogging/Newsletters	Public Service Announcements

SOFTWARE: Adobe CS4 (Illustrator/InDesign/Photoshop), Microsoft Office Suite, Access, QuickBooks, HTML

Related Jobs/Careers:
(Office Coordinator, Office Specialist, Events Coordinator, Marketing Coordinator)

RÉSUMÉ #5: Marketing – Communications – Administration (2011 U.S. Retail: $299)

WOW! RÉSUMÉS 2011-2012: Great Jobs...Extra Income...Happiness...

jimweston
@wowresumes.net

JAMES WESTON
787 Beauford Street; Mobile, Alabama 35816

Cell: 205-123-4567

Objective

Advertising Operations Manager for Online or Print/Electronic Environments

Profile

- 7+ Years' Experience in Online Advertising, Weekly Print Media and TV Production
- Know-how and technical skills in digital advertising operations, search engine optimization
- Record of Performance, Excellence and Quantifiable Bottom-Line Results in all hired positions
- Work well in fast-paced environments, with high energy and abilities to prioritize and follow up
- Outstanding managerial skills with knowledge of personnel functions in diverse cultural settings
- Willing to relocate to establish new online editions of established media or new ventures or startups

Work History

Southern Expressions Media, LLC, Mobile, AL
DIGITAL ADVERTISING OPERATIONS MANAGER, 2008 - Present
- Manage all aspects of online advertising for Southern Expressions Media, specializing in banner ads and online traffic for Southern's 10 websites, 5 national and regional blogs and multiple partner sites
- Execute the hiring, training and managing of 10-person Digital Operations Team
- Launch new campaigns and provide daily performance and inventory analysis
- Approve and complete clients' RFPs (Request For Proposals)
- Implement, track, and troubleshoot all files, including jpg, gif and swf
- Troubleshoot issues with clickTAGs and ActionScripts
- Implement third part tags built in HTML, iframe or Javascript
- Work daily with Heads of Sales, Marketing, Production and Media departments
- Report directly to the Senior Director of Marketing and VP of New Media
- Represent Southern Expressions Media in conferences, seminars and conventions

Weinzer Productions Global, Phoenix, AZ
PAY-PER CLICK SPECIALIST/SALES COORDINATOR, 2005 - 2007
- Created landing pages, managed bids and wrote ad variations for client's online paid advertising
- Produced and analyzed account reports
- Managed Sales Department for one of Arizona's most successful Internet Marketing Agencies
- Interacted daily with CEO and VP regarding marketing and development of new business

Footloose Productions, Los Angeles, CA
PRODUCTION COORDINATOR, COURT TV, ASSOCIATE PRODUCER, Judge Alan Murray, 2003 – 2005
- Coordinated daily promotions of Court TV at Warner Brothers in the WB/Court TV Studios
- Screened, logged, delivered On-Air Promotions of Judge Alan Murray
- Collaborated with Editors and Executives at Warner Brothers to coordinate ISO requests

Wheatfield Daily Waves, Mobile, AL
ASSOCIATE EDITOR AND REPORTER, 2001 - 2003
- Edited copy and articles for College Daily Newspaper during daily semester publications

Industry Skills

- PC, Mac, MS Word, Excel, Outlook, Open AdStream 24/7, Real Media, Google Analytics, 3rd party tags including Atlas DMT, DART, Mediaplex, OpenX, Zedo, etc.
- Advanced Knowledge of new media and online advertising including Google Ad Words, Quantcast, ComScore, Facebook, MySpace and Twitter

Education

WHEATFIELD COLLEGE, Mobile, AL; *Bachelor of Arts in Communication Design and Media Arts*, 2003
Numerous Seminars, Classes and Conferences in Web Development and Social Media

Related Jobs/Careers:
(New Media, Advertising Manager)

RÉSUMÉ #6: Online Advertising or Print Advertising (2011 U.S. Retail: $299)

WOW! RÉSUMÉS 2011-2012: Great Jobs...Extra Income...Happiness...

CHAPTER 1: OFFICE and ADMINISTRATIVE RÉSUMÉS

LOUISE ANNE DIOKNO
ladiokno@wowresumes.net

123 Palisades Drive; Malibu, CA 90401
(310) 123-4567

OBJECTIVE: Employee Benefits Administrator/Analyst

HIGHLIGHTS OF QUALIFICATIONS

Good with figures & record keeping
Thrive on challenges, new opportunities for accomplishment and success in helping clients on what they need
Broad knowledge of employee fringe benefit products and packages
Commitment to professional growth and development in the employee fringe benefit field
Enjoy keeping busy, learning new skills, and developing systems to get the job done better and faster
Ability to work independently as well as a team player

AREAS OF EXPERTISE / EMPLOYMENT HISTORY

Employee Fringe Benefits
- 401-K, Profit Sharing, Group Disability, Health, and Life
- Non-Qualified Executive Benefit Compensation
- ERISA, IRS Compliance, and Workers' Compensation

Financial Planning
- Explored various investment options and structured plans consistent with experience, obligations, resources and risk temperament
- Implemented and periodically updated financial plans, keeping clients apprised of the status of their investments

Research, Analysis and Evaluation
- Researched and analyzed various investment instruments

Mutual Funds, Annuities and Insurance Products
- Analyzed market conditions affecting clients' current and future financial strategies
- Delivered presentations on various retirement plans and on mutual funds to professional practitioners and small corporations

Needs Assessment/Advising
- Successfully advised and counseled small business clients on financial strategy
- Developed trust and rapport through attentive listening and showing interest
- Established several groups of qualified pension plans, 401(k) savings plan and other benefit plans, ensuring ERISA and IRS compliance
- Maintained excellent client relationships, securing trust and confidence through providing complete, accurate and timely financial services

Systems and Applications
- Use SYSPRO, Microsoft Excel, Access, and Word on PC/Linux to generate spreadsheets

2008-Present	Financial Consultant	HEALTHTEX FINANCIAL SERVICES
2007-2008	Loan Consultant/Analyst	COAST PACIFIC FINANCIAL
2005-2007	Maintenance Database Program	THE FOOD & BEVERAGE JOURNAL
2001-2004	Accountant	THE FOOD & BEVERAGE JOURNAL
1998-2000	Cashier and Bookkeeper	THE CHURCH IN TAIPEI BOOKSTORE

EDUCATION

M.B.A., March 2004; Pepperdine University, Malibu, CA; Major in Corporate Finance.
Courses in Financial Management, Topics in Financial Management, Theory of Finance,
Financial Markets & Institutions, and Economics.
B.S., June 1998; University of San Francisco, San Francisco, CA; Major in Computer Science
Courses in Programming, Assembly Language, PLI, Mid-Size Corporation Accounting Packages, Databases, Basic HTML

Related Jobs/Careers:
(Retirement Planner, Claims Specialist, Financial Planner)

RÉSUMÉ #7: Employee Benefits Administrator (2011 U.S. Retail: $319)

WOW! RÉSUMÉS 2011-2012: Great Jobs...Extra Income...Happiness...

ROBERT MCHENRY

1234 Hummock Avenue, #123 ◆ East Orange, NJ 07625 ◆ (609) 123-4567 ◆ rmchenry@wowresumes.net

Temporary or Freelance Database Consultant-Analyst / Accounts & Billing Specialist

EDUCATION

Computer Learning Center, Trenton, New Jersey, Certificate in Programming, 2004
Newark City College of Business, AA Degree in Business Administration, 2001
IT Software Classes, LearnIt!, Paramus, New Jersey, 2001

QUALIFICATIONS & SKILLS

- ☑ Extensive experience working with large databases, datasets and data warehouses
- ☑ Developed expertise in performing data mapping/data modeling along with analytical abilities
- ☑ Excellent performance and acknowledged recognition in customer service and technical support
- ☑ Familiarity with varied industries including media, finance, publishing, high-technology and healthcare
- ☑ Outstanding communications and interpersonal skills with ability to produce clear reports and presentations

EMPLOYMENT HISTORY

EMPLOYER	Title	Basic Duties	Location	Date
Salesforce.com	Accounts Receivable Analyst	Analyzed Accounts Receivable; Performed Research & Audits	Orange, New Jersey	11/ 2010 to 5/2011
Chase Bank Wholesale Services	Database Analyst Data Team Leader	Managed & Directed Data Team; Researched databases & issues	New York, New York	1/2010 to 10/2010
Atlantic Media Publishing	Accounts - Collections Specialist	Executed collections activities; Set up new accounts/billing	Orange, New Jersey	3/2009 to 12/2009
Castle Services for Google.Com	Senior Billing Administrator	Executed cash applications into Accounting; Managed staff	Newark, New Jersey	1/2008 to 7/2008
Citibank Email/Messaging Systems	Senior Software Analyst	Maintained Bank's Email System; Produced MIS reports & plans	New York, New York	6/2007 to 12/2007
WXXA Channel 23 Fox Affiliate	Credit & Collections Billing Supervisor	Oversaw all station billing; Prepared/designed credit reports	Albany, New York	11/2006 to 5/2007
State of New Jersey Consumer Credit Services	Credit Counseling Supervisor	Reviewed schedules/assignments; Trained & supervised 22 staff.	Trenton, New Jersey	3/2006 to 10/2006
Bank of America Retail Profitability	Database Consultant Team Leader	Analyzed data & generated stats; Performed analysis on datasets	White Plains, New York	2005 to 3/2006
Bank of America VM Systems Software	Database Specialist	Analyzed online MIS database; Installed & upgraded software	Elizabeth, New Jersey	2004 to 2005
Paid Prescriptions Medicare Services	Claims Processor	Screened & processed claims; Performed daily file maintenance	Newark, New Jersey	2003 to 2004
Community Rentals Property Management	Office Manager Rental Agent	Advertised rental units/vacancies; Prepared deposits & credit files	Paramus, New Jersey	2001 to 2003

PERFORMANCE EVALUATIONS (Sources Available)

"Robert McHenry completed our critical project before the contracted deadline and at peak performance."
"Rob is a mainstay who makes our organization more efficient, professional and humanistic."
"A prized recruit and a valuable contributor to our Database Team, 'Mac' earns his kudos deservedly."

Related Jobs/Careers:
(Temporary Office Pool, Office Specialist, Claims Processor, Collections Specialist, Credit Counseling)
RÉSUMÉ #8: Freelance Database / Accounts Billing (2011 U.S. Retail: $329)

WOW! RÉSUMÉS 2011-2012: Great Jobs...Extra Income...Happiness...

JOSEPHINE V. DEMORAY
12345 Broussard Street #123 Baton Rouge, LA 70601
305-123-4567
jvdemoray@wowresumes.net

OBJECTIVE: A challenging career in the field of public relations or non-profits

---

EDUCATION:

McNeese State University Baton Rouge, LA
Bachelor of Arts in Public Relations, 2007
Minor in Broadcast Journalism; Academic Scholarship Recipient; Grade Point Average: 3.75 in major

---

EXPERIENCE:

KYTL FM, Baton Rouge, LA
Programs Coordinator / PR Director, 2007 to 2010
- Coordinated and expanded music format for an adult contemporary radio station
- Approved and organized all community service campaigns and programs
- Mastered critical communication skills and gained notable experience in broadcast news writing
- Created and implemented award-winning public relations for KYTL FM and sister station 710 AM

"Ms. DeMoray has fulfilled potential and abilities in public relations and promotions with the requisite personality to succeed and make a name for herself and the organization with whom she affiliates."

CAMP TWIN PINES, Lafayette, LA
Youth Counselor, Summers 2001 to 2006
- Aided mentally and/or physically challenged individuals in day-to-day endeavors in summer camps
- Exercised patience and compassion while learning to help others who are faced with special challenges

[De Moray] "is an excellent worker with outstanding character and the ability to adapt, learn and apply."

MCNEESE STATE UNIVERSITY, Baton Rouge, LA
Information Desk Manager, 2005 to 2007
- Disseminated information about the University and city of Baton Rouge to callers/visitors
- Managed petty cash fund, special program announcements, email and regular mail inquiries
- Team-player and participant in the excellent upkeep and key control of the Student Union complex
- Trained new employees in use of computers, including MS Office Software and POS System Terminals

---

NON-PROFITS EXPERIENCE:

LOUISIANA STATE CAPITAL PRESERVATION SOCIETY, Baton, Rouge, Louisiana
Docent and Assistant PR Director, Fundraiser Seasons 2005 to 2011
- Capital Museum Information Officer and Greeter on Fundraiser Weekends
- Analyzed marketing elements of Approved Programs from State of Louisiana Arts Fund
- Created and implemented Public Relations Plan for Private Foundations Campaign 2010

"Josephine is a talent and a godsend who knows about creativity, hard work and a can-do attitude."

Related Jobs/Careers:
(Museum Docent, Media Advertising, Radio Promotions, PR Specialist)

RÉSUMÉ #9: Public Relations / Non-Profit Administration (2011 U.S. Retail: $299)

WOW! RÉSUMÉS 2011-2012: Great Jobs...Extra Income...Happiness...

LILIAN A. DORNE

123 Biscayne Way, #123, Miami, FL 48510   Cell: (305) 123-4567   ladorne@wowresumes.net

Management Analyst / Business Developer

- ✓ Committed and engaged Business Development Expert with 12 years' experience working with start-up to medium size enterprises using Management Analysis and Technical Internet Research Skills
- ✓ Internet Research Skills include Data Mining, Search Engine Optimization, Search Engine Advertising, Lead Generation and Vertical Market Penetration.
- ✓ Analytical and Problem-Solving Skills applied to Organizations encompassing Communications, Information Flows, Operations and Projects, Inventory Control and Budgeting
- ✓ Training and orientation toward bottom-line results in such areas as Operational Efficiency, Staff Communications and Expense Management
- ✓ Administrative Expertise includes Creation of Reports, Proposals, Presentations; Employing Research and Methodologies; Coordinating and Monitoring Projects

EDUCATION

UNIVERSITY OF GEORGIA, **B.S., Business Administration**, 1996

FLORIDA STATE UNIVERSITY, **Master of Business Administration**, International Markets, 2005

Professional Experience

INTERBANKING LATIN AMERICAN CALL CENTERS, Miami, FL
Business Developer / Internet Researcher, 2008 – March 31, 2011 (End of Contract)
- o Lead Business Development Consultant in the development of a start up call center for American Banks operating in Mexico, Argentina, Chile and Peru; Oversaw training of executives and consultant staff; Developed and defined sales strategies and coordinated sales teams in 5 countries and 2 states
- o Penetrated and tapped vertical markets with email marketing, cold calling, branding and marketing; Started and increased call center referral partners; Implemented recruitment, training and development of call center employees using multicultural techniques and simulations; Generated ROI in 3 months

JENETECH Resources Management, Inc. Ft. Myers, FL
Management Analyst, 2005 - 2008
- o Identified opportunities to improve operation efficiency (including expense management, alternative approaches to technology); Recommended solutions and implemented as approved; Conducted operational effectiveness reviews to ensure functional or project systems were applied and functioning as designed
- o Coordinated and provided resolution to issues with legal, project finance and credit and other support groups; Reviewed staff communications and created methodology to streamline; Reviewed regional office budgets and recommended necessary changes for expense management; Monitored operations of regional offices to ensure each office operated according to Company procedures
- o Developed and updated functional/operational manuals outlining established methods of performing work in accordance with organizational policy; Monitored project developments to ensure scheduling and compliance with company procedures; Prepared proposals, quarterly reports and presentations

DEEP WATER HORIZON Energy Consortium, Inc. Houston, TX
Legal Assistant, 2001 - 2005
- o Extensive administration of contracts, subcontracts and study agreements for International Demand Side Management Company; Conferred with Project Managers to negotiate and draft contractual terms; Collaborated with Risk Management Group in maintaining required insurance and completion and filing of workers compensation, tax and related corporate filings
- o Responsible for obtaining and qualifying Company for General Contractor's Licenses in States of operation; Prepared Uniform Commercial Code forms for all projects; Oversaw closing of regional offices involving negotiations and termination of leases and contracts; Managed and maintained Company's asset portfolio

Fluent in Spanish and some Portuguese

Related Jobs/Careers:
(Internet Researcher, Call Center Consultant)
RÉSUMÉ #10: Management Analyst / Business Developer (2011 U.S. Retail: $319)

WOW! RÉSUMÉS 2011-2012: Great Jobs...Extra Income...Happiness...

BLANK PAGE

-FOR NOTES-

CHAPTER 2:

<u>SALES and MARKETING RÉSUMÉS</u>

11 Model *WOW!* Résumés
(52 Job Titles)

<u>CREATE YOUR OWN RÉSUMÉ</u>:

If you are doing your own Résumé in the Occupational Category of <u>Sales and Marketing</u>, you can choose from among the *WOW!* Résumés in this Chapter modeling the wording, styles, formatting, bullets, borders, etc. You can also model any of the elements in the other *WOW!* Résumés in this Book.

Complete the Guides in the Appendices including the *WOW!* Action Verbs and specific targeted Keywords (that must be researched) to fully customize and create a unique and powerful *WOW!* Résumé!

If you have purchased this Book (and thus become an automatic 1-year Member of wowresumes.net) you can get Free unrestricted downloads (Word or PDF Files) of up to 5 *WOW!* Résumés in addition to a Free download of the Guides in the Appendices for you to print out or edit on your computer.

<u>DISCOUNTED RÉSUMÉ SERVICE</u>:

If you need help to create a *WOW!* Résumé call 888-503-3133 or go to wowresumes.net to work with professional Résumé Writers who practice *WOW!* Résumé principles. Book purchasers have up to one year to avail of a 30% Instant Discount on any *WOW!* Résumé or other *WOW!* Résumé products such as *WOW!*-Card® Résumés, as well as other benefits including <u>Free Résumé Posting</u> on the ever-growing wowresumes.net Website and <u>Updating from Twitter, Facebook, LinkedIn & Google Profiles</u>. Members get <u>Free Updates for 1 year</u> on their Main Résumé and <u>up to 90% Discounts</u> on additional (2nd, 3rd, 4th, etc.) Customized Résumés to target Specific Jobs, Careers, Industries or Special Urgent Applications.

*See the Back Cover for *WOW!* Résumé Service & Free Membership Information*

WOW! RÉSUMÉS 2011-2012: Great Jobs...Extra Income...Happiness...

The Top 2 Largest Occupations in the United States

Retail salespersons assist customers in finding what they are looking for, whether the product be shoes, computers, clothing or automobiles. Cashiers work in supermarkets, department stores, gasoline service stations, movie theaters, restaurants and many other businesses. On the higher end of the sales/marketing continuum, Sales and Marketing Managers coordinate their companies' market research, marketing strategies, sales, advertising, promotion, pricing, product development and public relations activities.

Sales and Marketing are large employment sectors of the U.S. economy. In fact the two largest occupations, Retail Salespersons and Cashiers are Sales Occupations. As of May 2009, there were 4,209,500 Retail Salespersons and 3,439,380 Cashiers in the United States. There were some 346,900 Sales Managers and 175,600 Marketing Managers (2009 Bureau of Labor Statistics, U.S. Department of Labor figures).

Earnings and Outlook

While Retail Salespersons and Cashiers, many of whom work part-time, only get annual mean wages of $24,630 and $19,030 respectively (Bureau of Labor Statistics, figures as of May 2009), Marketing and Sales (including Advertising, Promotions and Public Relations) Managers can command above average compensation: as of May 2008 (Bureau of Labor Statistics) median annual wages were $108,580 for Marketing Managers, $97,260 for Sales Managers and $80,220 for Advertising and Promotions Managers.

Retail Sales and Cashier jobs often have no education requirements beyond a high school diploma and involve mostly on-the-job training. However, having a college degree (or a great deal of experience) may help in moving into management positions.

For the more highly-sought Sales and Marketing Manager positions, employers often prefer a bachelor's or master's degree in Business with an emphasis in Marketing. Also highly recommended to land a job in the very competitive sales/marketing management field is the completion of an internship while the eventual job-seeker is in school.

The outlook for hiring for the next 5 to 8 years is good for Retail Salespersons since there is a large yearly turnover. Opportunities for Cashiers (for full-time and part-time jobs) are also good because of the need to replace the large number of workers who leave Cashiering (as the economy improves and as wages continue to be low, often starting at minimum wage.)

The prospects for the overall employment of Sales and Marketing Managers are expected to increase by 13% through 2018 (about as fast as average, according to Bureau of Labor Statistics). Demand for Sales and Marketing Managers will be spurred by competition for a growing number of goods and services, both domestic and international, and as advertising and marketing media, including the internet, evolve.

This Chapter covers *WOW!* Résumés for Stockbroker; Real Estate Sales; Insurance Sales; Industrial and Medical Equipment Sales; as well as Résumés for Restaurant Manager; Hotel Manager and Retail Manager. Related Occupations include Advertising Sales Agents; Market Researchers and Demonstrators; and Product Promoters.

WOW! RÉSUMÉS 2011-2012: Great Jobs...Extra Income...Happiness...

Teo (Taylor) Soong

312-123-4567

1234 Ogden Avenue #123; Chicago, IL 60601

teosoong@wowresumes.net

MBA in Marketing and Finance with Sales and International Experience

HIGHLIGHTS OF SKILLS:

- Fluent in Korean, English, Japanese, and some Chinese
- Outstanding leadership, communication, analytical, and computer skills
- Research and academic focus on Finance, Real Estate, and Marketing (MBA)
- Practical experience includes hospitality, construction, education and publishing
- Workforce diversity exposure in large world cities of Chicago, Los Angeles, Tokyo and Seoul

EXPERIENCE:

Property and Marketing Manager, Savoy Hotel and Construction Co., Seoul, Korea Jan. 2008 - Feb. 2011
- Coordinated advertising and public relations
- Performed financial and investment analyses for company's hotel holdings
- Prepared business plans and market feasibility studies for proposed commercial projects
- Assisted Director of Property Operations in instituting and implementing cost analysis programs

Consultant, Rosenthal Manufacturing Company, Chicago, IL Aug. - Dec. 2005
- Consulted on taxation and investment in six Asian countries
- Researched and reported on business practices in Asian countries
- Identified potential markets and distribution channels in Asia

English Teacher/Consultant, Teheranro Language Center, Seoul, Korea May - July 2004
- Consulted with businessmen/students interested in working/studying abroad
- Presented seminars on North American accounting systems and financial environments
- Coordinated advertising, class scheduling, and multi-level testing

Sales Representative, Asahi Newspaper Company, Tokyo, Japan Sept. 2002 - June 2003
- Marketed Asahi Newspaper (English Edition) to foreigners residing in Tokyo
- Increased circulation by 15%

EDUCATION:

University of Illinois, Urbana-Champaign, IL May 2007
Master of Business Administration
- Concentration: Marketing, GPA: 4.3/5.0

University of Southern California, Los Angeles, CA May 2002
Bachelor of Science in Business Administration
- Concentration: Finance and Marketing, GPA: 3.74/4.0
- Leadership & Outstanding Senior Award, May 2002

Waseda University, Tokyo, Japan Sept. 1991 - Aug. 2001
Junior Year Study Abroad Program in Japanese Studies, GPA: 3.6/4.0
- Lived with a Japanese family for 12 months

Anthony School, Los Angeles, CA April - June 2003
- Independent Study Program in California Real Estate Laws, Practice and Management

Related Jobs/Careers:
(Multilingual Consultant, Sales Representative)

RÉSUMÉ #11: MBA in Marketing with International Sales Experience (2011 U.S. Retail: $299)

WOW! RÉSUMÉS 2011-2012: Great Jobs...Extra Income...Happiness...

ARTEMUS BAINES NEWSOME

123 Clinton Road, # 12 • Sunnyvale, CA 94625

(408) 123-4567 • artbnewsome@wowresumes.net

STOCKBROKER
PROFESSIONAL SALES
OUTSTANDING CLIENT BENEFITS

CAREER HIGHLIGHTS

▲ Professional and technical/product knowledge to serve customers and achieve client goals
▲ Outstanding team player who is honest, reliable, detail-oriented, self-motivated with enthusiasm
▲ Focused sales abilities in prospecting, qualifying, problem-solving, client-building and CLOSING
▲ Record-setting or record-breaking achievements in all career sales positions for self and company
▲ Committed to constant improvement in sales and life skills through countless seminars/trainings
▲ Incentive driven; Musters physical stamina, and mental and intellectual abilities for top performance
▲ Adept at dealing with varied clientele from middle to upscale from multiple cultures and backgrounds
▲ Track record of quantifiable success in sales, marketing and management across industries/economies

PROFESSIONAL FINANCE & SECURITIES EXPERIENCE

A.G. Edwards, San Diego, CA
STOCKBROKER, 2007 to 2010
⊙ Executed trades for new and established clients in a volatile market exploiting new opportunities in emerging sectors
⊙ Monitored special client portfolios earmarked for changes and reviews employing statistical risk and income analyses
⊙ Advised clients recruited from AG Edwards financial and retirement planning seminars making low-risk recommendations
⊙ Conducted due diligence and informational meetings in-house and across departments for new FINRA regulations
⊙ Excelled as top sales performer (top 5% in new accounts) in district despite economic downturn and market volatility

Wells Fargo Advisors, LLC, San Francisco, CA
FINANCIAL RESEARCHER, 2004 to 2006
⊙ Conducted research on equity statistical databases and performed accuracy analysis related to 3rd party systems
⊙ Produced and disseminated stock and bond related documents and earnings estimates for research department

TECHNICAL/FINANCE SKILLS & ABILITIES

Financial Analysis	Technical Research	Portfolio Reviews
Market Sectoring	Stock Index Funds	Bond Index Funds
Foreign Exchanges	Currency Arbitrage	Hedge Funds Analysis
Retirement Programs	Debt Instruments	Industry Analysis

WOW! RÉSUMÉS 2011-2012: Great Jobs...Extra Income...Happiness...

ARTEMUS BAINES NEWSOME   Page Two

artbnewsome@wowresumes.net

EDUCATION & TRAINING

University of Pennsylvania, Wharton School of Business, Philadelphia, PA, MBA with concentration in Finance, 2006
University of California at San Diego, San Diego, CA, B.S. Degree in Mathematics with minor in Statistics, 2003
CURRENT SECURITIES LICENSURE:
Series 6 - Investment Company and Variable Contracts Products Representative
Series 7 - General Securities Registered Representative
Series 65 - Registered Investment Advisor
Management: Completed numerous Management Training Programs including FINRA Regulations

ADDITIONAL PROFESSIONAL SALES EXPERIENCE & ACHIEVEMENTS

Leather Center, San Jose, CA
STORE MANAGER, 2001 - 2003
⊙ Executed with exemplary standards the hiring, training and termination of personnel in quality furniture outlet
⊙ Performed bookkeeping and inventory functions; Excelled in sales: Led and broke store records for personal sales
⊙ Achieved number one sales ranking in a company that included over 34 showrooms across the United States

Leather Factory, San Jose, CA
SALES MANAGER, 2000 - 2001
⊙ Sold furniture and accessories; Promoted to Sales Manager within 3 months of hiring
⊙ Managed sales team to top-level production and morale instrumental in attainment of 200% increase in store sales
⊙ Maintained personal sales record of triple average production during all sales periods

Art Van Furniture, Taylor, MI
SALES REPRESENTATIVE, 1999
⊙ Sold furniture and household accessories in new market territory for family-owned retailer
⊙ Leader in sales for wood-care products in June 1999 as well as breaking corporate record in overall sales

Red Carpet South Coast, La Jolla, CA
REAL ESTATE SALES, 1995 - 1997 and 1998 - 1999
⊙ Sold commercial and residential properties, and served as Management Specialist; Listing Leader in May 1989
⊙ Recognized and awarded as Million Dollar Producer in 1996 and 1997; Three-time Member of the President's Club

Century 21 Gaslight, San Diego, CA
REAL ESTATE AGENT, 1994 - 1995
⊙ Sold residential and commercial property; Achieved Top Lister in 1995

Related Jobs/Careers:
(Financial Researcher, Securities Representative, Store Manager)
RÉSUMÉ #12: Stockbroker and Professional Sales (Star) Performer [Page 2 of 2] (2011 U.S. Retail: $349)

WOW! RÉSUMÉS 2011-2012: Great Jobs...Extra Income...Happiness...

Nathaniel Jackman

1234 Murberry Drive #123
Santa Clara, California 95051

(408) 123-4567
nat88jackman@wowresumes.net

CUSTOMER SERVICE / SOCIAL MEDIA / SEARCH ENGINE / INTERNET MARKETING

"Mr. Jackman is as advertised: a turn-around artist!"

"Jackman's work makes the difference between profits and losing out to the competition."

Nathaniel Jackman is ethical, bottom-line driven and is mission-critical to our operations!"

-SAMPLE CLIENT REVIEWS & COMPANY ASSESSMENTS-

BENEFITS TO COMPANY

➢ Adapt quickly to industry conditions to seize market opportunities ≺

➢ Improve website growth for specific revenue targets and budgets ≺

➢ Improve company's client relations with on-line functionalities ≺

➢ Optimize internal digital communications through secure means ≺

➢ Maximize bottom-line with efficient use of advertising/marketing budgets ≺

➢ Prolong product and service cycles by creating extra off-shelf inventory ≺

➢ Troubleshoot online problems and make appropriate recommendations ≺

KEY WORDS / COMPETENCIES

SEO (Search Engine Optimization)
SEM (Search Engine Marketing)
PPC (Pay Per Click) Advertising and Programs
CRM (Customer Relationship Management)
Beta Testing and Analysis
Lead Generation
Conversion Tactics (Visitors to Leads and/or Sales)
Internet Strategy Development
Social Media Optimization
Positive ROI (Return On Investment)

WORK EXPERIENCE

FORMULEX, Sunnyvale, CA
Director of SEO (Search Engine Optimization), 2010 to Present
- Work with Fortune 500 companies to gain positive ROI from search engine optimization marketing
- Manage 10 in-house staff and 30 overseas; Develop internal system for managing SEO campaigns
- Manage 250 Search Engine Optimization Clients including Microsoft, Intel, Cisco and Siemens-USA

TURNBULL TOUR PROMOTIONS, San Jose, CA
Online Marketing Consultant, 2008 to 2009
- Redesigned website from scratch to obtain a more search engine friendly URL structure and design
- Created successful marketing programs including Email, satellite site implementation and social media
- Grew online sales from $3 million to $8 million in one year maximizing investments in new software

WOW! RÉSUMÉS 2011-2012: Great Jobs...Extra Income...Happiness...

Nathaniel Jackman   nat88jackman@wowresumes.net

Page 2

WORK EXPERIENCE (Continued)

INFINETICS, Anaheim, CA
E-Commerce Manager, 2006 to 2008
- Online marketing management inclusive of SEO, SEM, E-mail, comparison shopping feeds and promotions
- Instituted E-commerce strategy and platform design, hardware and software integration and logistics
- Designed systems and employed analytics to track customer behavior and search/email patterns

FREETIME ACCESS, Santa Ana, CA
SEO Specialist, 2005 to 2006
- Enhanced and marketed 200+ real estate agent clients including link analysis and keyword optimization
- Worked with clients to develop strategic marketing plans which included Pay-Per-Click campaigns
- Found and developed local partners and advertisers for maximum client exposure to surrounding cities

WESTWAY CONSULTING, Irvine, CA
Lead Consultant, 2004 to 2005
- Successfully applied expertise in on-and off-page optimization, developing ethical methodologies
- Excelled in placement results on all major search engines optimizing web sites to top rankings
- Upgraded client web sites in their usability and functionality to improve user experience

MASTER INSURANCE SERVICES, Inglewood, CA
SEO Specialist, 2003 to 2004
- Transformed brand-new website from getting zero health insurance leads to getting 30 leads daily
- Instrumental in making website a top 5 ranking in visitors in very competitive health insurance market

EDUCATION

BA/EB, Business Administration/e-Business, Masters Institute, San Jose, CA – 2001 to 2003
AAS, Multimedia Communications, Los Angeles City College, Los Angeles, CA – 1999 to 2001
Film and TV/Marketing Courses, University of Southern California, L.A., CA – 1998 to 1999

TECHNICAL SUMMARY

Operating Systems: PC, Macintosh and UNIX Platforms
Software and Languages: Web 2.0, HTML 4.0, DHTML, ASP, PHP, Java Script, Microsoft Word, Microsoft Power Point, Microsoft Project Plan, Microsoft Excel, Flash, Fireworks, Dreamweaver, Illustrator, Photo Shop, Image Ready, QuarkXPress, ACT, Microsoft Outlook, ACT, Microsoft Project, Acrobat (PDF), Netscape, Microsoft IE, Firefox, Safari, Bing, Droid Google, Twitter

Related Jobs/Careers:
(Search Engine Optimization Specialist, E-Commerce Marketing Consultant)

WOW! RÉSUMÉS 2011-2012: Great Jobs...Extra Income...Happiness...

RICHARD W. DePAMO

rwdepamo@wowresumes.net

1234 Harbor Blvd. #123; Long Beach, CA 90541   (310) 123-4567

CAREER OBJECTIVE

A sales and/or management position with a growing company where my diverse experience and abilities can be effectively utilized

EDUCATION & TRAINING

University of Nevada, Las Vegas; B.S. Degree in Restaurant and Hospitality, 2007

Morningside College, Sioux City, Iowa; Liberal Arts, 2002 - 2004

California Culinary School: Management & Cooking Classes; Food Safety Certification, Current

PROFESSIONAL EXPERIENCE

ELEPHANT BAR & GRILL, Long Beach, CA
General Manager, 2009 to Present
* Successfully manage high-volume restaurant and bar featured as "Top Pick" in Long Beach Weekly
* Consistently excel sales and profit budget while decreasing cost and stabilizing payroll
* Directly supervise all aspects of restaurant and bar operations while leading a team of 60+

IL POSTRIO, Newport Beach, CA
General Manager, 2007 to 2009
* Turned around fortunes of upscale restaurant that regained its standing as "Top 100 in L.A. Area"
* Improved efficiency, profitability and increased client base with hiring of new chef and staff
* Planned and personally supervised special events, ensuring customer satisfaction and rave reviews

RUTH'S CHRIS STEAK HOUSE, Las Vegas, NV
General Manager, 2005 to 2007
* Managed successfully Las Vegas' #1 Off The Strip Steak House responsible for day-to-day operations
* Hired new chef, and two new assistant managers and reviewed all training/employee development

MORTON'S OF CHICAGO, Sioux City, Iowa
Assistant Manager/Wine Steward, 2002 to 2004
* Developed personnel and supervised 25 employees on weekday shifts and bar staff
* Performed effectively functions in purchasing, inventory control of beverages, beer and liquor

MCDONALDS RESTAURANTS, Kansas City, Missouri
Manager/Assistant Manager, 2000 to 2002
* Management and supervision of 40 employees including payroll and customer relations
* Promoted after top rank completion of Management Training Program and Burger University

STEAK & ALE RESTAURANT, Kansas City, Missouri
Food Server, 1998 to 2000
* Provided exceptional service with following of regulars; Consistently top seller in wine and specials

QUALIFICATIONS SUMMARY

* Proven track record leading a restaurant's direction to improved sales profitability and growth
* Excel at strategizing, cost cutting and quality control, maximizing profits with innovative programs
* Extensive knowledge of food and wines, experience in special events, catering and handling celebrities
* Over 10 years' experience in management/supervision of diverse workforce in dynamic environments
* Superlative in personnel development, inventory control, promotions, planning, budgeting forecasting
* Over 15 years of successful personal sales, customer service, public relations, advertising and marketing
* Thorough professionalism, integrity, industriousness, business acumen and due diligence re: regulations

Related Jobs/Careers:
(Food Service Management, Hospitality Manager)

RÉSUMÉ #14: Restaurant Management or Restaurant Sales (2011 U.S. Retail: $319)

WOW! RÉSUMÉS 2011-2012: Great Jobs...Extra Income...Happiness...

Tyne L. Montgomery

| 1234 Caminito East Lane | La Jolla, California 92037 | (619) 123-4567 | tynemontgomery@wowresumes.net |

Sales, Merchandising and Management in Upscale Retailing
Proven Sales Specialist in Luxury Brands and Upscale Consumer Products with ability to close transactions, perform accounting tasks, execute promotions and display advertising and ultimately manage and train personnel

Experience

Neiman Marcus, San Diego, California
Louis Vuitton Sales Specialist, February 2008 to Present
- Oversaw seven figure department
- Negotiated stock levels with buyers
- Acted as a liaison between factory and consumer
- Department ranked number six out of twenty-five stores
- Trended 73.4% over last year

Bloomingdales, San Diego, California
Merchandise Coordinator, Cosmetics Department, 2006 - 2008
- Aided manager in overseeing staff of twenty
- Recognized as department of the year
- Coordinated inventory levels from various vendors
- Input purchase orders from vendors to buying office
- Analyzed and developed departments within cosmetic and fragrance areas

Nordstrom's, San Diego, California
Merchandise Coordinator, Men's Furnishings and Clothing Department, 2003 - 2006
- Assisted manager in overseeing staff of eight
- Conducted intensive training to store personnel for point-of-sale terminal
- Formulated and delivered business strategies directed towards maximizing growth in the department
- Maintained inventory control

Sheridan, Stamford, Connecticut
Co-manager / Sales Associate, 2002 - 2003
- Sold bed linens and interior furnishings
- Recognized as the top volume producer
- Prepared visuals for front window and other displays

Adrienne Vittadini, Inc., New York, New York
Production Assistant, 2000 - 2002
- Oversaw shipping for both the dress and sport lines
- Purchased and shipped necessary trim i.e. buttons, lace, and fabric for factories
- Administered correspondence with domestic and international factories
- Provided customer service and handled complaints
- Opened domestic and international letters of credit
- Administered applications for design copyrights

Education

Pine Manor College, Chestnut Hill, Massachusetts
B.A. Marketing, Minor in Visual Arts, May 2000

Related Jobs/Careers:
(Luxury Products Marketing, Retail Sales, Retail Manager)
RÉSUMÉ #15: Upscale Retailing Management / Upscale Merchandising (2011 U.S. Retail: $299)

WOW! RÉSUMÉS 2011-2012: Great Jobs...Extra Income...Happiness...

ABE L. OKSUNA

1234 Saguaro Road No. 123
Phoenix, AZ 89015-1234
(602) 123-4567
abeoksuna@wowresumes.net

> ► High-caliber management executive
> ► Current in cutting edge concepts of international operations
> ► Sales experience in serving international clientele and multicultural markets
> ► MBA Scholar with knowledge in telecommunications, marketing and strategy

PROFILE

- o Upper management executive with proven experience building top-producing Profit center – modeled nationally
- o Globally-oriented with graduate work in international marketing/operations and telecommunications
- o Demonstrated presentation and interpersonal skills in a various settings including Korea, China, Singapore, India
- o Proven ability to increase revenues and profit through development and implementation of sales strategies
- o State-of-the-art knowledge of telecommunications industry with interactions among new international players

PROFESSIONAL EXPERIENCE

OASIS MANAGEMENT COMPANY 2005 - Present
Fast-track promotion with retail profit center ($1 million revenues) linked with 40 nationwide affiliates; Promoted through a series of increasingly responsible positions based on bottom-line performance and global strategies
Manager (2005 - Present)
Hold full responsibility for entire retail operation -- including product positioning and pricing, promotional strategy, inventory control, employee training, and employee relations; Analyzed consumer behavior/needs, and operational problems with the following results:
• Significantly increased market share and referral base by analyzing overall market and actively developing global strategy-developed multilingual and multicultural promotional strategies to international customers--currently 80% from the Pacific Rim
• Initiated regular promotional calendar and special events calendar increasing revenue from repeat customer patronage 71%-- system modeled in over in over 30 affiliates nationwide
• Analyzed retail inventory and introduced "real time" measures resulting in more effective selling space: 45% turnaround within 10 days
Assistant Manager (2003 - 2005)
Recruited as in-house consultant to profit centers within retail chain; Presented management training sessions on Increasing Revenues, Staff Productivity, and Reducing Expenses Methodology
• Averaged a 44% increase of revenue and a 21% increase in profits in six retail centers--developed strategic documents
• Trained employees in appropriate sales presentation skills -- developed training documents
Sales Associate (2001 - 2003)
Served local community and visiting international clientele; Recruited to train new sales associates in store policies and selling strategies
• Earned highest sales commission as first-year "rookie"
• Maintained monthly sales in top 10%-- retail chain-wide

EDUCATION

Completed MBA and BS degrees a full year ahead of schedule; Funded entire education
THUNDERBIRD UNIVERSITY, 2000, *MBA in International Management*
Noteworthy: "Motivational Needs in Different Cultures to Increase Productivity in a Global Business Environment"--Analysis of Global Strategies of Omega Corporation, an International Medical Supply Enterprise
THUNDERBIRD UNIVERSITY, 1998, *M.S. Telecommunications Management*
Thesis: Designed advanced network, utilizing traffic engineering, which optimized switching systems and resulted in > 70% dollar savings
UNIVERSITY OF SOUTHWESTERN LOUISIANA, 1996, *B.S. Marketing*

PROFESSIONAL AFFILIATIONS

◆ World Affairs Council   ◆ International Trade Council   ◆ Commonwealth Club

Related Jobs/Careers:
(Management Consultant, Marketing Consultant)
RÉSUMÉ #16: International Sales/Marketing – Multinational Management (2011 U.S. Retail: $349)

WOW! RÉSUMÉS 2011-2012: Great Jobs...Extra Income...Happiness...

**MANAGER IN
HOSPITALITY
CUSTOMER SERVICE
RETAIL OR CORPORATE**

JOLIETTE MINTEK
123 Natoma Street; Portland, OR 88103
(503) 123-4567
joliettemintek@wowresumes.net

COMPETENCIES:
- ✓ Customer Relationships
- ✓ Corporate Mission
- ✓ Bottom-Line Results
- ✓ Inventory Control
- ✓ Training
- ✓ Front Office Systems
- ✓ Back Office Accounting
- ✓ Loss Prevention

Experience
JAY JACOBS, Portland, OR
2007 – 2010, *Manager*
- Achieved store financial results of 25% profitability; Daily opening / closing bookwork
- Supervision of seven employees included recruitment and selection of support staff
- Evaluation of employees on monthly performance reviews
- Sales/customer service supervision for excellence and performance
- Trained and developed all subordinates through challenging work and delegation
- Conducted motivational store meetings and executed sales rallies
- Visual presentation/merchandise content including new technology
- Identified merchandise needs and communicated to buyers
- Loss prevention measures encompassed proficiency and accuracy of store POS Systems
- Planned payroll effectively and insured accuracy on payroll procedures
- Demonstrated commitment to shrinkage control and reduction
- Insured proficient and accurate markdowns/discounts

"Ms. Mintek makes concrete the concept of 'team' and leads the troops by example."

RITZ CARLTON HOTEL, Half Moon Bay, CA
2005 – 2007, *Assistant Manager / Senior Desk Clerk*
- Promoted through the ranks from Desk Clerk to Supervisor to Assistant Manager
- Excelled in customer service with multiple (3) Employee-of-the-Month Awards
- Assisted in the expansion of the Spa & Luxury Division of Front Desk Operations
- Functioned as Manager on Duty during weekends and holidays
- Integral in the execution of marketing and promotions that increased hotel sales
- Offered Manager positions at Ritz Carlton Los Angeles and Ritz Carton Lake Las Vegas

"Joliette Mintek executed the bottom-line results that the company planned, budgeted and achieved."

MAURICES, Great Falls, MT
2002 - 2005, *Assistant Regional Manager*
- Sales/Customer Service for 2nd largest department store in Montana
- Top producer in own personal sales and increased by 35% store net revenues
- Demonstrated product knowledge and promoted current sales/events promotions
- Management skills instrumental in reducing turnover 60% and increasing morale
- Daily opening and closing bookwork; Recruitment of employees; PR scheduling
- Visual presentation/merchandise content recognized by Local Merchant Association
- Completed merchandising moves and made appropriate adjustments when necessary
- Analyzed departmental performance; Planned and participated in store fashion shows
- Re-analyzed Loss Prevention Programs to reduce leakage and shoplifting to near zero
- Proficient and accurate on store register; Launched display overhauls and changes
- Inventory control resulted in reducing overhead and more efficient markdowns/discounts

"With commitment and execution of the Ritz credos of 'Customer Front and Center' and 'Whatever It Takes', Ms. Mintek makes guests, visitors, co-employees and management feel 'Top of the Ritz'"

ABOVE ARE SOME
PERFORMANCE
EVALUATIONS

Education
University of Nevada at Las Vegas, Las Vegas, NV
Bachelor of Arts Degree in Business & Retail Management, 2002

REFERENCES
AVAILABLE
FOR REVIEW

Community
Member/Fundraiser, Citizens For A Viable Downtown Portland, 2007 to Present

WOW! RÉSUMÉS 2011-2012: Great Jobs...Extra Income...Happiness...

STEWART CRESTON

1234 Belt Line Road #123, Dallas, TX 75221 ★ (512) 123-4567 ★ crestontex@wowresumes.net

CAREER OBJECTIVE: To obtain a position that maximizes my competitive spirit and energetic personality, utilizing my business experience, sales skills and lessons in athletics and life to enhance advancement and financial rewards for the organization, myself and the community.

PROFESSIONAL INSURANCE EXPERIENCE

SOUTHWEST INSURANCE COMPANY, Irving, Texas (2001 – Present)
- Fast-track promotion, sales and management exposure; Promoted through a series of managerial levels: 6 management levels in 6 years in Life area, 2 management levels in 2 years in Fire and Casualty area and immediate attainment of management level in Automobile area
- Continuous achievement of performance goals rewarded by compensation and awards, and integral participation in team objectives and Company missions

SOUTHWEST MUTUAL AUTOMOBILE CO, Dallas County Region
Senior Agency Field Specialist (2009 - 2010)
- ☑ Agency Management level position newly created due to Southwest restructuring; Selected from top 7% of qualified candidates

SOUTHWEST FIRE AND CASUALTY CO/DALLAS & FORTH WORTH SERVICE CENTERS
Fire Claims Representative and Fire Claims Specialist (2006 - 2009)
- ☑ Two management level positions in two years; Enhanced knowledge and experience in a different area of the company, keeping salary level

SOUTHWEST LIFE INSURANCE CO/OKLAHOMA-KANSAS REGIONAL OFFICE
Supervisor 3 and Assistant Superintendent (2002 - 2005)

SOUTHWEST LIFE INSURANCE CO.IMISSOURI-KANSAS REGIONAL OFFICE
Trainee, Supervisor 1, Supervisor 2, and Supervisor 3 (2000 - 2002)
- ☑ Youngest person in company to attain "Management Promotability Review Program"; Progressed and rapidly achieved successive management promotions derived from superior performance, development of superior leadership skills, and unrelenting dedication to training and improvement

SALES AND MANAGERIAL EXPOSURE

- ☑ Licensed by the States of Texas and Oklahoma as a Life Agent and a Fire & Casualty Broker/Agent; Assisted agents with prospecting, needs analysis, solicitation, competitive obstacles, and presentation of Insurance Products; Accountable for an operation consisting of 5 supervisors and 26 support level employees servicing all of the Life Insurance needs for a 2-state region

COMMUNITY INVOLVEMENT

- ☑ Participated in Southwest's Action Network and Speaker's Bureau; Regularly volunteer time to United Way, Big Brothers/ Big Sisters, Special Olympics and other community and civic activities

TRAINING AND SELF-EDUCATION

- ☑ State Certified to conduct Instructional, Technical, and Marketing Seminars; Employee Hiring, Training, and Development; Affirmative Action and Diversity Management; Cost Control and Expense Budgeting; Compliance w/Procedural, Financial, IRS, and State Auditing; Decentralization; Service Industry Exposure and Direct Consumer Contact; Managed Growth
- ☑ Attendance and participation in numerous seminars/courses in Sales, Marketing; Peak Performance, and Personal Excellence

EDUCATION

B.S. in Business Administration / UNIVERSITY OF TEXAS AT AUSTIN, 2000
Full Athletic Football Scholarship - All-American, Conference and District Honors
Major: Marketing Management

OTHER COLLEGE HONORS: Spencer-Rogers Respect Award; Honor Roll; College Orientation Leader; Captain and #1 Interior Lineman of the Varsity Football Squad; Four-year Varsity Letterman; Assistant Offensive Line Coach

Related Jobs/Careers:
(Insurance Claims, Life Insurance Sales, Liability Insurance)

RÉSUMÉ #18: Insurance Sales / Insurance Management / Insurance Training (2011 U.S. Retail: $349)

WOW! RÉSUMÉS 2011-2012: Great Jobs...Extra Income...Happiness...

CHAPTER 2: SALES and MARKETING RÉSUMÉS

Martha G. Gunther

1234 Magnolia Blvd. #123
Burbank, CA 91501

(818) 123-4567
mggunther@wowresumes.net

CAREER PROFILE:

Over 10 years' experience in the medical industry including 6 years of exceptional professional sales performance for well-respected companies in Midwestern & Western U.S.

"Ms. Gunther's achievements stem from her work ethic, intelligence and ability to meet the demands of changing times."
-From Recent Performance Evaluation-

PROFESSIONAL EXPERIENCE

CALPRO, INC., Pasadena, California 2006 - Present
Sales Representative / Field Trainer

SALES ACCOMPLISHMENTS:
- Sales Representative of the Month 6 times (2008 - 2010)
- President's Award Winner 2009
- Quarterly Sales Performance Award 3 times
- Tripled volume of business in own Southern California territory
- Requested and received Orange County territory, continuing top performance of over $1.2M growth in 3 1/2 months

OPPORTUNITIES / PROMOTIONS:
- Field Trainer for Los Angeles County (one of 3 people chosen)
- Leadership Committee Member (chosen by Head of Marketing and Sales)

WATSON AND ASSOCIATES, Springfield, Missouri, 1999 - 2005
Sales Representative
ACHIEVEMENTS & MEDIAN RANKING/PERFORMANCE AMONG 41 REGIONAL REPS:
- Sales and service of Medical/Surgical supplies to Hospitals (single use products): #3
- Sales and service of Video equipment and instrumentation for Laparoscopy: #5
- Sales and service of the Birtcher Argon Beam Coagulation and Electro cautery machines: #1
- New Territory: Western Missouri (Springfield, Kansas City): Granted extra territory
- Contacted key decision-makers such as Surgeons and Administrators: Ahead of schedule
- Provided follow up contact and in-service training: Letters of Commendation
- Developed communication with non-using Hospitals: Protocol recognized by Management
- Established realistic goals for development of business targets: On target
- Represented Company line's at State Conventions of ENT Surgeons, Ophthalmologists, The American College of Surgeons Convention, and the National AORN Convention: Awarded Merit Citation
- Evaluated new product lines for the Company: Evaluations used by Marketing

PROFESSIONAL STRENGTHS

- Energetic person with excellent achievement drive, striving to continue to be successful in sales
- Highly organized and well developed integrity-selling approach with excellent work ethics and follow-through
- Strong critical listening and advanced problem-solving skills allowing customers to realize true value of business
- Holistic perspective and approach to analyze a potential total account conversion and long term relationship

EDUCATION AND TRAINING

University of Missouri, Columbia, Missouri; *Bachelor of Arts in Communications*, May 1998
Boone County Technical College; Surgical Technologist
Sales Training Course in "Integrity Selling"

Related Jobs/Careers:
(Medical Technology Sales, Healthcare Technology Marketing)

RÉSUMÉ #19: Medical Equipment Sales / Sales Trainer (2011 U.S. Retail: $329)

WOW! RÉSUMÉS 2011-2012: Great Jobs...Extra Income...Happiness...

ERNEST C. BOCKEN

775-123-4567
erniebocken@wowresumes.net

Account Executive or Lobbyist for a Multi-National Energy Company

---

HIGHLIGHTS OF SKILLS, KNOWLEDGE AND ABILITIES

- ✓ Thorough understanding of advertising and promotions in the petroleum industry
- ✓ Research and state-of the-art knowledge in the growing new fields of natural gas and clean coal
- ✓ Familiarity with international energy industry including Russia, Canada, Mexico, Venezuela and Brazil
- ✓ Experience and interaction with energy lobbyists in the Western U.S. States and the Congress of the United States

---

EXPERIENCE

BBRD Worldwide, Reno, Nevada
Account Executive Manager for Elko Oil Account, 2004 to 2010
- Developed advertising materials for local placement during key market promotions
- Devised and accessed competitive advertising expenditure study
- Maintained and reconciled media and special events budgets
- Designed and presented advertising seminars for business and sales representatives in Elko Oil's Marketing Training Program
- Supervised summer interns participating in Elko Oil's cooperative education program and create program curriculum
- Represented Elko Oil at national automotive conventions
- Responded to Elko Oil's consumer mail, addressing concerns and comments

Tolbert and Mitcham Advertising, Inc., Seattle, Washington
Account Executive/Print Media Buyer/Traffic Manager, 1999 to 2003
- Developed and implemented annual advertising strategy and budgets
- Created and presented campaign strategies to clients
- Purchased print media for local and regional accounts
- Compiled and presented job estimates
- Instituted computerized traffic, media and billing systems

United States Senate, Washington, D.C.
Intern for Senator Patty Murray of Washington State, Fall/Summer 1998
- Coordinated campaign press release recording sessions
- Oversaw distribution of audio release tapes to state markets
- Conducted research project examining future job availability for Washington State citizens
- Compiled, analyzed and presented project's statistical findings

---

EDUCATION

University of Washington, Pullman, Washington
Bachelor of Business Administration degree in International Business, 1998
Minor in Political Science, Dean's List for six consecutive semesters.
Fluent in Spanish and some Portuguese and French.
Conferences and Symposia on Energy including New Exploration Technologies

LETTERS OF RECOMMENDATIONS AND REFERENCES: Available upon request

12345 Exhibition Road #123 ▪ Reno, Nevada 89512 ▪ erniebocken@wowresumes.net

Related Jobs/Careers:
(Energy Sales, Multinational Sales)

RÉSUMÉ #20: Account Executive/Industrial Sales/Lobbyist (2011 U.S. Retail: $299)

WOW! RÉSUMÉS 2011-2012: Great Jobs...Extra Income...Happiness...

Catherine Sulmani

1234 Federal Blvd. #123; Denver, CO 80211
303-123-4567
csulmani@wowresumes.net

Real Estate Specialist (Agent or Broker or Analyst)
Special Events
Marketing / Community Relations

Competencies Include:

Real Estate Contracts	Property Financing	Surveying / Appraising
Open Houses	Sales Brochures	Corporate Clients
Newsletters	Property Research	Market Analysis
Client Database Management	Escrows	Social Media
Telemarketing Campaigns	Press Releases	Data Mining

PROFESSIONAL HIGHLIGHTS:

Real Estate Experience
► Represented multi-million dollar realty firm, which developed housing tracts, managed > 1500 properties
► Planned grand opening of a new 75-home subdivision and supervised tours of subdivision
► Familiarity and technical skills in financing, distressed property portfolios, sales/dispositions

Special Events
► Coordinated events, vendor positioning, food prep and presentation, A/V, theme and design, break down
► Implemented planners' event strategy including appearance, staffing needs, catering and client requests
► Updated promotions/public relations by creating a marketing plan including LinkedIn, Facebook, Twitter

Community Relations
► Implemented proper set up for special events such as Food Drives & Toss for Tots for NFL Football Team
► Composed biographies for the Community Relations Department 2006-2007 media guide and programs
► Handled charity donations and coordinated appearance requests; Managed fan inquiries via mail and email

WORK EXPERIENCE:
Northern Colorado State Bank; Boulder, CO; *REO Processor*; 2010 - Present
Events for the 21st Century, Evergreen, CO; *Special Events Director*; 2008 - 2009
Pulte Homes, Las Vegas, NV, *New Homes Representative*; 2007-2008
Denver Broncos, National Football League Franchise, Denver, CO; *Community Relations*; 2005 - 2007
Tobias & Company, Real Estate Brokers, Denver, CO; *Real Estate Specialist/Manager*; 2001 - 2005

EDUCATION:
Bachelor of Business Administration; Boulder University, Boulder, CO, 2000
Licenses: Colorado & Nevada Real Estate Licenses, Current; Colorado Broker's License, 2003 - 2007
Computer Skills include: Microsoft Office Suite; REO Maestro; Constant Contact, Adobe Acrobat

COMMUNITY:
Member of Denver Chamber of Commerce & Citizens for a Better Denver; Company Coordinator for United Way

---

Related Jobs/Careers:
(New Homes Sales, Special Events Director, Community Relations)
RÉSUMÉ #21: Real Estate Sales / Special Events / Real Estate Marketing (2011 U.S. Retail: $269)

WOW! RÉSUMÉS 2011-2012: Great Jobs...Extra Income...Happiness...

BLANK PAGE

-FOR NOTES-

CHAPTER 3:

ACCOUNTING and FINANCE RÉSUMÉS

11 Model *WOW!* Résumés
(46 Job Titles)

CREATE YOUR OWN RÉSUMÉ:

If you are doing your own Résumé in the Occupational Category of Accounting and Finance, you can choose from among the *WOW!* Résumés in this Chapter modeling the wording, styles, formatting, bullets, borders, etc. You can also model any of the elements in the other *WOW!* Résumés in this Book.

Complete the Guides in the Appendices including the *WOW!* Action Verbs and specific targeted Keywords (that must be researched) to fully customize and create a unique and powerful *WOW!* Résumé!

If you have purchased this Book (and thus become an automatic 1-year Member of wowresumes.net) you can get Free unrestricted downloads (Word or PDF Files) of up to 5 *WOW!* Résumés in addition to a Free download of the Guides in the Appendices for you to print out or edit on your computer.

DISCOUNTED RÉSUMÉ SERVICE:

If you need help to create a *WOW!* Résumé call 888-503-3133 or go to wowresumes.net to work with professional Résumé Writers who practice *WOW!* Résumé principles. Book purchasers have up to one year to avail of a 30% Instant Discount on any *WOW!* Résumé or other *WOW!* Résumé products such as *WOW!*-Card® Résumés, as well as other benefits including Free Résumé Posting on the ever-growing wowresumes.net Website and Updating from Twitter, Facebook, LinkedIn & Google Profiles. Members get Free Updates for 1 year on their Main Résumé and up to 90% Discounts on additional (2nd, 3rd, 4th, etc.) Customized Résumés to target Specific Jobs, Careers, Industries or Special Urgent Applications.

*See the Back Cover for *WOW!* Résumé Service & Free Membership Information*

WOW! RÉSUMÉS 2011-2012: Great Jobs...Extra Income...Happiness...

CHAPTER 3: ACCOUNTING and FINANCE RÉSUMÉS

Financial Record-Keepers and Critical Analysts for Global Transactions

This Chapter covers the major occupations of Accounting-Bookkeeping-Auditing Clerks, Accountants-Auditors, Financial Analysts, Financial Managers and Banking.

Accounting-Bookkeeping-Auditing Clerks are financial record-keepers across industries. These financial clerks update and maintain accounting records, including expenditures, receipts, accounts payable and receivable, and profit and loss. In small business, bookkeepers and bookkeeping clerks are often responsible for some or all of the enterprise's accounts known as the general ledger. Considered the 12th largest occupation in the United States, there were some 2,063,800 Accounting-Bookkeeping-Auditing Clerks in 2008 (Bureau of Labor Statistics, U.S. Department of Labor).

Accountants and Auditors are charged with the responsibility of ensuring that businesses are run efficiently, public records kept accurately and taxes filed and paid on time. Accountants and Auditors also analyze and communicate financial information for various organizations such as companies, Federal, State and local governments as well as individual clients. The four major fields of accounting and auditing include public accounting, management accounting, government accounting, and auditing. In 2008, there were 1,290,600 Accountants and Auditors (Bureau of Labor Statistics, U.S. Department of Labor).

Financial analysts guide businesses and individuals in making investment decisions by assessing the performance of stocks, bonds, commodities and other types of investments. Financial Analysts are also called Securities Analysts and Investment Analysts who work for banks, insurance companies, mutual and pension funds, securities firms, business media and other businesses. There were some 250,600 Financial Analysts in the U.S. in 2008 (Bureau of Labor Statistics, U.S. Department of Labor).

Financial Managers oversee the preparation of financial reports, direct investment activities, and implement cash management strategies, as well as develop strategies and implement the long-term goals of their employing organizations. Almost every company, government agency and various types of organizations employs one or more Financial Managers. In 2008, according to the Bureau of Labor Statistics, U.S. Department of Labor, there were some 539,300 Financial Managers in the U.S.

Banking which employs multiple occupations (including those mentioned above along with Loan Specialists, Computer Specialists, Customer Service Representatives and Administrative Assistants) has an overall employment level of 1,842,000 in the U.S. (in 2008 according to the Bureau of Labor Statistics, U.S. Department of Labor).

While Accounting-Bookkeeping-Auditing Clerks and the lower-end positions in Banking may only have a high school diploma as the minimum requirement, the other major upper-level positions in this Category of Accounting and Finance require bachelor's or master's degrees in specialized fields as well as requiring licensure, certification and continuing education for Accountants, Auditors, Financial Analysts (especially in Securities and Financial Planning). In Banking, extensive experience and long-service can be pathways to management, in lieu of or in addition to formal education and training.

WOW! RÉSUMÉS 2011-2012: Great Jobs...Extra Income...Happiness...

CHAPTER 3: ACCOUNTING and FINANCE RÉSUMÉS

Compensation and Job Prospects

In the lower-end positions of Accounting and Finance (Banking), earnings are relatively low: in May 2008, the median annual wages of bookkeeping, accounting and auditing clerks were $32,510 (Bureau of Labor Statistics, U.S. Department of Labor), below the national median average wage. Earnings of nonsupervisory (non-management employees) averaged $605 per week in 2008 (Bureau of Labor Statistics), compared with $798 for workers in the finance and insurance and $608 for workers throughout the private sector. Banking wages vary widely by occupation where scope of responsibilities, experience, length of service as well as location and size of the bank being factors in salary levels.

As for Financial Analysts, median annual wages, excluding bonuses, were $73,150 as of May 2008 (Bureau of Labor Statistics) which was more than double the national median wage. Annual performance bonuses are quite common and can be a very significant part of the total compensation for Financial Analysts.

Financial Managers, excluding annual bonuses and stock options, earned on average $99,330 as of May 2008 (Bureau of Labor Statistics). The highest earners as of May 2008 (excluding bonuses and other compensation) were Financial Managers in Securities and Commodity Brokerage ($134,940) and the Financial Managers of Companies and Enterprises ($115,520).

According to the Bureau of Labor Statistics, the median annual wages of wage and salary Accountants and Auditors were $59,430 in May 2008. The middle half of this group earned between $45,900 and $78,210; the bottom 10 percent earned less than $36,720; the top 10 percent earned more than $102,380.

For Accounting-Bookkeeping-Auditing Clerks, job growth is projected to be about as fast as average due to the large size of the occupation with accounting, bookkeeping and auditing clerks expected to retire or change occupations. The same rate of growth is projected by the Bureau of Labor Statistics for Accountants and Auditors, with individuals possessing master's degrees and expertise in specialized areas such as international business, international financial reporting standards or current legislation having advantages in getting the best accounting and auditing positions.

For Financial Analysts and Financial Managers, there will be employment growth but there will be strong competition for these high-paying jobs. Candidates with expertise, training and education (especially master's degrees) in both accounting and finance will have the best prospects, as well as those candidates who have an understanding of international finance, derivatives, complex financial instruments and complex financial transactions.

While there will also be competition for the best high-paying Banking positions, there will be favorable job opportunities for office, administrative support and customer service representative jobs in Banking because of the size of the industry with relatively high turnover.

The *WOW!* Model Résumés in this Chapter include International Investment Banker; Bank Manger/Trainer; Staff Accountant; Self-Employed CPA; Underwriting/Compliance Auditor; and Financial Analyst/Consultant with Master's Degree in International Business.

WOW! RÉSUMÉS 2011-2012: Great Jobs...Extra Income...Happiness...

CHAPTER 3: ACCOUNTING and FINANCE RÉSUMÉS

JOHN WEN TRAN

1234 Magnolia Avenue
Riverside, CA 91822

(909) 123-4567
jwtran@wowresumes.net

INVESTMENT BANKING / ASSET MANAGEMENT / FINANCIAL ANALYSIS

CAREER PROFILE

★ 8 Years of excellence and increasing responsibility in banking and finance
★ Expert in relationship building emphasizing consultation & negotiations
★ Strong leadership and team building with ability to meet priorities/challenges
★ Results-orientation & great follow-through in customer service and client rapport
★ Performance-driven with motivation to excel personally and organizationally
★ Skilled in financial analysis, financial modeling, research & quantitative methods
★ Well versed in multicultural settings with strong language & cultural aptitudes

EDUCATION

Master of Business Administration, Finance Emphasis
California State University Fullerton, Fullerton, CA 2008

Bachelor of Science in Economics, Minor in Accounting
California State University East Bay, Hayward, CA, 2003

PROFESSIONAL EXPERIENCE

Inland Empire Proline, Riverside, CA
Finance and Accounting Consultant, 2008 to Present
❏ Assist President with financial modeling, budgeting and forecasting
❏ Perform internal control analysis of cash flow and ensure accounting accuracy

Bank of America, Walnut Creek, CA
Personal and Small Business Banker, 2007 - 2008
❏ Managed and deepened relationships with high value customers
❏ Performed complex account research and management of new accounts

World Savings/Wachovia Bank, Oakland, CA
Mortgage Loan Specialist / Loan Manager, 2004 - 2007
❏ Managed multiple projects & deadlines, originating over $50 in volume
❏ Partnered with underwriting, QA & Customer Care to decision 200+ loans

Telemar Financial, Fremont, CA
Futures and Options Specialist, 2003 - 2004
❏ Traded open contracts in dynamic & volatile markets making split second decisions
❏ Meticulously analyzed global markets with real world applications and results

Ameriquest Mortgage, South San Francisco, CA
Loan Consultant / Team Leader, 2001 - 2003
❏ Consistently ranked among the Top 3 Salespersons in Gross Profits & Units

SPECIAL SKILLS

Fluent in English, Vietnamese and Mandarin
Computer Proficiency: MS Office, Impact, Calyx, Salesforce, Lotus Notes, Genesys, Capital Asset pricing Model (CAPM) and Capital Budgeting with NPV IRR, MIRR, ROI, PI, DO/DU, Portfolio Management & Other Proprietary Software

---

Related Jobs/Careers:
(Personal Banker, Loan Consultant, Financial Analyst)

RÉSUMÉ #22: Investment Banking / Asset Management (2011 U.S. Retail: $299)

WOW! RÉSUMÉS 2011-2012: Great Jobs...Extra Income...Happiness...

Katarina V. Wilsmeier

123 Burroughs Road, Tarzana, CA 91702 ♦ 818.123.4567 ♦ katarinavw@wowresumes.net

BANKER / TRADER: BONDS – CURRENCY – INVESTMENT PORTFOLIOS
Licensed Series 7 and 63

Profile:
- Outstanding communication skills honed by exposure to business and multi-cultures, markets, languages and international travel
- Top performer in sales, client building, development and maintenance. Passionate in learning new personal and technical skills
- Enjoy working with other people. A good team member, bringing energy and enthusiasm into department al and company efforts
- Excellent "idea-person" -- adept at creating order out of chaos. Able to take a thought from the idea stage through to completion
- Meticulous and systematic in research and "number crunching" --gather, collate, classify info about figures, people and scenarios
- Refined problem-solving orientation -- able to isolate and clearly describe a problem in order that steps can be taken to rectify it

Professional Skills / Achievements:
- Developed business in banking, mortgages and investments including hedge funds, growing departmental revenue 21% year over year
- Managed $200 million in client assets, establishing portfolio rebalancing strategies and making recommendations to meet client goals
- Placed daily equity and mutual fund trades for clients up to $11 million with portfolio analyses, asset allocations and S&P ratings
- Sold municipal bonds, advised clients on asset allocations and the construction of portfolios generating commission in top 10%
- Presented retirement solutions to San Fernando Unified School district (Southern California) helping company win 1 of 3 contracts
- Performed daily interest rate yield curve models based on Fed funds, LIBOR, Commercial paper and 90 day Eurodollar futures
- Reconciled global security trades settlement with corresponding foreign currency trades and prepared trade ticket for F/X contracts
- Processed and confirmed fixed income trade settlements and allocations including MBS, ABS, and Treasuries; Ran daily reports
- Confirmed credit default swaps trades via DTCC as well as amounts, dates for full terminations; Executed management directions
- Translated English documents into German for an office of 50 people; Via established protocols, performed international wire transfers

Employment HIstory:

Union Bank Capital Management, Los Angeles, CA; 3/2010 to Present	*Trader, Fixed Income Settlements*
Lincoln Financial, Phoenix, AZ, 2008 to 2010	*Benefits Counselor, Pension Funds*
Charles Schwab, San Francisco, CA, 2007 to 2008	*Investments Specialist/Broker*
Wells Fargo Advisors, Los Angeles, CA 2006 to 2007	*Trader, Interest Rate Derivatives*
Citigroup Private Bank, Baltimore, Maryland, 2004 to 2005	*Relationship Officer*
Hypo-Bank, Munich, Germany; 2001 to 2002	*International Money Transfer Clerk*
Gwinner & Ulrich Publishers, Munich, Germany; 2000 to 2001	*Student Apprentice*

Education:
UNIVERSITY OF MARYLAND, College Park, Maryland
Bachelor of Arts degree in Finance 2005

ELLY-HEUSE REALSCHULE (HIGH SCHOOL), Munich, Germany, Diploma 2000

COMPUTER PROFICIENCIES: Microsoft Word and PowerPoint;
Bloomberg, SEI, PORTIA, TPG, AXYS, Advanced Excel including financial modeling forward rates and duration

Fluently speak, read and write German

Related Jobs/Careers:
(Bond Trader, Exchange Arbitrager)
RÉSUMÉ #23: International Investment Banker / Currency Trader (2011 U.S. Retail: $299)

WOW! RÉSUMÉS 2011-2012: Great Jobs...Extra Income...Happiness...

ROBERT DALEY

1234 Stockton St. #123 ◆ San Francisco, CA 94101 ◆ (415) 123-4567 ◆ rdaley@wowresumes.net

FINANCIAL ANALYST / CONSULTANT
International and Legal Experience

PROFESSIONAL EXPERIENCE

Commerce and Industry Bank, San Francisco, CA
California bank, with over $65 Billion in assets (affiliated with Agricultural Bank of China, largest capitalized bank in the world)

Financial Analyst (2008 - Present)
- Analyze companies with revenues ranging from $2MM to $500MM, in technology, real estate, retail and insurance
- Assess risks to Bank posed by clients, based on analyses of financial statements, collateral, and industries; Analyses carried out through direct contact with clients and research through credit and industry publications
- Perform advanced modeling of client financial statements, including pro forma and sensitivity analyses
- Propose effective means of mitigating client risk through credit structures which are mutually beneficial to client and Bank
- Present deals at senior level (Bank executives); Presentations outline risks to Bank of credits and factors which mitigate risks
- Assist in marketing efforts of loan officers, including presentations to prospective and existing clients

Winthrop, Carlson & O'Donnell, Attorneys At Law, San Francisco, CA
Prominent insurance defense firm with nationwide offices
Marketing Assistant (Summer 2005)
- Developed marketing plan and created firm brochures and assisted with newsletters
- Performed support duties in client research, public relations and media campaigns

Paralegal (Summers 2002 to 2005)
- Assisted the Director of Asbestos Litigation and provided day-of-court deliveries for Litigation Team Leader
- Summarized depositions / categorized discovery / reviewed medical records / researched general databases
- Prepared legal briefs and delivered logistical support for outside attorneys and expert witnesses/staff

EDUCATION

Shanghai University, Shanghai, China
Master of Science in International Business, September 2008

Monterey Institute of International Studies, Monterey, CA
Master of Business Administration: International Management (May 2004)
◆ International Finance, Economics and Accounting

University of Portland, Portland, Oregon
Bachelor of Arts: Political Science (December, 2001)
◆ Law and International Politics

SKILLS & ACHIEVEMENTS

- Exposure to foreign markets and clientele specializing in coastal China provinces, Hong Kong and Taiwan
- Excellent communication and relationship building skills with special expertise to contribute to company growth
- Developed foreign market business plan for contract food service company (J & L Service Company)
- Master's thesis was purchased by the Small Business Administration; Published studies in Shanghai
- Certificate: Advanced Training for Service Abroad (August, 2006): Language – Mandarin

COMPUTER PROFICIENCIES

Microsoft Excel, Powerpoint, Microsoft Forecaster, CODA –Financials, Acumatica Customer Management Suite, Exact Globe, Ajera PORTFOLIO, Budget Masetro, Deltek Costpoint, Power OLAP, Alibaba China (world's largest B2B auctioning website)

Related Jobs/Careers:
(International Banking, International Finance)
RÉSUMÉ #24: Financial Analyst / International Business Consultant (2011 U.S. Retail: $319)

WOW! RÉSUMÉS 2011-2012: Great Jobs...Extra Income...Happiness...

SHIRLEY A. TONG

123 Sandburg Lane • Chicago, IL 60601 • (312) 123-4567 • satong@wowresumes.net

| MANAGER-TRAINER IN BANKING, FINANCE, MARKETING |

■ SUMMARY OF QUALIFICATIONS

- □ Small business and entrepreneurial skills includes part-time network marketing
- □ Guerilla marketing skills critical for shoe-string budgets and tough economic conditions
- □ Broad knowledge and over 10 years' experience in financial institutions and credit markets
- □ Instrumental in growing $40M-$92M in base accounts in very competitive niche and traditional markets
- □ Management abilities, proven decision-making, and strong interpersonal skills with clients and co-workers
- □ Adept at achieving balance between authority and accountability, developing and implementing strategies/plans
- □ Skilled at team building to generate quantifiable results; Committed to personal growth & organizational excellence

■ PROFESSIONAL EXPERIENCE

Independent Distributor, 2009 to Present
Zrii Nutriveda Health Products, Oak Park, IL
- ➢ Generate average of $950 per month in income (growing 20% each quarter from start) with "down line" of 35+

Marketing Consultant, 2008 to Present
Tong & Associates, Chicago, IL
- ➢ Train and mentor small businesses and entrepreneurs with cost-effective and innovative promotional marketing

Financial Consultant, January 2006 to 2008
A & A Financial Management, Chicago, IL
- ➢ Built new business banking relationships and excelled in consulting on varied banking issues

Branch Manager/ Vice President, March 2002 to December 2005
Great Continental Bank - Southside Branch, Chicago, IL
- ➢ Developed sales for a $40M base branch in new area for Great Continental
- ➢ Opened most business accounts in region and increased checking base by 120%

Branch Manager/Vice President, December 2000 to March 2002
Great Continental Bank - West Jolene Branch, Jolene, IL
- ➢ Revitalized sales, service, and management of a $92M base branch with 13 employees
- ➢ Consistently exceeded company goals in product upselling and account solutions

Branch Manager/Vice President, July 1997 to December 2000
Great Continental Bank - Lincoln Park Branch, Lincoln Park, IL
- ➢ Expanded production of operations in a $70M base branch with 14 employees
- ➢ Made branch number 1 in revenues in regional district; Met 100% of quarterly goals

Credit Analyst, Dealer Operation Center, Financial Services, July 1995 to June 1997
First National Bank of St. Louis, St. Louis, MO
- ➢ Interacted successfully with over 300 auto dealers in Missouri; Analyzed financial statements
- ➢ Wrote credit authorizations, and recommended lines of credit; Maintained excellent rapport with dealers

■ EDUCATION & TRAINING

Washington University, St. Louis St. Louis, MO
Master of Business Administration in Finance, 1995

Washington University, St. Louis St. Louis, MO
Bachelor of Science in Marketing, 1992

Computer Proficiencies include: MS Office Suite, QuickBooks for the Web, BusinessWorks, BusinessVision 32

Related Jobs/Careers:
(Credit Analyst, Finance-Marketing Trainer)
RÉSUMÉ #25: Bank Branch Manager / Banking Trainer (2011 U.S. Retail: $319)

EVELYN H. SHANKAR

1000 Beacon Street ◆ Boston MA 02134 ◆ 617.123.3457 ◆ ehshankar@wowresumes.net

OBJECTIVE: Position in bookkeeping / accounting / banking for a progressive organization seeking to expand into underserved communities and new markets

PROFESSIONAL PROFILE
Detail-minded...extremely hard-working (have worked equivalent to 2 full-time jobs)...team contributor...committed to efficiency and quality...highly organized...excellent communications...results-driven attitude

OFFICE/ACCOUNTING SKILLS
Full charge bookkeeping: income statements; general ledger; payroll; tax statements; accounts receivable; accounts payable; bank reconciliation; computerized accounting; PC and Mac;
Excel; TimeSlips; QuickBooks Pro; BillPoint; MAS 90; Litigation Advisor; LEDES; DacEasy; FilemakerPro; Word

PROFESSIONAL EXPERIENCE
CITIZENS BANK, Boston, MA
Bank Teller/Customer Service Representative, 2008 to Present
⊙ Part-Time to Full-Time Position at downtown Boston Financial Center Branch
⊙ Handle cash, cash drawer, deposits, other accounts including consumer loans
⊙ Balance at end of day; Provide efficient, friendly customer service

QUINCY MARKET FRESH FISH COMPANY, Boston MA
Office Manager/Bookkeeper, 2005 to 2008
⊙ Multi-faceted position in a young growing firm ($5-$6 Million Annual Gross Sales)
⊙ Performed full charge bookkeeping: data entry, filing, report generation
⊙ Maintained accounts payable and accounts receivable
⊙ Administered payroll, involving documentation of employees' hours, schedules, etc.
⊙ Reconciled company bank account, assisting owner in handling extra business account responsibilities
⊙ Worked closely with company CPA to maintain all accounting procedures and reporting (including tax) requirements

JONES, MARQUEZ & ASSOCIATES, Oakland, CA
Billing Coordinator, 2003 to 2005
⊙ Excelled as Billing Clerk and quickly promoted to Coordinator for law firm specializing in product liability cases

THOMSON-BERKINS, South San Francisco, CA
Billing Coordinator, 2001 to 2003
⊙ Executed with efficiency and quality billing and job costing duties for an environmental consulting firm

LEGAL BAY PRESS, Redwood City, CA
Accounts Receivable, 2001 to 2004
⊙ Performed with merit as Data Entry Clerk / Accounts Specialist for 5 publications: invoicing, tracking, reconciliations

FIRST INTERSTATE BANK, San Francisco, CA
General Office Clerk/Computer Operator, 2000 to 2001
⊙ Entry level positions where business, technical, and interpersonal skills were obtained

EDUCATION
Tufts University, Medford, Massachusetts – **Bachelor of Arts in French**, 2000
Heald Business College, San Francisco, CA: **Financial Accounting, Managerial Accounting, and Taxation**, 2004

Related Jobs/Careers:
(Bank Teller, Billing Coordinator, Customer Service Representative)
RÉSUMÉ #26: Bookkeeper / Accounting Specialist (2011 U.S. Retail: $299)

WOW! RÉSUMÉS 2011-2012: Great Jobs...Extra Income...Happiness...

SAMUEL CHAN-GOMEZ

1234 Shaw Avenue #123 ▪ Fresno, CA 98168 ▪ 209-123-4567 ▪ schangomez@wowresumes.net

TARGET & OVERVIEW

Top Objectives: Accounts Management / Customer Service / Sales Support

PROFILE—Detail-minded...excellent written and oral communication skills...a team player...committed to quality results...highly organized...positive attitude...punctual and reliable...assertive but diplomatic...self-motivated...fast learner...honest

ACCOUNTING SKILLS—Profit and loss statements...general ledger...payroll...accounts receivable/collections...accounts payable...bank reconciliations...inventory management...database creation...spreadsheet data entry

COMPUTER PROFICIENCIES—Microsoft Word; Excel; Access; M.Y.O.B. Software Suite; Peachtree Complete Accounting; QuickBooks; SBT Fox Pro

EDUCATION

Merced College, Merced, CA
Certificate in Bookkeeping, 2007

Heald Business College, Fresno, CA
Associate Degree in Business, 2005

EXPERIENCE

➤Accounting

Merced County Sheriff's Department, Merced, CA
Accounting Clerk, 3/2010 to Present
→Data entry and processing in payroll department of 250 employees

Central Valley Medical Group, Fresno, CA
Accounts Specialist, 7/2008 to 2/2010
→Processed paperwork related to receivables/payables and insurance claims

➤Customer Service

California State Automobile Association, Stockton, CA
Claims Coordinator / Customer Service. 1/2007 to 6/2008
→Handled liability claims, written and recorded statements, policy payments

➤Collections

Frontier Communications, Fresno, CA
Credit Representative, 8/2005 to 8/2006
→Monitored collections of database of 3000 in Northern & Central California

➤Data Entry

Frontier Communications, Fresno, CA
New Accounts, 2/2005 to 3/2006
→Received and processed credit card and automatic payments

➤Sales Support

Big 5 Sporting Goods, Stockton, CA
Shipping and Receiving Specialist / Sales Clerk, 2001 to 2003
→Controlled inventories and stocking
→Performed sales and cashiering the last 6 months of job before schooling

Related Jobs/Careers:
(Collections, Data Entry, Accounting Clerk, Sales Support)

RÉSUMÉ #27: Accounts Management / Customer Service (2011 U.S. Retail: $299)

WOW! RÉSUMÉS 2011-2012: Great Jobs...Extra Income...Happiness...

ANDRES M. ORTEGA - CPA, MBA

1234 Lamar Road #123   ◆   Austin TX 78711   ◆   (512) 123-4567   ◆   amortega@wowresumes.net

PROFESSIONAL SUMMARY

- ❖ Over fifteen years of hands-on executive-level experience for small to mid-sized companies
- ❖ Directed accounting, financial analyses and reporting to management and regulatory agencies
- ❖ Varied industries include medical devices, food services, telecom, high technology and media
- ❖ Background encompasses Big 4 public accounting with Ernst & Young and roles with start-ups
- ❖ Performed turnarounds, post-IPO growth at private companies and subsidiaries of corporations
- ❖ Functional expertise includes cash management, cost accounting, ERP systems, budgets/forecasting
- ❖ Proven communication skills and management expertise with commitment to integrity and excellence

PROFESSIONAL EXPERIENCE

Andres M. Ortega Consultancy, Inc., Austin, TX, February 2009 to Present
Provide financial, accounting and advisory services to clients
- ➢ Internet customer prospecting company - Improve accounting and reporting for factored receivables
- ➢ Employee health services and testing company - Manage financial reporting to streamline operations
- ➢ SaaS based utility and power monitoring company - Interim Controller and Vice President

Digicon Satellite Systems, Mobile, Alabama
Manufacturer of high tech products and web services for the automobile and trucking industry
Controller, 2007 to 2009
- ➢ Developed accounting process for calculating warranty and sales return costs, reducing annual costs by over $1.2M compared to previous estimated methods and negotiations with auditors
- ➢ Implemented electronic deposit system to accelerate usage of $100M in annual check receipts
- ➢ Teamed with other company personnel to integrate accounting for European based SaaS venture
- ➢ Monitored cash balances and invested funds to obtain high yield while maintaining safety and liquidity
- ➢ Prepared tax schedules and audit support for multi-state tax and federal income tax filings yearly

Techlogix Telecom, Houston, TX
VC backed, high-tech, start-up manufacturer of telecom-network subsystems for Texas Instruments
Controller, 2005 to 2007
- ➢ Maintained a 5-person operations accounting staff while annualized revenue grew for $15K to $20M
- ➢ Managed operational cash requirements through four rounds of financing exceeding $45M while serving under five interim and permanent CFOs during three year period
- ➢ Implemented accounting process to integrate COGS and inventory with financial reporting

Andres M. Ortega Consultancy, Inc., Austin, TX, February 2002 to 2005
Provided financial, accounting, management and tax services to clients
- ➢ Faralex, a server manufacturer – Advisor: cleaned up records and developed accounting process
- ➢ Rio Grande Foods – Maintained company's financial models and prepared actual vs. budget reporting
- ➢ Tele-Cash, an internet software start-up with operations in U.S. and Mexico - Interim Controller

WOW! RÉSUMÉS 2011-2012: Great Jobs...Extra Income...Happiness...

ANDRES M. ORTEGA

amortega@wowresumes.net
--Page Two--

Sun Orthopedics Technology, Coral Gables, Florida
Staff Accountant/Accounting Manager/Controller, 1995 to 2002
➢ Directed handling of a full ERP system from A/P through G/L, monthly closes, financials, maintaining standard cost, executing cost roll-ups, updating costs and reporting variances
➢ Teamed with third parties to convert local manufacturing accounting system to corporate wide ERP system, QAD MFG-PRO
➢ Over 70 on-time, monthly and six annual closes under Ernst & Young Audit
➢ Implemented monthly financial reporting package enabling company to maximize profitable growth while annual revenue increased from $5M to $35M
➢ Started parts cycle count program from $10M raw material inventory resulting in identifying 6% excess inventory and $750k reduction in purchases
➢ Provided key accounting, due diligence and Ernst & Young audit support for $38M sale of company

Ruiz and Jackson, CPAs, Tampa, Florida
Cost Accountant, 1994 to 1995
➢ Prepared financial statements and analyzed cost of sales, gross profit, inventory & intercompany transactions

---

EDUCATION and TRAINING

CERTIFIED PUBLIC ACCOUNTANT, State of Texas

University of Miami, Miami, Florida – Master in Business Administration, 2000

Auburn University, Auburn, Alabama- B. S. Accounting Degree, 1993

A 2 Z Edumatics Seminar Series: Texas State Labor Law and Payroll Taxation, 2010

Texas Society of Controllers & CPAs: Strategic Planning for Multinationals, 2009

COMPUTER KNOWLEDGE & PRACTICE:
➢ CONTROL (KCI), Budget Maestro, QAD/MFG-PRO, Navision and MAS 500
➢ Microsoft Word, PowerPoint, Access, Outlook, Excel

Related Jobs/Careers:
(Cost Accountant, Controller)

WOW! RÉSUMÉS 2011-2012: Great Jobs...Extra Income...Happiness...

CHAPTER 3: ACCOUNTING and FINANCE RÉSUMÉS

Henry J. Moorer

123 Central Avenue   •   Buffalo, NY 12205   •   (518) 123-4567   •   hankjm@wowresumes.net

-----◆-----

Specialist/Supervisor in Accounts and Credit Collections

Highly motivated enthusiastic professional with documented track record of results and performance in accounts and credit collections. Excellent in communications and the ability to execute win-win-win negotiations with customers in challenging and emotional circumstances. Committed to integrity and accountability. Exemplary work ethic with a sense of balance. Ability to train and motivate personnel refining their telephone, communications and negotiation skills. Willing to accept responsibilities beyond immediate job duties to benefit the team and company.

---◆----◆----◆---

Bachelor of Arts in English, COLUMBIA UNIVERSITY, New York, NY, 2000
CITY COLLEGE OF ALBANY, Albany, NY, 2003 - 2005:
Courses in Accounting, Management and Computers

COMPUTER EXPERTISE
Acumatica Customer Management Suite (CRM), SYSPRO 6.0, Envision Series, CollectPro, MS Office Suite

Professional Experience

DEBT COUNSELORS OF AMERICA, Buffalo, NY
Collections Specialist / Supervisor, 2008 to Present
o   Contact customers by phone, email corporate form letters in remedy of delinquency
o   Authority to write off small amounts to correct general ledger; Monitor internal controls of collections
o   Maintain close communications with sales and accounting of client companies
o   Input in recruiting of new staff; In charge of training new hires and supervision of 12 collectors

NANTASCOT BANK, Schenectady, NY
International Loan / Collections Specialist, 2005 to 2007
o   Coordinated full loan service functions to International Corporate, Commercial, and Correspondent Units
o   Researched and resolved customer problems and inquiries; Processed in/out documentary collections
o   Maintained and updated all loan and loan-related documentation, including foreign tax credit system

ANTHONY PEARL FURNITURE, Albany, NY
Credit Collector (part-time), 2003 to 2005
o   Telephone collections of past due accounts
o   Advised customers in regard to their account status and payment options
o   Credit bureau and fraud account functions. Successfully collected 75% of assigned accounts

NYC FIRST INSURANCE SERVICES, New York, NY
Claims Clerk / Customer Service, 2002 to 2003
o   Processed Homeowners, Commercial Property and Automobile Claims
o   Executed Flood, Wind, Fire and Vandalism Damage Report Acknowledgements
o   Handled loss notices, new claims, adjuster assignments and inventory loss forms

CHEMICAL BANK, New York, NY and Albany, NY
Trade Services Assistant, 2000 to 2002
o   Assisted and informed Trade Portfolio customers regarding debits and credits to their accounts
o   Managed customer files using Acumatica CRM; Maintained mailing lists for bank-sponsored seminars

Related Jobs/Careers:
(International Loans, Credit Collections)
RÉSUMÉ #29: Accounts Specialist / Accounting Supervisor (2011 U.S. Retail: $299)

WOW! RÉSUMÉS 2011-2012: Great Jobs...Extra Income...Happiness...

KEVIN AUSMUS
KEVINAUSMUS@WOWRESUMES.NET

1234 Post Street
Hanford, CT 06902
(203) 123-4567

CERTIFIED PUBLIC ACCOUNTANT / DIRECTOR OF ACCOUNTING-AUDITING

CAREER HISTORY:

DELOITTE TOUCH TOHMATSU
An International Firm of Certified Public Accountants

Audit Manager
> Hanford, CT (9/2008 to Present)
> Paris, France (9/2001 to 8/2008)
> New York, NY (1/1995 to 9/2001)

Staff Assistant, Senior Accountant, Supervisor - New York (1/1995 - 9/2001)

Responsible for auditing and diverse financial, operational and ongoing advisory services to multinational corporations

Director of Accounting and Auditing - Paris (9/2001 - 8/2008)

Managed and coordinated the main office's auditing, accounting and financial reporting, including establishing and maintaining effective internal controls to ensure quality of work and adherence to policies and procedures and guiding 75 professionals in correctly applying U.S. and European professional standards

Industry experience includes manufacturing (wire and cable, consumer products, electronic components, precision timepieces, heavy machinery, shipbuilding, textile products), oil and gas, import/export, publishing, real estate, financial services, insurance, entertainment, legal services, etc.

Representative experience includes the following:

►**Administration**
- Planned, budgeted and controlled audit work on five continents, directing up to 25 managers and other professionals at multiple-locations
- Administered a 20-person accounting and auditing support function
- Directed company employees such as internal auditors, accounting department personnel and analysts performing audit-related work

►**Planning**
- Prepared and implemented the Paris office's annual Action Plan

►**Budgeting**
- Developed corporation's multi-divisional six-month operating budget

►**Budgeting and Collection**
- Managed receivables, established billing terms, forecasted cash flows and recommended adjustments and write-offs

►**EDP**
- Developed EDP recommendations and consulted on implementation
- Guided management in centralizing and computerizing its accounting

WOW! RÉSUMÉS 2011-2012: Great Jobs...Extra Income...Happiness...

_____

KEVIN AUSMUS...Page 2

►**Cost Accounting**	• Reviewed cost accounting and inventory systems at plants, analyzed the data (including variances) generated by these systems and recommended system improvements
►**Analytical/ Financial**	• Employed budget/actual comparisons and ratio and trend analysis to identify items requiring follow-up • Performed acquisition reviews, lease versus purchase studies, reviews of property insurance coverage, compliance with loan agreements, etc. • Reviewed contracts and extracted relevant financial information
►**Accounting**	• Consulted with financial executives on the impact of completed or contemplated transactions and of new professional and SEC pronouncements • Standardized the consolidation of a $4 billion diversified corporation and trained corporate accounting personnel to perform the mechanics
►**Tax**	• Prepared or reviewed complex book/tax reconciliations • Reviewed tax returns for consistency with the financial statements
►**SEC/Financial Reporting**	• Prepared or reviewed annual and interim financial statements for reporting to management, shareholders and the SEC • Conducted technical reviews of diverse SEC filings and financial statements in the New York Report Review Department • Directed the review of financial statements prepared under U.S. and diverse European accounting principles

EDUCATION:	• MBA with distinction (first in class), Columbia University – 1995
	  Finance and Quantitative Methods
	
	• BS, University of Houston – 1993
	  Accounting

PROFESSIONAL:	• American Institute of Certified Public Accountants • New York State and Connecticut Societies of CPAs
COMMUNITY:	• Advisor, Junior Achievement • Area Coordinator, United Way
LANGUAGES:	• Fluent in English and French, and some Dutch

WOW! RÉSUMÉS 2011-2012: Great Jobs...Extra Income...Happiness...

Michaela T. Krukow, CPA, MBA

1234 Wacouta Street #123 • St. Paul, MN 55101 • 612.123.4567
mtkrukow@wowresumes.net

Versatile Accountancy

Staff Accountant ◆ *Auditor* ◆ *Financial Analyst*

Well-rounded experience in accountancy with strengths in cost accounting, reconciliations and reporting

Outstanding track record in implementing initiatives and improvements to enhance accounting systems

Adept at pinpointing discrepancies and errors to prevent continuing and costly unnecessary expenditures

Excellent analytical skills in areas of budgeting, forecasting and income streams to assist decision-making

Highly motivated, self-disciplined with drive to accept challenges and to thrive in diverse, dynamic settings

Core Competencies

Audits & Financial Statements	Systems Debugging
Accounts Receivables/Collections	General Ledger Accounting
Accounts Payables/Inventory Control	Records/System Automation
Financial Reconciliations	Audit Review Procedures
Strategic Financial Analysis	Regulatory Compliance
Financial Research Projects	Tax Planning & Preparation

Professional Experience

American Federal Bank, St. Paul, MN
Senior Staff Accountant, 2008 to Present

- Prepare Annual Report's investment schedules and notes disclosure
- Initiate audit schedules and analysis for audits and quarterly reviews
- Finalize annual budget, writing accounting policies and procedures on investments, loans, cash reconciliations and American Federal Bank Parent Corporation's accounting activities
- Ensure accounting practices and internal controls on investments, loans in accordance with Generally Accepted Accounting Principles (GAAP)
- Review and approve accounts payable vouchers
- Process purchases and sales of securities and daily Federal trading activities
- Analyze and reconcile daily Federal Reserve trading activities, monthly cash, expenses (actual vs. budget), investment and loan accounts
- Cross train all accounting associates in general accounting duties
- Interface with Bank Examiners and Tax Accountants during annual audits
- Prepare and post investment journal entries into SYSPRO Accounting Software
- Handle the closing of American Federal Bank's Subsidiary Company activities through Axapta Software

WOW! RÉSUMÉS 2011-2012: Great Jobs...Extra Income...Happiness...

Page Two   Michaela T. Krukow, CPA, MBA

AmeriMed Devices, Milwaukee, WI
Senior Consulting Financial Analyst, 2005 to 2007

- Initiated the setting up of accounting procedures on Purchase Price Variance and provide assistance in setting up a forecasting model on Purchase Price Variance
- Documented policies and procedures on Material Finance for AmeriMed's North American sites
- Ensured the forecasting and accounting procedures on Purchase Price Variance and Inventory to be in compliance with Sarbanes-Oxley and GAAP
- Reviewed Purchase Price Variance agreements in customers' contracts and determined exchange rate impacts on Inventory and Purchase Price Variance
- Analyzed and reconciled General Ledger and Sub ledger accounts for Canada and Mexico product lines
- Prepared and posted journal entries into Great Plains ERP Software

Moskowitz, Kuiper, Ross & Co., LLC, CPAs, Chicago, IL
Staff Auditor, 2004 to 2005

- Completed quarterly and annual financial statements (compilation, review and certification)
- Carried out functions of audit testing and analytic review
- Reviewed major balance sheet and income statement accounts
- Scrutinized various industries including real estate, hedge funds, manufacturing and public relations
- Executed fiduciary accounting and tax preparation

Tyson, Briggs & Company LLP (Sub-Contractor of Ernst & Young), Chicago, IL
Staff Auditor, 2003 to 2004

- Participated in the planning of audit, performing procedures to determine components of internal control
- Selected procedures to be performed and assessed control risk and determined materiality
- Performed a variety of auditing procedures and techniques to transactions and balances in the financial statements to determine existence, reasonableness and/or valuation
- Prepared working papers documenting the work performed including the completion of full disclosures

Dinatrix Manufacturing (Subsidiary of 3M Corporation), Burlington, WI
Staff / Senior Accountant, 1998 to 2001

- Reconciled balance sheet and income statement accounts
- Prepared property tax, sales and use tax returns
- Performed consolidations, currency translation, payroll processing and monthly close cycles
- Processed 401K payment administration, Section 125 healthcare expense and reimbursements

---

Education

Ohio State University, Columbus, Ohio
Master of Business Administration, 2003

University of Wisconsin, Madison, Wisconsin
Bachelor of Arts, Majors in History and Accounting, 1998

COMPUTER EXPERTISE:
Great Plains (Era Platinum and Era Explorer); MFG/PRO (QAD); ADP; FAS; ATB; Axapta, Reportsmith; Tax; Gosystem Engagement Tax; CCH Tax Researcher; BNA Tax Projection; Microsoft Word; PowerPoint; Excel; QuickBooks

---

Related Jobs/Careers:
(Staff Auditor, Senior Accountant)

WOW! RÉSUMÉS 2011-2012: Great Jobs...Extra Income...Happiness...

<u>CHAPTER 3: ACCOUNTING and FINANCE RÉSUMÉS</u>

JULIA SANCHEZ

1234 E. Camelback Road • Phoenix, AZ 85026 • (602) 123-4567 • jsanchez@wowresumes.net

Seeking a career position in the fields of

Underwriting & Auditing

BANK-----MORTGAGE-----COMPLIANCE

AREAS OF EXPERTISE

COMPLIANCE: Intensive 3 years of underwriting and regulatory compliance auditing/administration
ANALYSIS: Current on new regulations to ensure bank departments update policies and procedures
PROJECTS: Vendor management includes creating/implementing policies, procedures and maintenance
AUDITS: Monitor, prepare and review SAR, audit loan files for HMDA and CTR violations (from retail)
ADMINISTRATION: Ensure management including Directors are delivered current regulatory information

Professional Experience

HERITAGE BANK, FSB, Phoenix, AZ
Compliance Administrator/Analyst, 8/2007 to Present
• Excel in performance and results in all aspects of regulatory compliance and analysis for community bank

PUEBLO MEDICAL INSTRUMENTS, Scottsdale, AZ
Senior Internal Auditor, 1/2006 to 8/2007
• Supervised financial and operational audits of construction projects, subsidiaries and special projects

CB COMMERCIAL, Tempe, AZ
Commercial Real Estate Underwriter, 2003 to 2005
• Performed credit analyses and underwriting of income-producing commercial real estate

RBS, Bridgeport, CT
Loan Review Analyst (Consumer Lending), 2002 to 2003
• Conducted monthly loan reviews, prepared month-end reports and presented findings to Loan Review

HALIBURTON, Riyadh, Saudi Arabia
Project Auditor, 2000 to 2002
• Audited and coordinated payments of 54 pipeline construction contractors
• Project successfully completed within <u>$2 billion</u> budget; Processed $7 million to $25+ million invoices

WEBSTER BANK, Waterbury, CT
Mortgage Loan Processor, 1998 to 2000
• Prepared mortgage loan files, using Desktop Originator and Gemstone underwriting programs

Education

SACRED HEART UNIVERSITY, Fairfield, Connecticut
Bachelor of Science Degree in Business Administration, 2000

CERTIFICATION
Certified Public Accountant, State of Arizona, 2003
Certified Internal Auditor Examination, Passed, May, 2005
FHA/VA Underwriting Training class – Certificate, 2008

Computer Skills

Excel, Outlook, PowerPoint, Word, Point/Calyx, Desktop Underwriter, AS400, Impact, Encompass, SYSPRO

Related Jobs/Careers:
(Internal Auditor, Compliance Administrator)

RÉSUMÉ #32: Mortgage Underwriting / Bank Compliance (2011 U.S. Retail: $299)

WOW! RÉSUMÉS 2011-2012: Great Jobs...Extra Income...Happiness...

BLANK PAGE

-FOR NOTES-

CHAPTER 4:

<u>HIGH TECH and ENGINEERING RÉSUMÉS</u>

14 Model *WOW!* Résumés
(49 Job Titles)

<u>CREATE YOUR OWN RÉSUMÉ</u>:

If you are doing your own Résumé in the Occupational Category of <u>High Tech and Engineering</u>, you can choose from among the *WOW!* Résumés in this Chapter modeling the wording, styles, formatting, bullets, borders, etc. You can also model any of the elements in the other *WOW!* Résumés in this Book.

Complete the Guides in the Appendices including the *WOW!* Action Verbs and specific targeted Keywords (that must be researched) to fully customize and create a unique and powerful *WOW!* Résumé!

If you have purchased this Book (and thus become an automatic 1-year Member of wowresumes.net) you can get Free unrestricted downloads (Word or PDF Files) of up to 5 *WOW!* Résumés in addition to a Free download of the Guides in the Appendices for you to print out or edit on your computer.

<u>DISCOUNTED RÉSUMÉ SERVICE</u>:

If you need help to create a *WOW!* Résumé call 888-503-3133 or go to wowresumes.net to work with professional Résumé Writers who practice *WOW!* Résumé principles. Book purchasers have up to one year to avail of a 30% Instant Discount on any *WOW!* Résumé or other *WOW!* Résumé products such as *WOW!*-Card® Résumés, as well as other benefits including <u>Free Résumé Posting</u> on the ever-growing wowresumes.net Website and <u>Updating from Twitter, Facebook, LinkedIn & Google Profiles</u>. Members get <u>Free Updates for 1 year</u> on their Main Résumé and <u>up to 90% Discounts</u> on additional (2nd, 3rd, 4th, etc.) Customized Résumés to target Specific Jobs, Careers, Industries or Special Urgent Applications.

*See the Back Cover for *WOW!* Résumé Service & Free Membership Information*

WOW! RÉSUMÉS 2011-2012: Great Jobs...Extra Income...Happiness...

<u>CHAPTER 4: HIGH TECH and ENGINEERING RÉSUMÉS</u>

High Technology Rules

Information Technology (IT) is now prevalent everywhere in the modern world: information products and services that affect every aspect of communications, business, government and everyday life. Information Technology Workers (from Data Entry Clerks to Computer Network Administrators to Systems Analysts to Telecommunications Specialists to MIS Directors to Technical Support and Sales) assist individuals and organizations share and store information through computer networks and systems, the Internet and computer databases. Computer Network, Systems, and Database Administrators held some 961,200 jobs in the United States in 2008 (Bureau of Labor Statistics, U.S. Department of Labor). Of this nearly 1 million "high-tech" technical job-holders: 339,500 were Network and Computer Systems Administrators, 120,400 were Database Administrators, 292,000 were Network and Data Communications Analysts, and some 209,300 were "Computer Specialists".

Related to the prominence of science and high technology, Engineers apply the principles of science and mathematics to develop economical solutions to technical problems. The work of Engineers is the link between scientific advances and the commercial applications that meet societal, business and consumer needs. Engineers held some 1.6 million jobs in the U.S. in 2008. The <u>largest</u> Engineering specialties include Civil Engineers (278,400); Mechanical Engineers (238,700); Industrial Engineers (214,800); Electrical Engineers (157,800); Electronics Engineers, <u>except Computer</u> (143,700); Computer Hardware Engineers (74,700); Aerospace Engineers (71,600); Environmental Engineers (54,300); Chemical Engineers (31,700); Health and Safety Engineers (25,700); Materials Engineers (24,400); Petroleum Engineers (21,900); Nuclear Engineers (16,900); Biomedical Engineers (16,000); and "Other" Specialty Engineers (183,200).

For Information Technology (IT), training and education vary by occupation. Network and Computer Systems Administrators are often required to have a bachelor's degree in such fields as Computer Science, Information Science or Management Information Systems (MIS) or other degrees supplemented with experience and computer courses such as Computer Programming, Computer Engineering, Mathematics and Statistics. For Network Architect and Database Administrator jobs, some employers prefer candidates to hold a Master's in Business Administration (MBA). For Webmasters, certification and/or an associate degree may be sufficient although more advance positions may require a computer-related bachelor's degree.

Engineers almost always enter their respective occupation with a bachelor's degree in their engineering specialty, though some basic research jobs may require a graduate degree. Engineers offering their services directly to public must be licensed (required in all 50 States and the District of Columbia to become Professional Engineers or PEs).

Future Outlook

The job outlook in the United States for Computer Network, Systems, and Database Administrators is projected by the U.S. Department of Labor to grow by 30 percent through 2018 with growth varying by specialty (23% for Network and Computer Systems Administrator; 20% for Database Administrators; 53% for Network Systems and Data Communications Analysts). Positions for Web Administrators and Web Developers are projected to be 13%. Growth for all occupations will be somewhat lowered by offshore outsourcing especially to countries such as India, the Philippines, Indonesia and Malaysia.

WOW! RÉSUMÉS 2011-2012: Great Jobs...Extra Income...Happiness...

CHAPTER 4: HIGH TECH and ENGINEERING RÉSUMÉS

The job prospects in the United States in engineering are expected by the U.S. Department of Labor to be good with growth as fast as the average (11% through 2018) for all engineering occupations, varying by specialty. Biomedical Engineers are expected to experience the fastest growth at 72% while Civil Engineers are expected to have the greatest numerical increase from 278,400 to about 345,200 by 2018.

Engineering Earnings

Engineers earn some of the highest STARTING salaries among Bachelor degree holders ranging from $52,048 for Civil Engineers, to $58,766 for Mechanical Engineers, to $64,902 for Chemical Engineers, to $83,121 for Petroleum Engineers (as of July 2009, even in the midst of the U.S. economic recession, according to the Bureau of Labor Statistics, U.S. Department of Labor).

The *WOW!* Model Résumés in this Chapter include Webmaster Developer; Graphics Artist; MIS Director; Help Desk Computer Support; Social Network Specialist; Electrical Engineer; Quality Assurance Engineer; Studio/Audio Engineer; Construction Engineer/Estimator; Biotechnology Laboratory Technician; as well as Biotechnologist/Environmental Scientist.

SUDHIR JAISWAL DESHPANDE

1234 Bluffs Parkway
Colorado Springs, CO 80202

(303) 123-4567
sjdesh@wowresumes.net

ELECTRICAL ENGINEER

Lasers ◈ ***Control Systems*** ◈ ***Systems Design***

EDUCATION

Graduate Level Research at University of Colorado at Colorado Springs: Laser & Optics, 2008 -2010

Virginia Polytechnic Institute and State University, Blacksburg, VA
Bachelor of Science, Electrical Engineering, 2007
Concentration in Lasers & Control Systems

TECHNICAL SKILLS/KNOWLEDGE

Magnetic Resonance Imaging ◈ Diffraction, Fourier Optics and Imaging
Antennas: Design and Applications ◈ Computational Models & Methods
Optimization Methods for Systems and Control ◈ Digital Image Processing
COMPUTER PROFICIENCY: Orcad PSpice, Matlab, Simulink, Multisim, Cadence Virtuoso, AutoCAD
MS Project, MS Excel, MS Visio, Photoshop, Flash
PROGRAMMING: C/C++, Visual Basic, Assembly, PHP, Verilog & VHDL

ACADEMIC PROJECTS

Focusing System for Lenslet Array:
- Developed unique motor controlling circuitry to enable smart actuation
- Wrote custom software in Matlab (DAC) to control actuation

Digital Thermometer:
- Handled all aspects of display including programming and circuitry

Audio Sample Rate Converter:
- Coded from scratch in Matlab and without the use of tool boxes

ENGINEERING EXPERIENCE

U.S. AIR FORCE RESEARCH LABORATORY, Colorado Springs, CO
Electrical Engineering Researcher, 2009 to 2010
- Developed a laser profilometer with user programmable resolution on the micron scale for use in defense applications
- Wrote a standalone Matlab program that acted as a data logger to help diagnose a problematic laser; Fixed electronics

RELATED EXPERIENCE

FUJIFILM DIMATIX, Los Angeles, CA
Engineering Intern, 2007 to 2008
- Assisted Senior Engineer with hardware testing on fluid level sensor prototypes; Performed and documented tests
- Updated wetted components of ink jetting stands to meet solvent specs; Gained experience with class 100 clean room

LICENSURE

Electrical Contractor's License, State of Colorado, License No. COG-123456
Passed the Fundamentals of Engineering (FE) examination

Related Jobs/Careers:
(Electrical Designer, Research Engineering)

RÉSUMÉ #33: Electrical Engineer-Lasers / Control Systems (2011 U.S. Retail: $299)

WOW! RÉSUMÉS 2011-2012: Great Jobs...Extra Income...Happiness...

CHAPTER 4: HIGH TECH and ENGINEERING RÉSUMÉS

MARJORIE CHAN

1234 Douglas Blvd.
Roseville, CA 95678

(916) 123-4567
marjchan@wowresumes.net

OUTSTANDING CHEMIST
Research • Education • Analysis • Process Control

EDUCATION

Master of Science in Chemistry with Honors, University of California, Davis, 2008

Bachelor of Science in Chemistry (ACS Certified), San Francisco State University, 2004

HIGHLIGHTS OF QUALIFICATIONS

➢ 6 years of training and education established in diverse research environments
➢ Keen intuition, gifted at assessing the needs of and communicating well with people
➢ Passionate interest in science and the application of knowledge in everyday life
➢ Outstanding skills in analysis, research and lab technologies applied with discipline
➢ Adept at computational work utilizing ChemDraw, Mathematica, LaTeX and UNIX

RELEVANT SKILLS & EXPERIENCE

RESEARCH TRAINING
As research assistant
➢ Collaborated on synthesis of phosphocitrate including molecular modeling/dynamics:
  • Evaluated NMR spectra to detect and quantify product and its derivatives
  • Investigated IR and UV-VIS spectra to, verify connectivity and bond types
  • Performed numerous literature synthesis and successfully amended synthesis approach
  • Computed most stable structural conformations of phosphocitrate
  • Proposed incorporation of Ab Initio calculations to find global structural minia
As student assistant
➢ Aided research for mass spectroscopy graduate group:
  • Computed structural minia for sucrose molecule on UNIX/VAX system
  • Determined fragmentation peaks for sucrose in Mass Spectrometer
  • Broadened synthesis skills working two quarters in an inorganic laboratory
As chemistry tutor
➢ Tutored groups of 4 to 6 students in inorganic and physical chemistry:
  • Demystified learning techniques relying primarily on memorization
  • Incorporated the use of basic physical principles
  • Successfully interpreted quantum chemistry to non-scientists in private tutoring

EMPLOYMENT HISTORY

2009-Present	Math Tutor	Kumon Learning	Roseville, CA
2008 (Summer)	Flower Harvester	California Everlasting	Dunnigan, CA
2007	Tutor	UCD Tutorial Center	Davis, CA
2006-2007	Research Asst.	UCD Chemistry Dept.	Davis, CA
2005-2006	Student Asst. II	UCD Nutrition Dept.	Davis, CA

Related Jobs/Careers:
(Chemistry Educator, Chemical Analysis)

RÉSUMÉ #34: Research Chemist / Chemical Process Control (2011 U.S. Retail: $299)

WOW! RÉSUMÉS 2011-2012: Great Jobs...Extra Income...Happiness...

CHAPTER 4: HIGH TECH and ENGINEERING RÉSUMÉS

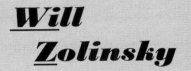

Will Zolinsky

1234 Buena Vista Street #123

Burbank, CA 91522

(818) 123-4567

wizgraphicz@wowresumes.net

MULTI-MEDIA GRAPHICS ARTIST / ILLUSTRATOR / FASHION DESIGNER

SKILLS

Adobe Illustrator
HTML
Photoshop
XHTML
InDesign
CSS Basic
Dreamweaver
Excel
Flash
Word
PowerPoint
Acrobat
ActionScript
After Effects
Cinema 4D
Quark
Avid HD
Final Cut
Pro HD
Media 100
VizRT
Pro Tools
RED Software
Combustion
Motion
DVD Studio Pro
Pilot Software
Curious Maps
Type 50 WPM

INDUSTRIES/MEDIA

Fashion
Television
Film
Comics
Architecture
Advertisement
Social Media
Photography

PROFESSIONAL WORK

SAMPLE CLIENTS, COMPANIES/ORGANIZATIONS IN NY & LA:

Stylesight.Com: Active Wear Fashion
Freelancer – Image Editing / Retouching for Trend Forecast Capsule

Triple 5 Soul: Showroom Displays for T-Shirts
Illustrator and Graphic Designer

Isaac Morris: Advertising
Freelancer / Production Assistant

Bill Donovan, Illustrator: Illustration & Photography
Personal Assistant

Gaarte.Com: Commercial Photographer/Web Developer
Freelance Illustrator / Retoucher

Fuse TV Network: Television
Assistant Broadcast Designer

Ritani New York: Advertising & Marketing
Photo Retoucher / Designer

Music Industry Online: Social Media & Music
Freelance Web Designer / Animator

Rosenberg Kolb Architects: Architecture
Marketing / Graphic Designer

Blue Man Group Productions: Film & Entertainment
After Effects Artist

EDUCATION

Stony Brook University, Stony Brook, New York
Bachelor of Arts in Studio Arts/Computer Graphics

University of Southern California, Los Angeles, CA:
Film, Photography and Computer Courses

Related Jobs/Careers:
(Multi Media, Fashion Designer)

RÉSUMÉ #35: Graphics Artist / Illustrator (2011 U.S. Retail: $299)

WOW! RÉSUMÉS 2011-2012: Great Jobs...Extra Income...Happiness...

WINTON S. KOO

1234 Linda Vista Lane #123   San Diego, CA 92101   (619) 123-4567

wskoo@wowresumes.net

Biotechnologist / Environmental Scientist / Chromatography Specialist

PROFILE HIGHLIGHTS

- Commitment and passion for clinical science and its commercial and social implications
- Highly effective and productive in working with a team with a problem-solving, goal-minded orientation
- In addition to diverse technical training, trained and experienced in Quality Control and Quality Assurance
- Extensive knowledge of biochemical techniques, analytical chemistry and success in biotech sales/support
- Excellent oral communication and written skills allowing effective interaction with people at all levels from technicians and scientists to lay people

PROFESSIONAL EXPERIENCE

COASTAL ANALYTICS, La Jolla, CA
Director of Operations, 2009 to Present
- Effectively consult with clients concerning a variety of novel scientific investigations and research
- Advise startups and established laboratories as to timely capital asset maintenance and acquisition
- Train staff and management in all aspects of analysis, instrument upkeep safety and regulations

TATLER-WILKING LABORATORIES, Thousand Oaks, CA
Chromatography Product Technologist, 2008 to 2009
- Engineered and developed new "state-of-the-art" portable UHPLC demo platform
- Completely revamped chromatography product demonstration space and cross-marketing material
- Advocated and reinforced post-sales support and created innovative "How To" Training Manuals

ALTON MEDWORKS, Calabasas, CA
Quality Control (QC) Chemist, 2007 to 2008
- Supervised team of 5 Analysts and 1 Compliance Officer, enhancing product analysis/testing
- Completed department-wide SOPs (Standard Operating Procedures) and advised R&D re designs/releases

WESTIX PHARMACEUTICALS, Sunnyvale, CA
Research Scientist, 2005 to 2007
- Managed 3500+ chemical compound library and updated application-wide toxicology data
- Co-wrote DrugMatrix chemogenomics research and bridged Informatics and Drug Discovery groups

TMILYX LABS INCORPORATED, Santa Clara, CA
Bioanalytical Chemist, 2002 to 2003
- Excelled at 24/7 analytics including instrument maintenance, performance monitoring and tuning
- Created validation reports to achieve compliance and delivered pK data in support of IND/NDA filings

TIMETRENDS BIOSCIENCES, San Diego, CA
Research Associate, 2001 to 2002
- Lead PCR and Gel Electrophoresis Analyst working under Dr. Manfred S. Liang and other scientists
- Advanced company's Satellite Science virtual research facility employing secured on-line data sharing
- Processed inter-departmental sera samples by Flow Cytometry; Implemented new research techniques

WOW! RÉSUMÉS 2011-2012: Great Jobs...Extra Income...Happiness...

WINTON S. KOO	wskoo@wowresumes.net	PAGE TWO

SPECIALIZED SKILLS

Liquid Chromatography [HPLC, UHPLC, IC, GPC/SEC, LC-MS]
Gas Chromatography [GC, HS-GC, TD-GC, GC-MS]
Flash Chromatography, solid Phase Extraction and Scale Organic Synthesis
PCR, Gel Electrophoresis and Flow Cytometry
Clinical Fields include Immunology, Serology, Hematology and Toxicology

EDUCATION

San Diego State University, San Diego, CA
Master of Science in Clinical Science, 2005

University of California at Berkeley, Berkeley, CA
Bachelor of Science in General Biology, 2001

AFFILIATIONS & LICENSES

American Chemical Society (ACS)
California Analytical Chemists Organization (CACO)
Association of Analytical Communities (AOAC)
California Association of Toxicologists (CAT)
Clinical laboratory Technologist (CA License 123456)
Medical Technologist (ASCP License 654321)

Related Jobs/Careers:
(Chromatography, Research Scientist)

WOW! RÉSUMÉS 2011-2012: Great Jobs...Extra Income...Happiness...

CHAPTER 4: HIGH TECH and ENGINEERING RÉSUMÉS

1234 56th Street; Indianapolis, IN 46204
(317) 123-4567
rrsingh@wowresumes.net

Randall Ramesh Singh

CAREER OBJECTIVE Mechanical Engineering Position in Construction / Manufacturing / Fabrication

PROFILE
♦ Dedicated to engineering discipline, results-oriented, and eager to learn
♦ Excellent problem-solving skills with capacity for leadership and team-building
♦ Outstanding computer, research, design and "roll up my sleeves" work ethic
♦ Avowed Practitioner of Sustainability Practices and Appropriate Technologies

EDUCATION
Valparaiso University, Valparaiso, IN
Master of Science in Mechanical Engineering, 5/2011

Punjab Technical University, Chandigarh Engineering College, Jalandhar, India
Bachelor in Technology, Mechanical Engineering, 2004

RELEVANT COURSES

Advanced Machine Design	Thermofluids Lab
Finite Element Methods	Vehicle Propulsion
Fluid Mechanics and Loading	Power Systems
Sustainable Energy Engineering	Tribology
Advanced Vibration Engineering	Computational Fluid Dynamics
Structural Integrity	Structural Mechanics
Management for Technology	Interfacing and Data Processing
Polymer Processing Technology	Risk and Reliability
Engineering Economics	Integrated Design / Manufacture

PROJECTS
♦ ROBOT COMPETITION: Designed/built robot to find and retrieve water on course
Awarded First Place

♦ PLUG-IN HYBRID ELECTRIC VEHICLE PROGRAM
Made presentations at Valparaiso for Nissan Motors as Program Ambassador

♦ HYDROELECTRIC WATERWHEEL
Stress Analysis and final drawing for Rural India NGO Pilot Program

SKILLS
♦ Computer Skills include SolidWorks, CATIA, Pro/Engineer, Mathcad, MATLAB
♦ Welding, joining and adhesives

WORK HISTORY
♦ DC DESIGN (INDIA): Worked with design team to customize vechicles for locals

♦ ZETO ENGINEERING LTD. (INDIA): Analysis of industrial processes/products

♦ PUNJAB TRACTOR LTD. (INDIA): HQ Manager for Marketing in 6 Indian States

ACTIVITIES
Volunteer Work for Engineers Without Borders, outside Jalandhar, India
Volunteer Math Tutor for Indianapolis Central High School

Related Jobs/Careers:
(Fabrication Engineer, Transportation Engineering)
RÉSUMÉ #37: Mechanical Engineer-Construction / Manufacturing (2011 U.S. Retail: $299)

DEMETRIUS JACKSON

1234 South Blvd. #123; Pontiac, MI 45195
(313) 123-4567
djacksonsounds@wowresumes.net

STUDIO & AUDIO ENGINEER

Technical Post-Production ◘ Talent Management ◘ Music Marketing & Promotions

Studio Business Development ◘ Agency & Representation

PROFILE

- 15+ Years' Experience in Music Industry
- Wide range of musical tastes and cultures
- Personable with outstanding networking savvy
- Knack to discover, nurture and refine talent
- Proficient in studio/audio arts and technologies

PROFESSIONAL ABILITIES

- Quick and efficient with Pro Tools HD software
- Adept in music and post-productions workflow/techniques
- Expert with soldering cables and other electronics
- Experienced Disc Jockey with basic knowledge of music theory
- Great ability to follow guidelines and interpret creative requests

EDUCATION

Detroit University, Detroit, MI
Multimedia Studies Program, 1999

Expression College for Digital Arts, Berkeley, CA
Bachelor of Applied Science, Sound Arts, 2002

TECHNICAL SKILLS

SSL 9000j	SSL 6000
Control 24	Neve VR
Icon D-Control	Yamaha DM-2000
Yamaha 02R	Yamaha SM20
Soundcraft SM 20	Tascam DM-3200
Pro Tools HD Operator Certified	Logic Studio Master Certified

PRESENT EMPLOYMENT

ASSISTANT ENGINEER, 3/2009 - Present
Ultrasonic Waves, Auburn Hills, MI
- Set up and break down mics and other gear
- Operate Pro Tools during tracking sessions
- Document setups, fill out recall sheets, general chores

PROFESSIONAL EXPERIENCE

SOUND ENGINEER, 2007
Anton Film Works, Detroit, MI
- Provided post-production sound services for 2 short movies

VOICE OVER RECORDING ARTIST, 2006
Alta Image Group, Detroit, MI
- Performed voice over recording for AT&T's new IVR System
- Recorded voice talent while on live conference calls with MIG

DIGITAL EDITOR / SOUND ENGINEER, 2005 & 2006
Luxam Motowners, Detroit, MI
- Recorded, mixed & mastered 2 completed CD album projects

CONSULTANT/OFFICE MANAGER, 2003 to 2005
Tactics Uptown, Oakland, CA
- Promoter and Marketer at Music Talent Agency

ENTREPRENEURIAL

OWNER/HEAD ENGINEER, 2007 to Present
Eastwood Studios, Pontiac, MI
- Execute engineering sessions and perform all duties to run studio

OWNER/ENGINEER/PERFORMER, 2002 to 2003
DJ the DJ Productions, Oakland, CA
- Owned and operated recording service and performed at clubs

BUSINESS APTITUDE

- Knowledgeable in the practical aspects of Intellectual Property
- Office management skills include accounting and receivables
- Experienced in telemarketing and email promotional campaigns
- Ability to raise small capital and community grants for local talent

AGENCY REPRESENTATION

- Agent for the Rapper, Bird Dogger, 2005 to 2009
- Agent for the Band, Yo Yo Mamacita, 2000 to 2002

Related Jobs/Careers:
(Talent Agent, Sound Engineer, Digital Editor)
RÉSUMÉ #38: Studio Technician / Audio Engineer / Music Business Developer (2011 U.S. Retail: $299)

WOW! RÉSUMÉS 2011-2012: Great Jobs...Extra Income...Happiness...

Svetlana Malkovich

1234 Colorado Blvd., #123
Pasadena, CA 90418

(818) 123-4567
lanamalkovich@wowresumes.net

Information Technology Quality Assurance Engineer

Qualifications Profile

✓ Wide spectrum of specialized expertise in IT Quality Assurance grounded in excellent technical & engineering education

✓ Extensive experience in varied industries impacted by the practice and strategic implementation of Information Technology

✓ Technical focus on the development and execution of both manual and automated tests to achieve mission critical goals: Functional, integration, interface, regression, stress, load, boundary, performance, acceptance, installation & usability

✓ Very knowledgeable in the software development lifecycle process, release management and defect tracking processes

✓ Adept and current in the science/advancement of test methodologies compatible with business and design specifications

✓ Consistently outstanding performance results in meeting of deliverables and adapting new business concepts thoroughly

Major Proficiencies

Analysis/Documentation of Test Results – Different Formats		SAP	PeopleSoft
Black Box Testing	Gray Box Testing	White Box Testing	Crystal Reports
Business Object	Systems Integration	Ecommerce	IBM WebSphere
ASP.NET	SQL Server	Sharepoint	Quality Center
Test Director	WinRunner	QuickTest Professional	LoadRunner
IBM Rational ClearQuest	IBM Rational ClearCase	Selenium	Perl
Microsoft Windows (XP)	UNIX	Mac OS	Oracle DB
SQLPLUS	Oracle Financials	Oracle ERP	Shell Programming
Java	FTP, TCP/IP protocols	HTML-Web	IVR
Toad	Citrix	Ajax	eChangeman

Education

University of California at Berkeley, Berkeley, CA
B.S. in Computer Science, 2002

Moscow Technical University, Moscow, Russia
M.S. in Aeronautical Engineering, 1993

Specialized Training

✓ UNIX, SQLPlus, Client/Server and Web Computing
✓ Oracle Financial Technical Foundations: successfully completed courses on Oracle Accounts Payable
✓ Oracle GL, Oracle Projects, Oracle Fixed Assets, Oracle Purchasing and Define Flexfields
✓ SAP: SAP Human Resources, SAP Master Data Management
✓ Cisco Networking Academy program: successfully completed curse on CISCO networking classes
✓ Covey Leadership Conferences: "First Things First" and "The 7 Habits of Highly Effective People"
✓ Community Classes and Meetups in Conversational and Written Mandarin (Already fluent in English and Russian)

WOW! RÉSUMÉS 2011-2012: Great Jobs...Extra Income...Happiness...

Svetlana Malkovich, **Page Two**

Professional Experience

➢ **ST. JUDE CHILDREN'S RESEARCH HOSPITAL**, Lancaster, CA
IT Specialist and Consultant (Part-time), 8/2010 to Present

PROJECT: Troubleshoot computer network and provide enhancements to database and inventory systems

SELECTED ACHIEVEMENTS:
- Analyzed organization's computer nets across departments and functions to determine inefficiencies and duplications
- Created accepted IT Project Plans in conformance to Budget and Goals of Board of Directors of Hospital and Foundation

....

➢ **LONGSHOREMAN'S UNION LOCAL NO. 2**, Long Beach, CA
QA Specialist, 1/8/2008 to 7/2010

PROJECT: Replacement of IT legacy system (Mapper/Unisys) with new, more user-friendly and web-based application

SELECTED ACHIEVEMENTS:
- Streamlined data entry processes on .Net Platform written primarily in C+; Validated results using SQL
- Formulated testing strategy and high level plans; Developed test staffing and infrastructure requirements
- Conducted functional, integration, system, regression, batch, performance and user acceptance tests
- Coordinated QA coverage with members of the development and business teams for on-going releases

....

➢ **WELLS FARGO BANK**, Walnut Creek, CA
QA Engineer , 2005 to 2007

PROJECT: Replacement of trade assignment with implementation of automated solutions for receipt and distribution

SELECTED ACHIEVEMENTS:
- Developed design specifications and coordinated testing across departments; Validated results using SQL scripts
- Documented business requirements for application changes and issues; Facilitated PAM upgrade from 6.55 to XG4

....

➢ **VERIZON WIRELESS COMMUNICATIONS**, Pleasanton, CA
QA Engineer, 2002 to 2005

PROJECT 3: Replacement of multiple legacy systems with ORACLE Financial Suite

SELECTED ACHIEVEMENTS:
- Reviewed design, conversion and interface specifications for Accounts Payable; Developed test plans & cases/test scripts
- Validated technical designs against business requirements and design documentation to generate state of the art systems

PROJECT 2: Developed system to perform all business functions of Human Resources, e.g. modules/reports/interfaces

SELECTED ACHIEVEMENTS:
- Conducted system integration and performance testing ensuring that design solutions met business requirements
- Performed technical data conversion and interface analysis; Built test plans and cases; Developed master plan

PROJECT 1: Developed web based system allowing employees to maintain hours, adjusted pay stubs (W4), etc.

SELECTED ACHIEVEMENTS:
- Managed comprehensive volume and stress tests for all software and hardware components
- Created global test plan from data analysis; Conducted load, volume and stress tests, sometimes simultaneously
- Facilitated meeting with Project Manager, Architect, Application System Engineers and Business Analysts

Related Jobs/Careers:
(IT Specialist)

WOW! RÉSUMÉS 2011-2012: Great Jobs...Extra Income...Happiness...

Leah Torrealba

1234 Stark Street #123
Portland, Oregon 97201
(503) 123-4567
leahtchica@wowresumes.net

(BIOTECHNOLOGY) LABORATORY TECHNICIAN

TECHNICAL SKILLS

Lab Operations
- Gram Staining and Characterization
- ELISA (immunoassay)
- Buffer Preparation
- Cell Culturing
- SDS-PAGE
- Streak Plating
- Serial Dilution
- PCR
- DNA Extraction/Isolation

Lab Equipment
- Gel Electrophoresis Assembly
- Microscopy
- pH Meter
- Autoclaving
- Thermal Cycler
- Pipetting
- Spectrophotometry
- Centrifuge
- Haemocytometer

Lab Practices
- Aseptic Technique
- Bioinformatics
- Good Manufacturing Practices (GMP)
- Standard Operating Procedures (SOP)

Diagnostic Tests
- Hematology
- Phlebotomy
- Blood Bank
- Bone Marrow Slides
- Urinalysis
- Coagulation
- Chemistry
- Serology

RELEVANT EXPERIENCE

Generalist Laboratory Technician, RIA Section, 2009 to Present
GlaxoSmithKline Clinical Laboratory, Portland, Oregon
- Execute thyroid panel testing (T3 uptake, T4, TSH)
- Perform early pregnancy tests, hepatitis screening & hormone tests
- Operate multichannel auto pipetting machine & gamma counter
- Process computer results transcription and document results

EDUCATION

BioHealth College, Salem, Oregon
Biotechnology Technician Certificate, 2008

Eastern Washington University, Cheney, Washington
Computer Classes in Microsoft Office and Liberal Arts, 2005 to 2007

Related Jobs/Careers:
(Laboratory Generalist, Laboratory Operations)

WOW! RÉSUMÉS 2011-2012: Great Jobs...Extra Income...Happiness...

Ralph W. May

1234 Fountain Ave #123   West Hollywood, CA 90045   (213) 123-4567

ralphwmay@wowresumes.net

Network / IT Manager-Analyst / Forensics

PROFILE

- ☑ Over 10 years' experience in the high tech industry focused on Networking and Computer Forensics
- ☑ Highly motivated, detailed and energetic professional able to meet deadlines and extreme pressure
- ☑ Outstanding interpersonal and communication skills with the ability to multitask and problem-solve
- ☑ Experience in operations, logistics, inventory and demand management, procurement & QA Testing
- ☑ Expert in Computer Forensics that have been mission-critical components to investigations/security

TECHNICAL SUMMARY

Operating Systems:
Windows Server NT/2000/2003/2008, Windows 3.x/95/98/Vista/7
Mac OS X / 9.2, Sun Solaris, Linux, UNIX, DOS, OS/2 Warp, Novell Netware
iPhone OS, Palm OS, Symbian UIQ, Android, Windows Mobile

Programming Tools:
Visual Basic, Visual InterDEV, HTML, DHTMS, ASP, JAVA, JavaScript
VBscript, ODBC, SQL, C/C++

Applications:
EnCase Forensic, EnCase Enterprise, EnCase Discovery, iConnect, kCura Relativity, Clearwell,
iPro, eCapture, Mobius, SilentRrunner, Forensic ToolKit, Exmerge, SafeBack, Veritas BackUp Exec,
SQL Plus, Toad for Oracle 9.61, HP Quality Center 9.2, MS Visio 2007, Crystal Report 7.0
NetMeeting, WebEx, WebEx Connect, MS Backoffice, MS Internet Information Server, MS Proxy Server
MS MapINFO, GFI MailEssentials, Great Plains, MAS90, QuickBooks Enterprise

Hardware: Servers, Blade Servers, Routers, Cisco Switches, Sonicwall, Watchguard Firewalls, Back Ups

EDUCATION

McGill University, Montreal, Quebec, Canada
Bachelor of Science Degrees in Statistics and Computer Science, 1999/2002

AWARDS

Outstanding Performance CAP Award, Cisco Systems, 2009
Federal Bureau of Investigation (FBI) Civilian Merit Award, 2006
Gap Corporation, Outstanding Teamwork Achievement Recognition, 2004

WOW! RÉSUMÉS 2011-2012: Great Jobs...Extra Income...Happiness...

Ralph W. May, Page Two

ralphwmay@wowresumes.net

PROFESSIONAL EXPERIENCE

RW MAY CONSULTING, INC., West Hollywood, CA
<u>Freelance Computer Forensic/IT Consultant</u>, 2009 to Present
✓ Designed and implemented the network/server environments to meet requirements of 2 web enterprises
✓ Connected iPhone and Android mobile devices to corporate mail environments along with backups
✓ Implemented and maintained an Exchange Server; Secured the network with a Sonic Firewall

CISCO SYSTEMS, San Jose, CA
<u>IT Analyst/Team Leader</u>, 2007 to 2009
✓ Developed Functional Spec Requirement documents engaging in QA testing for integration/functionality
✓ Collaborated with IT Teams to provide solutions to enable notifications to leverage Cisco frameworks
✓ Led team of 3 Specialists on 4 functional areas to provide out-of-box solution approaches/customizations
✓ Mentored Interns and led team trainings on adoption of wiki and Web 2.0 Tools with documented results
✓ Developed structured presentations and communications as a leader on the change management board

eINVESTIGATION SOLUTIONS, INC., Los Angeles, CA
<u>Computer Forensic/IT Specialist</u>, 2006 to 2007
✓ Assisted in expanding company from 2 to 4 offices with a Data Center, maintaining network and servers
✓ Implemented/maintained Microsoft Server 2005/2007, Exchange Server 2003/2007, Symantec Back Up
✓ Provided main technical support for Mac OS X, Encase and Forensic ToolKit and trained 2 Assistants
✓ Researched and created plans for VoIP technologies; Migrated the company to a VoIP Telecom system

HEWLETT PACKARD, Cupertino, CA
<u>Project Specialist</u>, 2004 to 2006
✓ Led Federal Bureau of Investigation (FBI) Project in the development and replacement of over 500 Cisco switches throughout 80 FBI U.S. and Puerto Rico locations
✓ Oversaw all aspects of the day-to-day management, offsite staging, installation, technical specifications and security clearance for FBI Project
✓ Designed, analyzed data integrity issues and warranty saving, saving HP $500,000 in warranty expenses

GAP CORPORATION, San Francisco, CA
<u>Logistics Planner</u>, 2003 to 2004
✓ Accomplished the analysis and enhancement of allocation/delivery tools in support of inventory goals
✓ Performed forecast, budget and delivery plans, communicating to Distribution and Finance departments
✓ Supported evolving store strategies, and execution and recapping of seasonal delivery frequency models

CERTIFICATIONS

CISSP (Certified Information Systems Security Professional) Certification, 2010
iConnect Administration Certification, 2009; EnCase Guidance Software Certification, 2007
AccessData Forensic Toolkit Certification, 2005

AFFILIATIONS

Association of Certified Fraud Examiners, Associate Member since 2003
L'Association International des Etudiants en Science Economique et Commerciales (AIESEC), 1997-2002

Related Jobs/Careers:
(IT Project Specialist, Computer Forensics)

WOW! RÉSUMÉS 2011-2012: Great Jobs...Extra Income...Happiness...

RICK DELHINGER
delhingerr@wowresumes.net

1234 Rosslyn Road • Houston, TX 77019 • (281) 123-4567

CONSTRUCTION MANAGER / ENGINEER / ESTIMATOR

CONSTRUCTION MANAGEMENT ABILITIES

△ Perform pre-construction site inspections; Track and schedule equipment, deliveries, timesheets, fixtures/materials
△ Ensure the achievement of quality control, the meeting of deadlines, and the harmony among workers/personnel
△ Coordinate Interior Build-outs consisting of Framing, Electrical, Plumbing, HVAC, Sheetrock, Painting, Ceilings, etc.
△ Coordinate Exterior Completion of Sidewalk, Drive, Parking, Fencing, Hardscape, Landscape, Outdoor Lighting, etc.
△ Supervise Project Foremen and Laborers; Hire and Schedule Subcontractors; Resolve field and production issues
△ Execute decisions on behalf of ownership/investors based on planning, problem-solving, regulations and leadership

ENGINEERING EXPERTISE

△ Perform drafting and drawing (AutoCAD) for Architectural, Electrical, Structural, Civil and Mechanical plans
△ Conduct on-site inspections during pre-construction, build-outs ensuring technical conformity to plans
△ Execute specific technical requirements of Operations and Maintenance (O & M) Manuals with management guide
△ Assist Project Manager, (Senior) Estimators, (Sub) Contractors in technical support and any necessary research
△ Handle and complete/review documentation such as drawing schedules, timesheets, and field and technical notes

ESTIMATION/ESTIMATION/MANUAL SKILLS

△ Analyze blueprints, specs, proposals and quotes to prepare time, cost, materials and labor estimates for bidding
△ Prepare preliminary estimates for planning purposes and detailed itemized estimates based on final plans and specs
△ Check plans/drawings and quantities for calculations accuracy; Assess cost effectiveness of products and services

WORK EXPERIENCE

Estimator/Supervisor, 2009 - Present: Excellent performance in analysis, estimation, costing and supervision
OUTDOOR, HORIZONS, Houston, TX: A large Southeast Texas commercial landscape contractor company

Project Manager, 2007 – 2009: Successfully oversaw to completion on budget 3 mid-sized developments
INTERCOASTAL MANAGEMENT GROUP, Port Arthur, TX: Construction Management of Warehouses/Industrials

Project Manager, 2006 – 2007: Managed and completed 2 simultaneous landscape and hardscape contracts
ABERJIAN & ASSOCIATES, Houston, TX: Award-winning landscape contractors with established builder history

Estimator, 2005 – 2006: Analyzed price proposals to determine price structures and assisted Project Manager
SANCHEZ & BRADFORD DRYWALL, Houston, TX: Subcontractor to Lennar Corporation and D.R. Horton

Assistant Project Manager, 2003 – 2005: Completed within budget and on schedule 2 adjoining motels
TXP CONSTRUCTION MANAGEMENT, Texas City, TX: Top ranked Commercial Contractors in Texas City

Project Manager, 2001 – 2003: Managed successful completion of 35 homes in Galena Park of South Houston
D.R. HORTON, Houston, TX: Well-run and highly profitable developer/builder in 25 states, based in Texas

EDUCATION

UNIVERSITY OF ST. THOMAS, Houston, Texas
Bachelor of Science in Construction Management, 2001

Computer Skills include MS Office (Word, Excel), AutoCAD, Accubid Change Order Pro 5, MS Project, Primavera

Related Jobs/Careers:
(Construction Estimator, Development Project Manager)
RÉSUMÉ #42: Construction Manager / Construction Engineer (2011 U.S. Retail: $329)

WOW! RÉSUMÉS 2011-2012: Great Jobs...Extra Income...Happiness...

<u>CHAPTER 4: HIGH TECH and ENGINEERING RÉSUMÉS</u>

(314) 123-4567   **LAWRENCE J. LINVILLE**   ljlinville@wowresumes.net
1234 S. Lindbergh Blvd.
St. Louis, MO 63131

MANAGEMENT INFORMATION SYSTEMS (MIS) DIRECTOR/CONSULTANT

IT'S ALL ABOUT PERFORMANCE

➢"In the Field" and "Absolutely Hands-On"; Proactive in effecting solutions to meet priorities and deliver profits◄
➢Great balance in managing people, projects and technologies (the ideal definition of MIS) that result in benefits◄
➢Work efficiently and effectively with documentable results at any moment in time to demonstrate worth/impact◄
➢Effectuate bottom-line results to cut costs, deliver performance and enhance Return-on-Investment sustainably◄

CAREER HIGHLIGHTS

➢15+ years of managing highly successful projects, building excellent and high-performing IT teams/enterprises◄
➢Special skill set of "hands-on" effective IT management, technology mastery, systems integration/best practices◄
➢Entrepreneurially and technically creative strategies with outstanding follow-through in multicultural settings◄
➢Pragmatic approaches to solving technical and organizational issues helping enterprises gain competitive edge◄
➢Varied industries include wholesale and retail products, telecommunications, call centers, banking, education◄
➢Advanced degrees (Master of Arts in Philosophy and Mathematics, Master of Business Administration - Finance)◄

TECHNICAL SKILLS

OPERATING SYSTEMS:
UNIX; Linux Flavors: CentOS, Red Hat 7.2/ES 3-4; Fedora FC4/FC5; Gentoo 2.6 15+;
Windows 2000/2003/2008; Mac OS x; Sun Solaris; Novell Netware

DATABASES:
Oracle 11i; Oracle R12; Remedy 5.0 SAP; PeopleSoft; MS Access; MS Project

HARDWARE:
Blade Servers; CISCO PIX Firewalls / VPN Concentrator; pfSense Firewalls; Coraid; VLANs; RAIDs

ACCOUNTING/FINANCE:
e-Business Suite; SYSPRO; MAS 500; Oracle Financials; One World (J.D. Edwards)

PROFESSIONAL EXPERIENCE

LENDING TREE.COM, St. Louis, Missouri
Provider of Internet search services through a combination of traffic aggregation and proprietary Websites
***Director of IT Operations**, 2008 to 2010
Responsibilities and Accomplishments:
➢ Aligned the IT goals with LendingTree.Com's core business and prioritized the projects presented to Operations
➢ Managed strategic relationships between IT and other departments and employees; Reported directly to CTO
➢ Created synergies and stabilized production environment; Reshaped IT policies, documentation and procedures
➢ Designed and managed a fully integrated Bugzilla / SVN / Wiki / MailMan / ViewVC "closed loop" code system
➢ Deployed cfengine / puppet meta-monitored Nagios-driven infrastructure for detailed monitoring/administration
➢ Effected strong focus on automation, version control, security and operational excellence in all eight data centers

WOW! RÉSUMÉS 2011-2012: Great Jobs...Extra Income...Happiness...

LAWRENCE J. LINVILLE
ljlinville@wowresumes.net
-Page Two-

PROFESSIONAL EXPERIENCE (continued)

RESTORATION HARDWARE, Columbia, Missouri
A specialty retailer of hardware, furniture, lighting, textiles and related merchandise in 30 states (105 locations)
Senior System Administrator / Consultant, 2006 to 2008
Responsibilities and Accomplishments:
➢ Designed the new generation of IT infrastructure and processes: ITIL, SAS70, IT Sarbanes-Oxley & OS controls
➢ Oversaw and successfully managed all Restoration Hardware e-Stores and updated corporate TIER 4 data center
➢ Enhanced IT SOX / Auditing; version control, change management board, problem management, version control
➢ Created automated MS DHCP/TFTP driven PXE-based installations of Solaris 10 with intelligent SVN framework

NORTH LAKES, INC., Chicago, Illinois
Wireless software maker in Midwest and Ontario, Canada
Director of Operations, 2004 to 2005
Responsibilities and Accomplishments:
➢ Documented 23% year-to year ROI increase as Director of critical IT operations for high volume wireless company
➢ Created automatic 30+ server updates and WorkTrack distribution/version control via use of custom Server tools
➢ Designed and implemented the "fault tolerant/self-healing" framework for multi-tier architecture within budget
➢ Established corporate-praised department policies and procedures for Service Level Agreements with all vendors

WEBTACTICAL SOLUTIONS, INC., Seattle Washington
B2B Data Processing / ASP / High End Lead Generation Call Center
Director of MIS, 1999 to 2002
Responsibilities and Accomplishments:
➢ Set up & managed multiple projects: B2B lead generation/telemarketing in heavy customer-driven environment
➢ Built a "super team" of 8 IT people; Redesigned the corporate data processing center from ground up within budget
➢ Architected and created a cluster of servers and scripts, policies and procedures to streamline & automate tasks
➢ Initiated, orchestrated & deployed telemarketing applications reducing production timeline from 2 weeks to 1 hour

DOTT CORPORATION, New York, New York
Designer and manufacturer of shoes, belts and leather accessories (210 employees)
Network Manager / EDI Administrator, 1997 to 1999
Responsibilities and Accomplishments:
➢ Supported corporate network and Electronic Data Interchange with Macy's, GAP, Target & other major vendors
➢ Provided daily updates, development & troubleshooting of complex corporate in-house built financial software
➢ Mastered and deployed new EDI standards for the factory environment, deploying WinFrame application suite

E-SYSTEMS, INCORPORATED, London, England
Installer of Local Area Networks and Electronic Data Interchanges throughout U.K.
MIS Director, 1995 to 1996
Responsibilities and Accomplishments:
➢ Reduced operating costs by 12% over 2 years; Negotiated a five-year service agreement, saving $75K/year
➢ Directed conversion from MAI/Basic 4 to IBM AS/400 3months ahead of schedule, saving $50K in costs

---

EDUCATION

SAINT LOUIS UNIVERSITY, JOHN COOK SCHOOL OF BUSINESS, St. Louis, Missouri
Master of Business Administration in Finance, 2004

TRINITY COLLEGE, OXFORD UNIVERSITY, Oxford, U.K.
Masters' Degrees in Philosophy and Mathematics, 1995

Related Jobs/Careers:
(Network Manager, Systems Administrator, MIS Consultant)

WOW! RÉSUMÉS 2011-2012: Great Jobs...Extra Income...Happiness...

CHAPTER 4: HIGH TECH and ENGINEERING RÉSUMÉS

Art J. Lopes, Jr.

| 1234 La Brea Ave #123 | (310) 123-4567 |
| Inglewood, CA 90301 | ajjunior@wowresumes.net |

DESKTOP / HELPDESK COMPUTER SUPPORT: TEMP OR PERMANENT

- Multiple certifications with 10 years of IT field experience, network management, network design and implementation
- Recognized excellence in desktop/helpdesk support abilities specializing in viruses, spyware, malware and remote support
- Technical support experience in various industries including telecommunications, investment banking and manufacturing
- Proven initiative, leadership and business skills in multicultural environments that contribute to organizational success

--------------AREAS OF EXPERTISE--------------

SOFTWARE:
Windows NT 4.0
Apple OS 8.x-10.x
ActivIdentity

Windows Server 2003/ 2008
Windows XP/7 (all versions)
MySQL, MS SQL 6.5/7.0
Securedoc Enterprise

Dial-up NT, Net IQ
Sametime/Remedy/Service Center
BlackBerry Desktop Manager 4.2 – 4.x
HD Encryption/SafeNet Token Utility

HARDWARE:
Compaq ProLiant

PC Setup & Deployments
HP Integrity

BlackBerry Setup & Deployments
Dell PowerEdge/Gateway 900 Series

NETWORK:

Active Directory

Network Infrastructure Design

--------------PROFESSIONAL EXPERIENCE--------------

COMPUTEMPS AGENCY, INC., Culver City, CA
Desktop / Network Support, 2 Contracts for Textile Manufacturer and Toys Distributor, 8/2010 to 7/2011
- Design and build custom server & workstations, upgrading & implementing existing hardware into new networks
- Maintain secured wireless solutions with installations of secured Virtual Private Networks using proprietary technologies

FEDERAL RESERVE BANK OF SAN FRANCISCO, San Francisco, CA
Help Desk / Desktop Technician, 2008 to 2010
- Provided critical 2nd level support to all NRAS (National Remote Access Software) clients including mobile applications
- Performed backup support for Level I when necessary and furnished dedicated support for Bank Senior Management

DEUTSCHE BANK NEW YORK, New York, NY
Help Desk Technician, Level I-II, 2003 to 2007
- Led multiple projects: the Bankers Trust and Deutsche Bank merger, and the migration process of Scudder Investments
- Supported and configured over 350 software applications using remote Timbuktu II Pro software, and software roll- outs

DHL WORLDWIDE DELIVERY, New York, NY
Help Desk Technician, Level I, 2001 to 2003
- Performed remote troubleshooting resolution or testing/analysis on all DHL computer systems, within client/server milieus
- Significant contributor in projects such as Resource Web Pages for Internal Users and for Internal Tech Support uses

INDUS INTERNATIONAL, Paramus, NJ
Desktop Support Specialist, 2000 to 2001
- Provided all levels of technical support to internal and worldwide clientele maintaining customer hardware/software

--------------EDUCATION--------------

University of Phoenix, Walnut Creek, CA: Bachelor of Science, Information Technology, 2008
CERTIFICATIONS: Microsoft Certified Professional – Windows Server 2003/2008; Systems Diagnostic Specialist, 2007;
Information Security Specialist, 2006;Networking Security Specialist, 2005; CompTIA A+ Certified, 2001 to Present

Related Jobs/Careers:
(Network Support, Tech Support, Help Desk Technician)

RÉSUMÉ #44: Help Desk / Computer Support (2011 U.S. Retail: $329)

WOW! RÉSUMÉS 2011-2012: Great Jobs...Extra Income...Happiness...

Janika Baldini

1234 Katella Ave. #123; Anaheim CA 92802; (714) 123-4567   janbaldini@wowresumes.net

WHAT I CAN OFFER A SOCIAL NETWORK OR INTERNET (MARKETING) COMPANY

❑ Unique combination of skill sets, experience and aptitude for technology, marketing and customer building

❑ Very successful formulating marketing strategy and social media approaches to exponentially grow business

❑ Strong and varied marketing experience with online, social media, entrepreneurial and mobile projects

❑ Well-rounded background and technical expertise from involvement with large corporations to start-ups

❑ Abiding commitment to the new era of the "social customer" to amplify offerings of new products/services

CAREER TRANSITION INTO MARKETING AND SOCIAL MEDIA STRATEGIES

❑ PROFESSIONAL EXPERIENCE

CROWDSWISE, INC., Fullerton, CA
A Social Media Marketing Referral Platform for Brands and Marketers
Director of Marketing, 8/2010 to Present
► Direct and execute all marketing activities including strategy, brand extension, lead generation and PR
► Plan, create and fully deploy company and product messaging geared towards brands and marketers
► Design and launch lead generation marketing strategies and campaigns with ROI benchmarking

XCERION AB, Linköping, Sweden
Hybrid Cloud Computing platform and "icloud" Cloud Computing Social Desktop and Storage Company
Marketing and Project Management Consultant, 6/2009 to 7/2010
► Created and implemented B2B and B2C marketing strategies covering online search, PR, SEO, Copy Writing, Social Media, Blogging and Mini-Site initiatives
► 300,000 new users captured and retained with customer relationship management approaches

ARDONNE, INC., Palo Alto, CA
Web to Mobile Content Technology Company
Marketing Manager, 7/2008 to 6/2009
► Headed product marketing for FastPicks, Ardonne's flagship product and service
► Designed and project-managed unique social network campaigns (including MySpace, Facebook, Twitter)
► Managed all company SEO and SEM activities with partner companies
► Directed all marketing efforts according to ROI and within budget that resulted in more than 125,000 registered users in 13-30 demographic over 6 month period

WHIZTIMES, Miami, FL
Mobile Media and Marketing Technology Firm
(Promoted) Vice President in Marketing and Business Development, 8/2006 to 6/2008
► Administered and executed sales and potential partner presentations, contracts and proposals
► Successfully launched NBA's Miami Heat's "Hot Hoopsters" mobile campaign to 2 million fan base
► Won bid and profitably introduced Fox Sports "real-time" mobile voting campaigns

WOW! RÉSUMÉS 2011-2012: Great Jobs...Extra Income...Happiness...

Janika Baldini

janbaldini@wowresumes.net   Page Two

PROFESSIONAL MARKETING EXPERIENCE
- Continued -

MASTIX, Atlanta, GA
Mobile Game Developer and Publisher
Marketing Director / IT Reviewer, 1/2006 to 8/2006
►Negotiated and handled relationships with partner brands for products including ESPN, X-Games, IMG
►Designed, wrote and managed several online sweepstakes in 2006 (ESPN Summer Games & Wimbledon)

RELATED PAST ACHIEVEMENTS AS SOFTWARE ENGINEER

☐ ADDITIONAL PROFESSIONAL EXPERIENCE

FACEBOOK, Palo Alto, CA
World's Pre-Eminent and Largest Capitalized Online Social Network
Web Applications Engineer, 4/2005 to 12/2005
►Co-developed or co-wrote various add on apps: "Places", "Photos", "Pulse"
►Developed with Mem Cache over 300 web servers
►Teamed with Product Developers to implement new functionality to existing framework
►Optimized legacy code to improve overall performance of applications
►System profiled to find bottlenecks and performed source control development
►Gained technical and cultural insights into social networking and mass behavior

MEGATEST/TERADYNE INC., San Jose, CA
Worldwide Manufacturer of Automated Test Equipment (ATE)
Software QA/Release/Build Engineer, 2002 to 2004
►Identified, tracked, debugged software defects and provided test feedback
►Developed automated test suites for new releases, verifications and system tests

EDUCATION & PROFESSIONAL DEVELOPMENT

GEORGIA TECH UNIVERSITY, Atlanta, Georgia
Master of Business Administration, Marketing, 2006

FLORIDA STATE UNIVERSITY, Tallahassee, Florida
Bachelor of Science in Computer Science, 2001

Social Media Marketing and Web 2.0 Conferences

CRM (CUSTOMER RELATIONSHIP MANAGEMENT), MARKETING AND IT SKILLS

PeopleSoft Enterprise CRM	Oracle e-Business Suite CRM
Oracle Financials	SYSPRO
SQL	Sybase
Microsoft Access	Microsoft Project
Apache Servers	Windows and Mac
Firewalls	HTML, XML, DHTML

Related Jobs/Careers:
(Social Network Marketing, Social Media, Facebook Applications)

WOW! RÉSUMÉS 2011-2012: Great Jobs...Extra Income...Happiness...

Manly Colombo
Web Master   Web Developer   Web Designer
(916) 123-4567

1234 Laguna Blvd. #123   Elk Grove, CA 95757

themanly@wowresumes.net

M A N L Y   C O L O M B O • C O M

SUMMARY:

✓ Responsible, mature, client-focused goals & benefits
✓ Tech skills learned academically & at high tech cos.
✓ Tremendous work ethic to meet budgets & deadlines
✓ Track record of innovation, leadership & management
✓ Management includes projects, people & technology
✓ Over 8 years in web design, development & marketing
✓ Experience with small businesses & start-up ventures
✓ Flexible, good listener with abilities to adapt and act
✓ Varied knowledge of industries include: Fashion, Law, Construction, Real Estate, Restaurant, Dentistry, etc.

CLIENTS & WEB SITES DEVELOPED:

☑ GreenTrikes.Com: Restaurant Delivery
☑ Peter Huber, DDS: Family Dentistry
☑ West Oakland Design, Inc: Architects
☑ O'Donnell Contractors: Construction
☑ Super Threads: Fashion Consignment
☑ Tantabaum & Associates, LLP: Law
☑ Clinton L.T. Wong, CPA: Accounting
☑ Laguna Lake Realty: Real Estate
☑ Zrii Ayurveda -- Silvia Fung: Wellness

TECH SKILLS:

PROGRAMMING:
⇨ ASP/PHP/SQL/MySQL, PERL/CGI, JavaScript
⇨ DHTML/HTML/CSS, UNIX, Linux, FileMaker
⇨ ColdFusion, Oracle, Java, C/C++

PLATFORMS:
⇨ Irix/SGI, Solaris/SUN, OS/Mac, Blackberry
⇨ Linux/DOS/WINDOWS/NT/XP

APPLICATIONS:
⇨ Photoshop, Dreamweaver, Flash, Illustrator
⇨ QuarkXPress, MS Office Suite, QuickBooks, etc.

BENEFITS FOR HIRING COMPANY/CLIENT:

► Quality consulting that leads to bottom-line profits
► Marketing strategies and campaigns for results
► Tech trouble shooting & guidance for performance
► Multiple services include copywriting & data entry
► Current on state-of-the-art web techniques
► Latest techniques in SEO and Web Marketing
► "Free" Product Catalogs, Social Networking
► Cost-effective reliable web hosting & e-commerce
► New automatic profit centers added to business
► Independent Contractor Agreement/No Payroll

EDUCATION & MISCELLANEOUS:

SAN JOSE STATE UNIVERSITY, San Jose, CA
B.S. in Computer Science, 2002

ORACLE UNIVERSITY, Palo Alto, CA
Training in Oracle Financials & CRM

LEARN IT, San Francisco, CA
Web Design & Web Programming

Math Tutor, Franklin High School, Elk Grove, CA

TESTIMONIALS:

"Manly gave our practice the high-tech boost we were looking for." - Dr. Peter Huber, Sacramento, CA

"Mr. Colombo worked on our team for almost 9 months, creating a powerful and winning image for our operations." - John O'Donnell, Contractor-Owner

"Manly Colombo is meticulous, extremely competent and a consummate professional." - T.J. Lawson, Attorney, Tantabaum & Associates, San Francisco

---

Related Jobs/Careers:
(Web Designer, Website Programmer)

RÉSUMÉ #46: Web Master / Web Developer - INDEPENDENT CONTRACTOR (2011 U.S. Retail: $319)

CHAPTER 5:

<u>HEALTHCARE, EDUCATION & MISCELLANEOUS</u> <u>RÉSUMÉS</u>

17 Model *WOW!* Résumés
(75 Job Titles)

<u>CREATE YOUR OWN RÉSUMÉ</u>:

If you are doing your own Résumé in the Occupational Categories of <u>Healthcare, Education & Miscellaneous</u>, you can choose from among the *WOW!* Résumés in this Chapter modeling the wording, styles, formatting, bullets, borders, etc. You can also model any of the elements in the other *WOW!* Résumés in this Book.

Complete the Guides in the Appendices including the *WOW!* Action Verbs and specific targeted Keywords (that must be researched) to fully customize and create a unique and powerful *WOW!* Résumé!

If you have purchased this Book (and thus become an automatic 1-year Member of wowresumes.net) you can get Free unrestricted downloads (Word or PDF Files) of up to 5 *WOW!* Résumés in addition to a Free download of the Guides in the Appendices for you to print out or edit on your computer.

<u>DISCOUNTED RÉSUMÉ SERVICE</u>:

If you need help to create a *WOW!* Résumé call 888-503-3133 or go to wowresumes.net to work with professional Résumé Writers who practice *WOW!* Résumé principles. Book purchasers have up to one year to avail of a 30% Instant Discount on any *WOW!* Résumé or other *WOW!* Résumé products such as *WOW!*-Card® Résumés, as well as other benefits including <u>Free Résumé Posting </u>on the ever-growing wowresumes.net Website and <u>Updating from Twitter, Facebook, LinkedIn & Google Profiles</u>. Members get <u>Free Updates for 1 year</u> on their Main Résumé and <u>up to 90% Discounts</u> on additional (2nd, 3rd, 4th, etc.) Customized Résumés to target Specific Jobs, Careers, Industries or Special Urgent Applications.

*See the Back Cover for *WOW!* Résumé Service & Free Membership Information*

WOW! RÉSUMÉS 2011-2012: Great Jobs...Extra Income...Happiness...

CHAPTER 5: HEALTHCARE, EDUCATION & MISCELLANEOUS RÉSUMÉS

Two Industries with 30 Million Total U.S. Jobs

This Chapter covers two of the largest industries in the United States (#1 Healthcare with 14.3 million jobs in 2008, & #2 Educational Services with 13.5 million jobs in 2008 – according to the Bureau of Labor Statistics, U.S. Department of Labor), and miscellaneous but important fields such as Entertainment and Media, Law, and Architecture.

The Healthcare industry combines medical technology and the human factor to diagnose, treat and administer care around the clock, responding to the needs of millions of people from newborns to the elderly to the terminally ill. According to the Department of Labor, there are some 595,800 establishments that make up the healthcare industry that vary in size, staffing and organizational structures: about 76% of these organizations are offices of physicians, dentists and other health care practitioners; hospitals are only 1% of all healthcare establishments but employ 35% of all workers in the industry. Nursing and residential care facilities at 11.4 % of all establishments are an important and growing segment of the health care industry employing almost 23% of all healthcare workers.

Healthcare also employs large numbers of workers in support and service occupations, and professional occupations including Physicians and Surgeons, Dentists and Registered Nurses (the 5th largest occupation in the U.S. with 2,583,770 in 2008).

The Educational Services industry is comprised of a variety of institutions that offer academic education, career and technical instruction, and other education and training to millions of students each year. The 13.5 million workers (2008) in educational services cover all aspects of education from teaching (47% of all workers in the industry are teachers) and counseling, to driving school buses to serving cafeteria food to administrative support, to managerial, to custodial, etc. Elementary School Teachers (excepting special education) numbered 1,544,300 in 2008, the 15th largest occupation in the United States according to the U.S. Department of Labor.

Entertainment and Media (broadly labeled by the U.S. Department of Labor as "Arts, Entertainment and Recreation") is a large industry that in 2008 employed almost exactly 2 million workers ranging from Actors and Athletes (Professional), to Coaches and Scouts, to Designers, Producers and Directors, to Dancers, to Media Personalities as well as various Service Occupations such as Security Guards, Cooks, Bartenders, Waiters/Waitresses, Amusement, Recreation and Casino Workers and Recreation and Fitness Workers.

Being a very litigious society, in the United States, the two main occupations in Law are substantial. There are some 759,200 Lawyers and 263,800 Paralegals and Legal Assistants. About 26 percent of Lawyers are self-employed either as partners in law firms or in solo practices. About 71 percent of Paralegals and Legal Assistants work in law firms. (2008 figures from U.S. Department of Labor)

Architects held about 141,200 jobs in 2008, 21 percent being self-employed and 68 percent in architectural, engineering and related services industry. Most Architects obtain their professional degrees through an academic Bachelor of Architecture program. Others earn a Master's degree after completing a Bachelor's degree from a different field. The median annual wages for wage-and-salary Architects were $70,320 (as of May 2008, BLS, U.S. Department of Labor). The lowest 10% earned less than $41,320 while the highest 10% earned more than $119,220.

WOW! RÉSUMÉS 2011-2012: Great Jobs...Extra Income...Happiness...

CHAPTER 5: HEALTHCARE, EDUCATION & MISCELLANEOUS RÉSUMÉS

Full Spectrum of Requirements, Wide Range of Earnings and Prospects

In the very large Healthcare industry, most workers have jobs that require less than 4 years of college education, but health diagnosing and professional treating practitioners are highly educated. Projected to generate almost 3 million new jobs through 2018, ten of the twenty fastest growing occupations are healthcare-related (50% for Home Health Aides; 46% for Personal and Home Care Aides; 40% for Medical Scientists; 39% for Physician Assistants; 38% for Skin Care Specialists; 36% for Physical Therapist Aides; 36% for Dental Hygienists; 36% for Dental Assistants; 34% for Medical Assistants; and 33% for Physical Therapist Assistants).

Wages vary widely in Healthcare from an annual median wage of $19,180 for Personal and Home Care Aides to $81,230 for Physician Assistants who of course assist Physicians who depending on specialty can earn more than $300,000 per year. The rapid growth in the elderly population is one of the main drivers to the job growth in the Healthcare industry.

Some of the most highly educated workers in the U.S. labor force are in the more than 13 million-strong Educational Services industry. About 64% of employees have at least a bachelor's degree (the minimum requirement for nearly all professional occupations in the industry). Many professional occupations in education also require a master's degree or doctorate, particularly for jobs at postsecondary institutions or in administration. Job growth in Educational Services is projected to grow about 12% through 2018 (as compared to 11% for all industries combined).

Education will have numerous openings due to its huge size and because the industry has a greater-than-average number of workers over age 55 in its various occupations set to retire, from janitors to education administrators. This age factor is also reflected in the wages/earnings of occupations in the Educational Services Industry – Education Administrators, Teachers, Counselors and Librarians – are higher than average for all occupations because Education workers tend to be older (salary seniority) and have higher levels of educational attainment. Median annual wages range from $22,700 for Teacher Assistants to $61,500 to Postsecondary Teachers.

Legal occupations will grow 15% through 2018 (with Paralegals and Legal Assistants expected to grow by 28%) but competition especially for Lawyers (90,000 increase) will be very "keen" according to the U.S. Department of Labor. Employment of Architects is projected to increase by 16% through 2018, with strong competition expected, especially for position at the most prestigious firms who are expanding internationally, especially to China and other fast developing countries.

According to the Bureau of Labor Statistics, in May 2008, Lawyers had a median annual wage of $110, 590 while Paralegals and Legal Assistants had an annual median income of $46,120.

As for Entertainment and Media, the U.S. Department of Labor projects a growth rate of 15.5% through 2018. There will be numerous openings in an industry that at the higher end features a very few megastars earning tens of millions of dollars per year to the majority of workers earning lower than average wages due to youth (45% of all workers in this industry are under 35 years old) and the seasonal nature of many industry jobs.

The *WOW!* Model Résumés in this Chapter include Registered (Travel) Nurse; Medical Doctor; Dental Hygienist; Massage Therapist; Medical Social Worker; Private Chef/Food Consultant; Actor/Dancer/Choreographer; Videographer; International Architect/Designer and Journalist.

WOW! RÉSUMÉS 2011-2012: Great Jobs...Extra Income...Happiness...

Yolanda Thomas

1234 Constitution Avenue #123   Washington D.C. 20041
(202) 123-4567   yolandathomas@wowresumes.net

ELEMENTARY SCHOOL TEACHER – GRADES K-5

PROFILE

✎ Youthful, dynamic and resourceful teacher dedicated to helping children achieve their academic and personal goals

✎ Committed educator employing innovative and established successful methods to attain a basis for lifelong learning

✎ Devoted promoter of scholastic and social development by combining fun, stimulation and challenge to be the best

✎ Adept at creating trust, positive behavior through encouragement and praise, and honoring individuality and culture

✎ Successful in producing results documented by test score improvements and enhancements in grades and conduct

CERTIFICATION

Washington D.C. Certification in Elementary Education (K-8) March 2006

Washington D.C. Certification in Early Childhood Education (K-6) December 2005

TEACHING EXPERIENCE

DAVIS ELEMENTARY SCHOOL (K-6), Washington D.C.
Fourth Grade Teacher, 2007 to Present
■ Implement all aspects of the academic curriculum in math, social studies and language arts

THURGOOD MARSHALL ELEMENTARY SCHOOL (K-6), Washington D.C.
First Grade / Fourth Grade Substitute Teacher, 2006 to 2007
■ Experience in team teaching and adapting curriculum for gifted students

SELCECTED ACHIEVEMENTS

★ Improved DC BAS and DC CAS Scores of <u>each</u> student in 4th grade class to Proficient or Advanced
★ Met with <u>every</u> student's parent(s) or guardian for Parent-Teacher Conferences (2008 – 2010)
★ Created a well-received and School District-recognized Fourth-Grade Orientation Night for Parents (2008)
★ Awarded *Excellence in Teaching Award Winner 2010* (Davis Elementary School Recipient)

ACTIVITIES

BIG BROTHERS BIG SISTERS, Washington D.C., Special Events Coordinator, 2009, 2010
DAVIS ELEMENTARY SCHOOL, Washington D.C., Social Committee Member, 2008 to Present
DISTRICT OF COLUMBIA PUBLIC SCHOOLS, Washington, D.C., PTA Member, 2007 to Present

EDUCATION

Emory University, Atlanta, Georgia, Bachelor of Arts in Educational Psychology, 2005

Howard University, Washington D.C., Certificate of Completion in Child Development & Elementary Education, 2006

Workshop: Practical Literacy Center, Vienna, Virginia: "Strengthening Reading & Writing Instructions", 2008
Seminar: TLC Continuing Education, Washington D.C.: "Maximize Your Student's and Your Own Math Skills", 2010

Related Jobs/Careers:
(Educator, Grammar School Teacher)

RÉSUMÉ #47: Teacher – Elementary School (2011 U.S. Retail: $299)

WOW! RÉSUMÉS 2011-2012: Great Jobs...Extra Income...Happiness...

CHAPTER 5: HEALTHCARE, EDUCATION & MISCELLANEOUS RÉSUMÉS

Mario De Carmine

1234 Warner Road # 123   ▪   Tempe, AZ 85281   ▪   (480) 123-4567   ▪   mariodc@wowresumes.net

---

■ PROFILE: CNA & PERSONAL CAREGIVER

→ Dedication to Career Focusing on Personal Care, Physical, Emotional and Spiritual Support
→ Skills and Training to Meet Mental Health and Social Service Needs to Elderly and Ill
→ Proficient in Providing Respite Care and Restorative Services to Clients and Patients
→ Attentiveness and Affinity for Delivering Wellness, Companionship Services and Rehabilitation
→ Background and Experience in Offering Hospice Patients and Families with Palliative Care

■ EMPLOYMENT HISTORY

PERSONAL CARE EXPERIENCE:
Personal Care Attendant / Administrative Assistant, 12/2010 to Present
TARAMED HEALTH CARE, Tempe, AZ
◆ Assist in physical therapy, exercises, stretches, ambulation and transport needs
◆ Schedule in-home visits, do filing and faxing, prepare paperwork and audit homes
◆ Assist with medication management; Do errands, meal preparation and cleaning chores

CLINICAL EXPERIENCE:
Certified Nurse Assistant, 2007 to 11/2010
DESERT SAMARITAN HEALTH CARE & REHABILITATION CENTER, Tempe, AZ
◆ Provided nursing care for the prevention of deformities and decubiti; Daily use of medical and ARJO equipment
◆ Coordinated patient care of cognitively impaired residents; Collected and reported baseline data upon admit/discharge
◆ Assisted with tube feedings; Monitored drip rates; Provided Foley care, enemas, colostomy changes, care of mature stomas
◆ Collected specimens and provided Residents with transfers using sliding board; Maintained airway clearance by oral suction

RELATED EXPERIENCE:
Executive Assistant, 2004 to 2006
CELEBRITY CLIENT (CONFIDENTIAL), New York, NY
◆ Provided executive-administrative support to Theatre Director/Producer/Actor
◆ Supervised personal finances, investments, handled household and estate affairs

Executive Assistant, 2002 to 2004
DELOITTE TOUCHE, New York, NY
◆ Provided executive-administrative support to Managing Director, 5 Senior Executives and Staff

■ EDUCATION

UNIVERSITY OF ARIZONA, Tucson, AZ
Certified Nurse Assistant Program, Certificate 3/2007

AMERICAN HEART ASSOCIATION, Phoenix, AZ, BLS Healthcare Provider, 2008
BERKELEY COLLEGE, New York, NY, Executive Secretarial Degree, 2002

■ ACCOMPLISHMENTS / IMPACT

Employee of the Month 5 times (2007 to 2010) and Employee of the Year (2009) at DESERT SAMARITAN
Cited and rewarded in Probate Court (New York) for "true, genuine and loving servitude" for the Estate of (CONFIDENTIAL)
Highly recommended by past and present clients for "outstanding service and personal care" and "being the best"

Related Jobs/Careers:
(Executive Assistant, Personal Attendant)

RÉSUMÉ #48: CNA-Certified Nursing Assistant / Personal Caregiver (2011 U.S. Retail: $299)

WOW! RÉSUMÉS 2011-2012: Great Jobs...Extra Income...Happiness...

CLARISSA PEREZ

1234 Rapid Run Road #123 • Cincinnati, OH 45203 • 513.123.4567
cperezmedasst@wowresumes.net

MEDICAL ASSISTANT
Competent, Compassionate, Industrious and Bilingual in Spanish/English

SKILL AREAS		
Back Office Medical	✓ Room Patients ✓ Pulmonary Function Tests ✓ Sterilization ✓ Autoclaving	✓ Take Vital Signs ✓ Taking Specimens ✓ Draw Blood/Venipuncture ✓ EKG, etc.
Front Office Medical	✓ Patient Processing ✓ Records Management ✓ Phones/Messaging ✓ Sending Specimens to Lab	✓ Appointments Management ✓ Prescription Refills ✓ Bookkeeping ✓ Insurance Verifications/Claims

EDUCATION

AMERICAN BUSINESS COLLEGE, Dayton, Ohio
Medical Assisting Degree, 2003

CINCINNATI CITY COLLEGE, Cincinnati, Ohio
Computer Classes and Business Courses, 2008 to 2010

RELEVANT EXPERIENCE

Medical Assistant/Intake Specialist, 2008 to Present
Blood Centers of Ohio, Cincinnati, Ohio
♦ Execute Hematocrit Checks, Check Vital Signs, Draw Blood
♦ Perform Automated Machine setups and monthly/quarterly cleanings
♦ Answer phones, make appointments and educate Donors on new/current regulations

"Ms. Perez is an outstanding employee and an even better person. She is a great asset."
- Elaine Bancroft, Office Manager, Blood Centers of Ohio: (513) 555-1000

Medical Assistant, 2003 to 2008
Medical Office of Arla de Guzman, M.D., Dayton, Ohio
♦ Excelled as Medical Assistant for Asthma & Allergy Specialist Physician
♦ Performed all Back Office duties including Vital Signs, Blood Draws & Allergy Tests
♦ Handled Front Office tasks including Phones, Insurance, Lab Orders & Office Supplies

More Reviews and References Available

"Patients and staff love Clarissa and she makes our office run like clockwork."
- Dr. Arla de Guzman: (937) 123-1000

Medical Assistant Extern, May to June 2003 (160 Hours)
Oakwood Medical Group, Dayton, Ohio

Related Jobs/Careers:
(Medical Intake Specialist, Medical Receptionist)

RÉSUMÉ #49: Medical Assistant (2011 U.S. Retail: $269)

WOW! RÉSUMÉS 2011-2012: Great Jobs...Extra Income...Happiness...

CHAPTER 5: HEALTHCARE, EDUCATION & MISCELLANEOUS RÉSUMÉS

Maxima "Maxie" Contreras, RN, BSN

(831) 123-4567
mcontrerasrn@wowresumes.net

1234 Cesar Chavez Way #123
Salinas, CA 93905

Qualifications Summary

☑ Internationally educated, tri-state (CA, NV, TX) licensed Travel Nurse with over 10 years of experience in direct patient care
☑ Outstanding clinical skills practiced and refined in hospitals, nursing homes, specialty clinics and acute/critical care settings
☑ Committed to deliver excellent patient care using a humanistic and holistic approach, emphasizing prevention and education
☑ Work extremely well as patient advocate with open lines of communication among all members of the health-care team/staff
☑ Dedicated to new learning and fresh experiences open to travel/relocate; Highly professional as organization's representative

Education/Licensure

B.S. Nursing, Cebu Doctors College, Cebu Philippines, 1998
Commission on Graduates of Foreign Nursing School Certificate, 2000
Registered Nurse – California, 2010; Registered Nurse – Nevada, 2010; Registered Nurse – Texas, 2008
Advanced Cardiac Life Support (ACLS), current; Advanced Trauma Life Support (ATLS), current

Professional Experience

Travel Nurse, 2010 to Present, ACCENT CARE NURSE STAFFING, Kaiser Hospital, San Jose, CA
❑ Care for patients (Med/Surgery Telemetry floor) acutely ill with many medical disorders from Diabetes Type 1 and 2, Pneumonia, Urinary Tract Infections, Cancer, Pancreatitis, MI, Abdominal, Orthopedic and Back Surgeries

Travel Nurse, 2008 to 2010, WESLEY/JOHNSON HEALTHCARE, Various Hospitals, San Diego, CA and Reno, NV
❑ Multiple assignments on Med/Surgery/Trauma Care Units: Cared for patients with multi-system problems and multiple diagnoses such as DM, uncontrolled, PNA, COPD, Pneumothorax; Performed IV insertions, Foley catheter & nasogastric tubes

Registered Nurse, Geriatric Care, 2004 to 2008, BRIARWOOD NURSING HOME, Houston, Texas
❑ As Senior Charge Nurse, provided nursing evaluations, initiated and implemented Plans of Care; Coordinated all aspects of patient care including medications, treatments and therapies using interdisciplinary team approach

Registered Nurse, Nurse Extern, 1998 to 2000, CEBU CITY ONCOLOGY CENTER / PI HEART CENTER, Cebu, Philippines

Selected Clinical Experience

✓Geriatric Care	✓ABG	✓Chronic Illness	✓Substance Addiction
✓IV Therapy	✓EKG	✓Coro Angiogram	✓Pacemaker Insertion
✓NGT/GT Insertion	✓Heparin Lock	✓Post-Op Therapy	✓Dialysis
✓Computer Charting	✓Meds Administration	✓Arrest Response	✓Diabetic Care

Testimonials (Sources upon Request)

"Nurse Contreras is consistently excellent with abilities to advocate for patients and represent our hospital with professionalism."

"Maxie Contreras rates an A+ as a Registered Nurse and A++ as a person, team member and caregiver."

"Extremely competent in clinical abilities, humane in personal interactions and excellent in communications."

Related Jobs/Careers:
(Geriatric Nurse, Foreign Degreed Nurse)

RÉSUMÉ #50: Registered Nurse / Travel Nurse (2011 U.S. Retail: $319)

WOW! RÉSUMÉS 2011-2012: Great Jobs...Extra Income...Happiness...

EVITA LIZA MOLIERE, M.D.

1234 South Rainbow Blvd. #123   •   Las Vegas, NV 89101
702-123-4567
elmolieremd@wowresumes.net

PRIMARY CARE / EMERGENCY / COMMUNITY PHYSICIAN
Career Summary

❑ Over 10 years' experience in Primary Care, Emergency Medicine and Community/Administrative Healthcare
❑ Superior clinical skills honed in multicultural, high-stress environments including daily and diverse rotations
❑ Outstanding interpersonal and communication skills highlighted by facility in English, Italian and Spanish
❑ Exposure and familiarity with general and unique medical conditions afflicting children, women and elderly
❑ Dedication to healthcare and preventative medicine including patient education and continuous training/learning

EDUCATION

University of Bologna School, Bologna, Italy

Doctor of Medicine, 1997
Graduate with High Honors

University of Nevada at Las Vegas, Las Vegas, NV

Post Graduate Studies, 2008 - 2009
Public Administration

Certifications

Advanced Cardiac Life Support (ACLS)
Advanced Trauma Life Support (ATLS)
American Board of Emergency Medicine (ABEM)
American Board of Family Medicine (ABFM)

Professional Licenses

Doctor of Medicine (MD) – State of Nevada
Doctor of Medicine (MD) – State of California
Doctor of Medicine (MD) – Bologna, Italy

PROFESSIONAL EXPERIENCE

"I enjoy and relish each work day that is often full of difficult cases because I connect with each person in a 'visceral' way".

Sunrise Community Medical Clinic, Las Vegas, Nevada
Primary Care Physician, 2008 to Present

■ Interact and treat disabled, medically complicated and HIV patients from at-risk and low-income groups
■ Practiced and dedicated to provide innovative and compassionate care to inner-city minority populations
■ Diagnose patients with a variety of acute conditions and deliver or arrange for immediate treatments
■ Implement preventative medicine programs to target individuals vulnerable to potential institutionalization
■ Team and cooperate with community leaders and other health care professionals for outreach & programs

WOW! RÉSUMÉS 2011-2012: Great Jobs...Extra Income...Happiness...

CHAPTER 5: HEALTHCARE, EDUCATION & MISCELLANEOUS RÉSUMÉS

EVITA LIZA MOLIERE, M.D.   elmolieremd@wowresumes.net

Professional Experience, Continued

ST. ROSE DOMINICAN HOSPITAL, Las Vegas, Nevada
Site Administrator & Primary Care Physician, 2003 to 2007
<u>75% of Position, Clinical; 25% of Position, Administrative</u>
- Conducted exams, ordered tests, prescribed medications and formulated treatments plans
- Provided preventive health care advice and psychosocial screenings and assessments
- Partnered with medical social worker, primary nurse case manager and medical assistants
- Oversaw general medical operations of site, including personnel, supervision and compliance

IBN AL BITAR HOSPITAL, MÉDICINS SANS FRONTIÈRES (MSF) / DOCTORS WITHOUT BORDERS, Baghdad, Iraq
Emergency Care Physician / Consultant, 2002 (7 months), 2007 (6months)
- Examined between 240 to 300 patients per 24 hour shift on rotation in ER and "policlinics"
- Implemented quality control and quality management practices according to ISO guidelines
- Conducted monthly seminars and case reports as foundation and recommendations for training

MISERICORDIA DI VAGLIA, Florence, Italy
Ambulance Physician, 2000 to 2002
- Performed duties as the only physician in non-profit clinic in suburban/outer Florence
- Responded to emergencies or urgent medical conditions such as stroke and cardiac cases
- Made house calls and provided information and consultation on general health issues/prevention

STENONE IMMIGRANT'S MEDICAL CENTER, Florence, Italy
General Practitioner, 1998 to 2000
- Consulted and treated immigrants from various countries from Middle East with diverse medical needs
- Applied principles and treatments in family practice of different social groups including children and elderly

---

RESEARCH/SCHOLARSHIP

"Chronic Fatigue Syndrome", Graduation Thesis, 1997
University of Bologna Medical School, Bologna, Italy

Malaki, J., and <u>Moliere, E.L.</u>, "PTSD (Post Traumatic Stress Disorder), Asthma and Allergies in School Age Children in Urban War Environments", presented at and published in the proceedings of The International Symposium of Emergency Medicine, Rome, Italy, December 5-7, Vol. 2, 2:18-41, 2002

"Emergency Care Sterilization Procedures", Co-Authored Bilingual Pamphlet approved by Iraqi Health Ministry, 2007

Related Jobs/Careers:
(Physician, Medical General Practitioner)

WOW! RÉSUMÉS 2011-2012: Great Jobs...Extra Income...Happiness...

CHAPTER 5: HEALTHCARE, EDUCATION & MISCELLANEOUS RÉSUMÉS

VINCHIA O. CHU
chiachu@wowresumes.net
915-123-4567

1234 Westwind Drive #123   El Paso, TX 79903

Part-Time or Full-Time
DENTAL HYGIENIST

CAREER PROFILE

☑ Ability to work well in fast-paced environments
☑ Training and personality to team with professionals
☑ Experience working with children and elderly

☑ Organized, highly motivated and detailed-oriented
☑ Outstanding communications skills and patient management
☑ Available to substitute on short notice and part-time

SKILLS & QUALIFICATIONS

Dental Hygiene Skills:

- Periodontal Assessment
- Oral Cancer Screening
- Scaling and Root Planning
- Irrigation

- Restorative/Aesthetic Screening
- Coronal Polishing
- Amalgam Polishing
- Nutritional Counseling

- Medical History Review
- Sealants and Fluoride Treatment
- Sub Gingival Curettage
- Patient Dental Education

Back/Front Office Qualifications:

- Setting up Patient Rooms
- General Office Management
- Insurance Claims/Verifications

- X-rays, Conventional, Digital, Panoramic
- Making and Confirming Appointments
- Updating Charts for Recall Patients

- Sterilization of Instruments
- Making Charts for New Patients
- Billing and Patient Relations

PROFESSIONAL EXPERIENCE

DOCTORS RODRIGUEZ AND CHANG GENERAL DENTISTRY, El Paso, TX
Registered Dental Hygienist, 7/2010 to Present
■ Excel in duties including health history reviews, probing, bitewings, prophylaxis, full scale debridement, SRP and Coronal Polishing

TOWN AND COUNTRY DENTISTRY, Los Angeles, CA
Registered Dental Hygienist, 9/2008 to 5/2010
■ Performed primary duties including histories, probing, digital bitewings, local anesthetic, prophylaxis, SRP and Fluoride Treatments

EDUCATION/LICENSURE/DEVELOPMENT

SANTA BARBARA CITY COLLEGE, Santa Barbara, CA
Associate of Science Degree in Dental Hygiene, 5/2007

CALIFORNIA STATE POLYTECHNIC UNIVERSITY AT POMONA, Pomona, CA
Bachelor of Science Degree in Computer Science, 5/2003

Texas Registered Dental Hygienist, (6/2010 – Current); California Registered Dental Hygienist (7/2008 – Current)
Licensed for Local Anesthesia, Nitrous Oxide, Tissue Curettage
CPR/BLS License (2/2008 – Current); Volunteer Dental Hygienist at El Paso Veteran's Administration (2010)

Related Jobs/Careers:
(Dental Office, Dental Assistant)

RÉSUMÉ #52: Dental Hygienist Part-Time/Full-Time (2011 U.S. Retail: $269)

WOW! RÉSUMÉS 2011-2012: Great Jobs...Extra Income...Happiness...

CHAPTER 5: HEALTHCARE, EDUCATION & MISCELLANEOUS RÉSUMÉS

Jaime R. Galarde
12134 Victoria Avenue #123
Riverside, CA 92503

Social Worker / Counselor
(951) 123-4567
jgalardeusa@wowresumes.net

SOCIAL WORK PHILOSOPHY

To enhance the quality of life for "at-risk" populations including the homeless, the poor and frail elderly, and other stressed and distressed groups in society, especially veterans: I believe personal caring is the key in providing community outreach. Through interdisciplinary approaches there can be prevention, intervention and life-enhancement. The costs to society are minimized with the implementation of cost-effective humane programs.

CAREER SUMMARY

- 10 years' experience as In-Patient Medical Social Worker, 4 years as Adult Day Health Care (ADHC) Social Worker
- Expertise in performing Individual Plan of Care (IPC) Assessments including 6-month Psychosocial Evaluations
- Adept at conducting group therapy sessions in various topics including fear, anxiety, anxiety, self-esteem, aging
- Advanced Degree (Master's in Social Work) and Research Experience in Sociology, fully Certified and Trained
- Administrative Skills include Microsoft Word, Excel, Access, PowerPoint, Internet, Typing 65 Words Per Minute

---

EXPERIENCE

Moreno Valley Health Center, *Moreno Valley, CA*   *2009 to Present*
MEDICAL SOCIAL WORKER

Duties:

- Complete psychosocial assessments for in-patients within 48 hours of admission
- Assist patients in general medicine, intensive care and the emergency room
- Work with Case Managers to ensure medical compliance; Make referrals for community resources

Impact/Accomplishments:

- Advocate for elderly clients especially non-English speaking seniors needing Access Services and housing
- Provide empathetic one-on-one interviews with medical patients, assisting them to make informed decisions

Rhoda Harriman Adult Day Care (ADHC), *Corona, CA*   *2007 to 2009*
ADHC SOCIAL WORKER

Duties:

- Provided social services, completed home visits & ensured medical criteria met Title 22 admission standards
- Completed according to Individual Plan of Care (IPC), initial , quarterly and 6-month psychosocial assessments
- Worked toward providing intervention which addressed problems identified on IPCs to enhance quality of life

Impact/Accomplishments:

- Successfully facilitated group therapy for participants on topics including function-decline and aging process
- Identified and provided counseling for clients with problems of loneliness, depression, alienation, isolation, etc.

WOW! RÉSUMÉS 2011-2012: Great Jobs...Extra Income...Happiness...

Jaime R. Galarde

jgalardeusa@wowresumes.net

Page Two

EXPERIENCE (Continued)

Kaiser Hospital, Los Angeles, CA   *2006 to 2007*
MEDICAL SOCIAL WORKER
Duties:
- Completed initial and 6-month psychosocial assessments for dialysis and cystic fibrosis patients
- Provided sensitive one-on-one initial assessment for dialysis (End Stage Renal Disease ESRD) patients
- Followed-up on communications and documentation for cystic fibrosis clinic patients, including referrals

Impact/Accomplishments:
- Ensured patient compliance by education on importance of maintaining their health with at-home procedures
- Excelled on Health Connect Software system, facilitating efficiencies and training new staff on computer system

San Bernardino Veteran Resource Center, San Bernardino, CA   *2002 to 2006*
READJUSTMENT SOCIAL WORKER
Duties:
- Worked w/multi-disciplinary team assisting combat vets make successful transition from military to civilian life
- Provided individual and group counseling, facilitated group therapy and provided community referrals and info
- Assisted individual veterans to regain mental health as well as stability in their homes, families and communities

Impact/Accomplishments:
- Taught well-received "Life Skills" Class to Veterans and their families that addressed financial/emotional issues
- Awarded Plaque of Accomplishments as Coordinator and Facilitator of Group Therapy for Veterans with PTSD

EDUCATION / CERTIFICATION / AFFILIATIONS

California State University, East Bay, Hayward, CA
MASTER'S DEGREE IN SOCIAL WORK (MSW), June 1999, G.P.A. 3.9/4.0

University of California at Santa Barbara, Santa Barbara, CA
BACHELOR OF SCIENCE (B.S.) IN SOCIOLOGY, June 1990

Riverside Junior College, Riverside, CA
CHEMICAL DEPENDENCY CERTIFICATE (June 2010) G.P.A. 3.7

Member, National Association of Social Workers (NASW) since 2000
Member, California Association of Alcohol/Drug Educators (CAADE)

Honorable Discharge from United States Army (1987)
Life-Time Member of Disabled American Veterans and Member of California Veterans
80% Service Connected Disabled Veteran

Related Jobs/Careers:
(Group Therapy Coordinator, Readjustment Counselor, Social Worker)
RÉSUMÉ #53: Medical Social Worker [Page 2 of 2] (2011 U.S. Retail: $349)

WOW! RÉSUMÉS 2011-2012: Great Jobs...Extra Income...Happiness...

CHAPTER 5: HEALTHCARE, EDUCATION & MISCELLANEOUS RÉSUMÉS

Zara
Saito

1234 Kapiolani Blvd. #123
Honolulu, HI 96813
(808) 123-4567
zarasmassage@wowresumes.net

MASSAGE / PHYSICAL THERAPIST & LIFE COACH

SKILLS

Swedish
Foot Reflexology
Deep Tissue
Polarity Therapy
Sports Massage
Acupressure
Neuromuscular
Shiatsu
Trigger Point
Aroma Therapy
Myofascial Release
Salt Glows
Paraffin for Hands & Feet
Cranial Sacral
Joint Mobilization
Hot & Cold Stone Therapy
Range of Motion
Body Clay Masks

RELATED SERVICES

Back, Arms & Legs Waxing
Body Wraps
Infrared Dry Sauna

PRICING/PROTOCOL

$80.00 Per Hour of Massage

$25 Per Hour Infrared Sauna

Nutrition/Life Coaching by
Appointment

Professionally Draped
during Massage

PROFESSIONAL WORK

ZaraS Bodies in Paradise, Honolulu, Hawaii
Massage Therapist / Life Coach, 2008 to Present
❧ Provide wondrous mobile/private services to local clients & tourists
❧ Formulate and administer nutrition/exercise/relaxation programs
❧ Coach, motivate and counsel professional and weekend athletes

University of Hawaii at West Oahu, Honolulu, Hawaii
Assistant Athletic Trainer, Women's Athletic Dept., 2006 to 2008
❧ Prepared athletes for games and practices including taping/bracing
❧ Administered active and passive manual therapeutic exercises
❧ Conferred with certified athletic trainers & staff re: treatments

Santa Fe School of Massage, Santa Fe, New Mexico
Massage Therapist / Instructor, 2003 to 2006
❧ Taught the practice and arts of Shiatsu and Swedish Massage
❧ Developed and practiced programs in mineral & stone therapies

Albuquerque Center of Physical Therapy, Albuquerque, New Mexico
Physical Therapist, 2001 to 2003
❧ Performed rehabilitative and occupational therapy treatments

CREDO/MODALITIES

"Body Heart and Soul in all Great Traditions of East and West"
Yoga
Meditation
Hypnotherapy
Biofeedback
Raw Foods Nutrition

EDUCATION

University of New Mexico, Albuquerque , New Mexico
Bachelor of Science in Physical Therapy, 2000

Santa Fe School of Massage, Santa Fe, New Mexico, Certificate, 1998
Acupuncture School of New Mexico, Santa Fe, NM, Certificate, 1993

Related Jobs/Careers:
(Athletic Trainer, Massage Instructor, Masseuse)
RÉSUMÉ #54: Massage Therapist / Physical Therapist / Life Coach (2011 U.S. Retail: $299)

WOW! RÉSUMÉS 2011-2012: Great Jobs...Extra Income...Happiness...

Marianne Dushert

1234 Canal Street   New Orleans, LA 70012   (504) 123-4567   mdushertchef@wowresumes.net

(Private) Chef / Manager / Consultant
◆◆◆◆◆

❙●❙ SUMMARY ❙●❙

- ◆ 20 Years Successful Experience in Food & Beverage Industry as Cook, Chef, Manager and Consultant
- ◆ Extremely hard working, dependable, knowledgeable and oriented toward greatness of team/organization
- ◆ Familiarity and expertise in high volume casual, fine dining, banquets and catering, country club and hotel
- ◆ Skilled in spread sheets, data transmittal, inventory, ordering/receiving, scheduling, cost control, menus
- ◆ Experience as Front of House Manager and as Back of House Supervisor in dynamic multicultural settings

❙●❙ HIGHLIGHTS ❙●❙

- ◆ Met consistent efficiencies in operations and business targets of (average) 30% to 33% food cost management
- ◆ Successfully participated, engaged and contributed to eight new restaurant openings (mostly as a Consultant)
- ◆ Mentored and co-developed under Argentinean, Austrian, English, German, Italian, Jewish and Swedish chefs
- ◆ In catering & banquets, achieved recognition for remote/multi-venue production with 4-7 simultaneous events
- ◆ In sales and management, attained 70% to 150% increase in sales and clientele in 2 high volume renovations
- ◆ In consulting and management services, innovated & implemented promotions to increase product/service sales

❙●❙ CAREER SKILLS

- ◆ Management expertise in products, personnel, technologies, purchasing
- ◆ Development and implementation of inventories (from $5K to $100+K)
- ◆ Computer Point of Sales Literacy, MS Office Suite, Squirrel, Aloha, Micros
- ◆ Menu Creations from Casual to Conference Center to Holiday to Fine Dining

❙●❙ BASIC SKILLS

- ◆ Serve Safe Certified with basic mastery of cooking philosophy and techniques
- ◆ Preparation of entrees for carry-outs, as well as portion packaging and storage
- ◆ Knowledge and preparation of exotic foods, including wild game and preserves

❙●❙ SPECIALTIES

- ◆ International and regional cuisines of Northern and Central Europe and Argentina
- ◆ American West and mountain wild game and South American seafood including riverside
- ◆ German and French baking/desserts/sauces, as well special/allergy specific diet foods

❙●❙ WORK HISTORY

THE UDDER FACTORY & FLAVORS, LLC, Great Falls, Montana
Food and Business Consultant, 8/2010 to Present
- ◆ Opened new restaurant in downtown Great Falls specializing in cheeses and Midwest cuisine

WOW! RÉSUMÉS 2011-2012: Great Jobs...Extra Income...Happiness...

Marianne Dushert
Page Two

mdushertchef@wowresumes.net

🍽 WORK HISTORY (continued)

RIVER BIRCH LODGE, Winston Salem, North Carolina
Executive Chef/Consultant, 6/2009 to 7/2010
◆ Wrote, priced and implemented menus, standardizing recipes; Hired/trained kitchen staff; Developed food cost analysis

WIT'S END RANCH, RESORT & SPA, Bayfield, Colorado
Executive Chef, 1/2008 to 5/2009
◆ Performed BOH at a 4-star level resort including hiring, training, scheduling, ordering, inventory and daily operations

THE FAMOUS STANLEY HOTEL, Estes Park, Colorado
Restaurant Manager, 10/2006 to 1/2008
◆ At 3-star level establishment hired/trained all FOH service staff and bartenders, increasing bar and food sales 30%

PEACEFUL VALLEY RANCH, Lyons, Colorado
Executive Chef/F&B Director, 3/2005 to 7/2005 and 3/2006 to 9/2006
◆ Expertly managed FOH/BOH staff, food and beverage departments; performing successful weddings & catered events

SCHULER'S RESTAURANT (EST. 1909), Marshall, Michigan
Interim Executive Chef, 5/2004 to 12/2004
◆ In AAA 3-Diamond upscale historic restaurant ($4m+/yr/sale) managed menus, purchasing, inventory and staff of 43

GULF MARINE YACHTS CHARTER & DINING CRUISES, New Orleans, Louisiana
Executive Chef, 5/2002 to 1/2004
◆ Developed menus, established and maintained purveyor accounts in fast-paced environment serving upscale clients

VARIOUS RESTAURANTS, HOTELS AND PRIVATE ESTATES, U.S., Europe, South America
Private Chef, Cook, Steward, Bookkeeper, Au Pair, Waitress, 1990 to 2002
◆ Excelled in varied food and beverage, and customer service positions, gaining practical and technical knowledge

🍽 TESTIMONIALS/REVIEWS

"... Ms. Dushert created one of the most exquisite cuisines I have relished on a professional writing trip. Her expertise of Colorado regional dishes is startling. The original gourmet combinations of trout and wild game were savory delights."
Eleanor Wallabee, Associate Editor, Southern Desires Magazine, El Paso, Texas

"Chef Dushert displays her passion for local cuisine inherited from the DNA of an iconoclastic grandmother. She has discovered a balance between exotic foods and local atmosphere. Her forte is a mix of Continental and Southwestern"
Alan Mann, Food Writer and Critic, Travel West America, Denver, Colorado

"Marianne Dushert is a talent and a treasure. She will be an asset and a performer for any organization who will be fortunate enough to nab her. She is gifted in a down-to-earth and reassuring way. She is both charming and competent."
Roy Admunson, Co-Owner and Partner, Alley Cat Bar & Grill, New Orleans, Louisiana

🍽 EDUCATION

LOUISIANA CULINARY ACADEMY, New Orleans, Louisiana
A.O.S. Degree, 1991

Related Jobs/Careers:
(Executive Chef, Restaurant Manager, Food & Beverage Director)

WOW! RÉSUMÉS 2011-2012: Great Jobs...Extra Income...Happiness...

Jackson Breyer

1234 Candelaria Road #123 ■ Albuquerque, NM 87109 ■ (505) 123-4567 ■ jackbreyer@wowresumes.net

VIDEOGRAPHER – PHOTOGRAPHER – GRAPHICS ARTIST

PROFESSIONAL SUMMARY

☑ 10 Creative Years as Motion Graphic Designer, Video Editor, Photographer

☑ Outstanding communications, organizational and business planning skills

☑ Award-winning Freelance Work and Management-Praised Company Work

☑ State-of-the-Art Technical Skills honed from education and practice/work

☑ Eager and able to work with, teach and learn from other Creative Artists

EXPERTISE & PROFICIENCIES

✓Superior abilities in Adobe Photoshop and After Effects
✓Strong skills in Final Cut Pro including color correction/audio mixing
✓Solid skills in compression for video and the web, H.264, FLV, F4V, etc.
✓Experienced in high definition, HDV, DVCPROHD formats
✓Highly proficient in flash development and animation
✓Well-practiced skills in shooting camera and recording audio
✓Knowledgeable and proven to hand code XHTML and CSS
✓Programs include Flash/AS2, Dreamweaver, CS5, Compressor, MS Office
✓Qualified and experienced in marketing, promotions & accounting

SELECTED FREELANCE JOBS

➥ Film & Documentary Shorts: *City of Enchantment*; *Spirits of the Ages* shown at University of New Mexico; *Running with Dogs*, comedy, 2006 to 2010

➥ Corporate Video and Multimedia Presentations: Wells Fargo, Bank of Albuquerque, Galles Chevrolet, Keshet Dance Company, 2007 to 2009

➥ Audio Editing: University of New Mexico Lobos NCAA Men's Basketball, 2009; Kob-TV4 Main Station, 2008 to 2009

➥ DVD Creation and Commercial Video Production: Mesa Wind Power DVD for national and global distribution, 2008

COMPANY EMPLOYMENT

➥ **NEW MEXICO STATE FAIR**, Albuquerque, New Mexico
Motion Graphic Designer/Senior Pro Ad Operator, 2005 to Present
Adroit at meeting State Fair Annual goals in dispensing over $100K of multimedia advertising and educational programs
Design, produce and animate original advertisements for pre-State Fair events and during Summer and Fall State Fair fortnights
Communicate, collaborate and coordinate with State Fair technicians, Management, State Officials and State Fair Corporate Sponsors

➥ **IMACHINATIONS MULTIMEDIA**, Pittsburgh, Pennsylvania
Multimedia Contractor, 2004 to 2005
Performed project management in web, motion graphics and video production; Contributed to company profitability and public relations

EDUCATION

CARNEGIE MELLON UNIVERSITY, Pittsburgh, Pennsylvania
Bachelor of Arts Degree in Cinema/Television, 1999

CENTRAL NEW MEXICO COMMUNITY COLLEGE, Albuquerque, New Mexico
Internet, Media and Arts Classes, 2007 to 2009

Related Jobs/Careers:
(Multimedia Artist, Graphics Artist)

WOW! RÉSUMÉS 2011-2012: Great Jobs...Extra Income...Happiness...

CHAPTER 5: HEALTHCARE, EDUCATION & MISCELLANEOUS RÉSUMÉS

Isaac Cole Jones   icjonesart@wowresumes.net

1234 East Hopkins Avenue #123   ❈   Aspen, CO 81611   ❈   (970) 123-4567

ACTOR   DANCER   CHOREOGRAPHER   PERFORMER   TEACHER

PROFILE

Dance →→ Afro-Haitian-Caribbean, Ballet, Modern, Jazz
Acting →→ Musical Theatre, Improvisation
Singing →→ Blues, Gospel, Jazz, Soul

EXPERIENCE

Dance:

2010	Choreographer for Aspen Music Festival "Mountain Climbers"
2009	Hip-Hop Performer in Brazilian Athletic Shoe Commercial By Blue Horizon Films for Azevedo Casting
2004 - 2008	Guest Artist appearances with Colorado Dance Theatre, Aspen, CO
2004	Performer in "Millennium Glitz" at Silver Legacy, Reno, NV

Theatre:

2009	Guest Choreographer for Winter Concert at Boulder High School, CO
2007	Solo Performance as "Bo Jangling" at Nevada State Fair, Reno, NV
2007	Featured as "Bo Jangling" at Lyon County Fair, Fernley, NV
2007	Guest Artist/Composer at Harrah's Music Exhibition, Reno, NV
2006	Guest Choreographer for "Westward Ho" at Boulder, CO Opera House

Teaching:

2009	Hip-Hop Instructor at School of the Arts, Boulder, CO
2008	Guest Instructor/Choreographer, School of the Arts, Boulder, CO
2003 - 2007	Jazz Instructor at Murray's Dance Studio, Denver, CO

EDUCATION

2003 - 2008	TRAINING & DEVELOPMENT: Willie Stums (Jazz); Dan Zmuda, Jorge Ruiz and Alberto Ligaya (Ballet)
1998 - 2001	The City University of New York (CUNY), New York, New York Musical Arts Major with Minor in Educational Psychology

Related Jobs/Careers:
(Choreographer, Dancer, Dance Instructor)

RÉSUMÉ #57: Actor / Creative Artist / Performer (2011 U.S. Retail: $299)

WOW! RÉSUMÉS 2011-2012: Great Jobs...Extra Income...Happiness...

Willie Suarez
suarezw@wowresumes.net

1234 Marietta Road #123   Atlanta, GA 30311   (404) 123-4567

SECURITY / LAW ENFORCEMENT
City   State   Federal   Private

PROFILE

★ Highly competent and rigorously trained professional dedicated to the discipline and career of security and law enforcement
★ Results-oriented performer in the "field" and office with management and supervisory experience able to work alone or in a team
★ Excellent analytical skills with refined and proven situational problem-solving skills executed in dynamic/pressure conditions
★ Repeatedly commended for consistently outstanding performance in the private/commercial sector as well as in the U.S. Army

AREAS OF STRENGTH

■ Investigative Techniques	■ Conflict Resolution	■ Emergency Response	■ Search & Seizure
■ Physical Security	■ Theft Prevention	■ Technical Surveillance	■ Anti-Terrorism
■ Training & Supervision	■ Resource Management	■ Physical Assessment	■ Budget Administration

PROFESSIONAL EXPERIENCE

SOUTH GUARD SECURITY, Atlanta, Georgia
Security Officer/Supervisor/Manager, 2007 to Present
■ Secure client facilities/properties including fire alarm and maintenance systems; Conduct investigations, training and supervision

CONSOLIDATED MASTER SECURITY SERVICES, Miami, Florida
Security Officer / Company Investigator-Auditor, 2005 to 2007
■ Conducted security patrols and surveillance in large warehouses/port facilities including emergency response & criminal interdictions

RELATED EXPERIENCE (UNITED STATES ARMY)

UNITED STATES ARMY & UNITED STATES ARMY RESERVE, Kandahar, Afghanistan & Fort Benning, Columbus, Georgia
First Lieutenant/Signal Officer, 2002 to 2003 and 2004 to 2005
■ Excelled as Platoon Leader in operations, communications, maintenance, supply, personnel and tactical deployments
■ Responsible for health, morale, training, discipline and safety of all Soldiers; Maintained equipment worth over $50 million

AWARDS & RECOGNITION

★ Army Commendation Medal; Army Achievement Medals (3)
★ Physical Fitness Badge / Platinum Physical Fitness Award

MILITARY EDUCATION

CECOM Certified in Advanced Routing, IT Networking, Cisco Routing & VOIP (Voice Over Internet Protocol)
Leadership Development and Assessment Course, (Signal Officer Basic Course), Airborne School, Combat Lifesaver Certified (2004)

(CIVILIAN) EDUCATION/CERTIFICATION

MERCER UNIVERSITY, Atlanta Georgia
B.A. in Political Science with concentration in Criminal Justice and a minor in Psychology, 2010

Georgia Guard Card certified through Bureau of Security and Investigative Services, Current

Cleared for Top Secret Information with Single Scope Background Investigation (TS/SSBI)

Related Jobs/Careers:
(Security Officer, Security Investigator, Anti-Terrorism)

RÉSUMÉ #58: Law Enforcement / Security Management w/Military Experience (2011 U.S. Retail: $299)

WOW! RÉSUMÉS 2011-2012: Great Jobs...Extra Income...Happiness...

CHAPTER 5: HEALTHCARE, EDUCATION & MISCELLANEOUS RÉSUMÉS

RUTHERFORD A. LIDDELL, J.D., M.B.A.

1234 Ledbetter Drive, Suite 100	Dallas, TX 75203 (214) 123-4000	rutherford@liddelatty.com

PROFILE / BACKGROUND

EMPLOYMENT & LABOR LAW

ATTORNEY   ARBITRATOR/MEDIATOR   LITIGATOR   EDUCATOR

Skilled litigation and consulting Attorney with extensive experience in state and federal courts in diverse areas of the law, specializing in Employment and Labor Law. Armed with an MBA and starting as a Human Resources Manager at Fortune 500 Firms Motorola and Texas Instruments, entered into Law Practice as private Attorney and have become Partner in top Dallas, Texas Labor Law Firms.

CORE EXPERTISE

Labor & Employment Law	Age Discrimination in Employment	Americans with Disabilities Act	Covenants Not To Compete
Disability Discrimination	Employment Breach of Contract	Employment Discrimination	Employment Termination
Equal Employment	Executive Severance Contracts	Family & Medical Leave Act	Sexual Harassment
Reductions in Force	Title VII Discrimination	Wrongful Termination	Wage and Hour Law
Whistleblower Litigation	Uniformed Services Employment and Reemployment Rights Act		Commercial Litigation

KEY ACCOMPLISHMENTS

AS ATTORNEY:
Appeared in over 100 United States, Texas and California court cases; litigated against Fortune 500 Corporations; Involved in high-profile cases that received national media attention such as *Mazola, et al v. Frontier* (employment sexual assault by a discharged employee), *Weston v. Planet Hollywood* (wrongful termination) and *In The Matter of TXZ* (equal employment in a Texas Maquiladora).

Successfully negotiated Law Firm's contracts; Provided effective input in grievance management, business unit productivity and employment planning; Resolved all discrimination complaints and charges and directed the Law Firm's Affirmative Action Plan (AAP).

AS ARBITRATOR/MEDIATOR:
Acted as Arbitrator as member of the American Arbitration Association's Labor Panel, a Hearing Officer for Texas State Board of Education, for California labor Relations Board and the U.S. Department of the Interior. Decisions have been published by Commerce Clearing House in its "Labor Arbitration Awards" series.

AS EDUCATOR:
Taught graduate and undergraduate level courses at Baylor University and teaches at Dallas Community College, Texas Immigration Center (gratis): Equal Employment/Employee Relations Law, Human Resources and Diversity, Labor Law and Labor Relations.

PROFESSIONAL EXERIENCE

Partner – Hartley, Mason, Sanchez & Torres, Dallas, TX	2005 to Present
Principal Attorney – Law Office of Rutherford Liddell, Irving, TX	2002 to 2005
Partner – Watkins & Chavez, Dallas, TX	2000 to 2002
Senior Litigation Associate – Turnbull, Kalinsky & Werth, Los Angeles, CA	1999 to 2000
Litigation Associate – Darnell, Muldowney & O'Dowd, Los Angeles, CA	1997 to 1999
Litigation Associate – Burnby & Jackson, San Marcos, CA	1995 to 1997
Litigation Associate – Munson, Leakey & Pavin, Irving, TX	1993 to 1995
Human Resources Manager - Motorola, Fullerton, CA, 1990	1989 to 1990
Claims & Benefits Manager – Texas Instruments, Austin, TX	1985 to 1988

EDUCATION / COMMUNITY

J.D., Baylor University School of Law, Waco, TX, 1993

M.B.A., Anderson School of Management, University of California at Los Angeles, Los Angeles, CA, 1990

B.A. Political Science, Minor in Spanish, Cum Laude, University of Texas at Austin, Austin, TX, 1985

Legal Advisor, Pro Bono, Magnet Schools Fair, Dallas Independent School District

Tutor in English, Career Counselor Volunteer, Maya Angelou High School, Dallas, TX

Related Jobs/Careers:
(Law Partner, Litigation Associate, Principal Attorney)

RÉSUMÉ #59: Lawyer with Specialty – 1 Page (2011 U.S. Retail: $349)

WOW! RÉSUMÉS 2011-2012: Great Jobs...Extra Income...Happiness...

CHAPTER 5: HEALTHCARE, EDUCATION & MISCELLANEOUS RÉSUMÉS

Ralph and Mirna Tamarak, On-Site Property Managers

rmtamarak@wowresumes.net   1234 Grand Avenue #123   Santa Ana, CA 92702   (714) 123-4567

MAINTENANCE AND TEAM PROPERTY MANAGEMENT

QUALIFICATIONS SUMMARY

Management (Mirna Tamarak):

✓ Accept and Screen Applications for Leasing
✓ Uphold and Enforce Property Rules
✓ Initiate Maintenance and Repair Work
✓ Place Advertising and Public Relations
✓ MS Office Computer Software Proficiency

✓ Collect Rent and Handle Trust Banking
✓ Handle Tenant Relations and Complaints
✓ Conduct Walk-through Unit Inspections
✓ Comply with Housing Laws/Regulations
✓ Licensed Real Estate Agent, CA DRE

Maintenance (Ralph Tamarak):

✓ General Maintenance and Cleaning
✓ Interior and Exterior Painting
✓ Remove Old Carpeting and Install New
✓ Install and Repair Unit Appliances

✓ Light plumbing and Electrical
✓ Maintain Landscaping and Grounds
✓ Light Repair and Patching
✓ Repair/Replace Faucets and Toilets

EXPERIENCE

GRAND AVENUE PALM APARTMENTS, Santa Ana, CA
On-site Maintenance/Property Managers (Husband & Wife), 2007 to Present
■ Perform excellent management and exemplary maintenance in 24-Unit Apartment Complex
■ Maintain 98% occupancy in the last 3 years retaining 100% on-time rental payments
■ Uphold value of real estate with high continuous income and first-rate property condition
  Compensation: Rent plus $1,200 per month

HOLLYWOOD HILLS PROPERTY GROUP, Los Angeles, CA
Property Manager (Mirna Tamarak), 2004 to 2007
■ Performed accounting, advertising, leasing, insurance, collections, tenant and sub-contractor interactions
■ Promoted to Full Manager from Leasing Agent and Assistant Property Manager upon outstanding performance

CALTRACK STORAGE, Inglewood, CA
Assistant Facilities Manager (Ralph Tamarak), 2003 to 2007
■ Assisted in managing and maintaining 43,000 square foot facility including security, fire, HVAC and offices

PERSONAL & PROFESSIONAL PROFILES

✓ Hard-working, honest, systematic and meticulous, with dedication to friendly professionalism
✓ Committed to organizational (property) success due to strong leasing, tenant relations and owner loyalty
✓ Serious team (husband & wife) devoted to achieve quick vacancy turnover (if any), cleanliness/safety
✓ Outstanding time management and follow-through dealing with maintenance & tenant issues promptly

EDUCATION & TRAINING

Mirna Tamarak:
Los Angeles City College, Los Angeles, CA: Associate Degree in Property Management, 2003
Real Estate Salesperson License, California Department of Real Estate, 2004

Ralph Tamarak:
Quadell Training Institute, Fullerton, CA: Certificate in Facilities Management, 1999

Related Jobs/Careers:
(Facilities Manager, Apartment Manager, Property Maintenance)

WOW! RÉSUMÉS 2011-2012: Great Jobs...Extra Income...Happiness...

CHAPTER 5: HEALTHCARE, EDUCATION & MISCELLANEOUS RÉSUMÉS

INTERNATIONAL ARCHITECT DESIGNER

V. R. Varaja

DrVarajaDesign@wowresumes.net

1234 Rue Airlie #1000	▪ Montréal, QC, Canada H5C 2W6 ▪	(877) 123-4500

PROFILE

⊙ Expert at fusing advanced technologies and the human scale for beautiful, healthy and functional built environments
⊙ Head of a firm that operates as a distributed office by forming project-based teams and collaborations worldwide
⊙ Utilize state-of-the-art 3D software tools from outside the field of architecture in order to create new realities
⊙ Conduct own research to evolve firm's design tools to foster creations that are both unexpected and thought-provoking
⊙ Master of Architecture and PhD in Urban Planning; Fluent in English and Hindi; Conversant/literate in French & Spanish

REPRESENTATIVE PROJECTS

Varaja, Targot & Kohl International Design (vtkintldesign.com), Montreal, New York, New Delhi

ARCHITECTURE

2007 – 2010: Designed and managed 2 projects in Quebec, Canada & New York, New York: >100k sq. m. / >USD200M

2009: Won nation-wide competition to design and manage new 1000 acre Jawaharail Nehru University Campus, New Delhi

2006 – 2009: Assisted Indian State of Madhya Pradesh to create and redesign 3 large contiguous townships & public sites

DESIGN

2009 – 2011 Commissioned to design proposals for display and furniture lines for La Maison Ogilvy, Montréal, Canada

2010: Designed LEED AP Certified Components for Temperate Zone Buildings: TEMPAbrane Invertible Building Membrane

2009: Designed Project Template for use by urban and village "architects" in India for township planning, design & build-out

ACCOMPLISHMENTS/INNOVATIONS

★ Add value to every client's goals, investments and desires by designing with excellence and being attuned to the technical, situational and socio-economic conditions of each project

★ Implement significant new approaches to architectural design with ground-breaking digital technologies, advanced materials and novel management practices

★ Lectures and Shows in U.S., Europe, China, India & Middle East

AWARDS

★ 2008, 2009, 2010: Named as #1 Design Firm in India

★ 2009 - 2011: Firm's "Retro-Avant-Garde" Design Show included in Museum of Modern Art (New York)

★ 2005: Firm's Display purchased for permanent collection by Board of Directors of Pompidou Museum (Paris, France)

★ 2000: Along with Partner, Hans Kohl 2 of Forty (Best US architects) under Forty (years old) by AIA

EDUCATION

McGill University, Montréal, Quebec, Canada, PhD in Urban Planning, 2003
Columbia University, New York, New York, M.A. in Architecture, 1998
Indian Institute of Technology Delhi Hauz Khas, New Delhi, India, B.S. in Computer Science, 1995

Related Jobs/Careers:
(Project Developer, Senior Architect, Urban Planner, Architect-Partner)

RÉSUMÉ #61: Architect / International Designer (2011 U.S. Retail: $349)

WOW! RÉSUMÉS 2011-2012: Great Jobs...Extra Income...Happiness...

Janice Marsalas

janmarsalas@wowresumes.net

1234 Chestnut St. #123; Philadelphia, PA 19093
(215) 123-4567

CAREER PROFILE: GRANTS/FUNDRAISING

◆ Organizational and consultative experience with successful record in securing grants and funding
◆ Extensive background in the non-profit sectors combined with expert familiarity in corporate operations
◆ Exceptional in communications skills honed by training in Multi/Cross-Cultural Conflict Resolution
◆ Developed proficiencies in Fundraising, Grant Reviews, Fund Development, Project Management & Events
◆ Affinity for the Creative and Dramatic Arts, Human Rights, International Relations and Environmentalism

EDUCATION

UNIVERSITY OF CALIFORNIA AT LOS ANGELES, Los Angeles, CA
Bachelor of Arts, International & Area Studies (Human Rights Emphasis), 2000

TEMPLE UNIVERSITY, Philadelphia, Pennsylvania
Law Courses and Mediation Training (including Ethics & Conflict Resolution), 2008 - 2009

RELEVANT EXPERIENCE

JANICE MARSALAS CONSULTANCY, Philadelphia, PA
Self-Employed, 2005 to Present
Please See Page Two (Areas Of Expertise) for Description and Details of Successful Consulting Experience

Kimmel Center for the Performing Arts, Philadelphia, PA
Booking Administrator, 2003 to 2005
■ Scheduled all uses of the Kimmel Center and affiliated facilities in liaison with administrators & presenters
■ Evaluated licensee requirements for services and personnel, including union stage crew, engineers & security
■ Performed contract administration, rental revenue accounting, usage recordkeeping and financial reporting

CIVIL WAR LIBRARY & MUSEUM, Philadelphia, PA
Special Events Coordinator, 2001 to 2003
■ Excelled in the promotion of the museum as a special events venue to corporations and convention industry
■ Managed events, including artists and facilities booking, contract administration, security & event supervision
■ Planned and directed exhibition and protocol activities, recognition events and liaison with PA Art Commission

---

J M **Janice Marsalas** – Page Two   janmarsalas@wowresumes.net

AREAS OF EXPERTISE

FUNDRAISING:

(2005 to Present)
Highlighted Organizations Served Successfully:

- Temple University
- Chester County, PA
- PA Healthcare Consortium
- Philadelphia Mayor's Office
- The City of Camden, New Jersey
- Northern Philadelphia Public Trust
- Camden Emergency Women's Services
- La Salle University
- Martin Luther King March
- Morrison Baptist Church
- DynaMight Community Group
- Frankford Hospital

FUND DEVELOPMENT:

- Management of grant proposals, interim and final grant reporting and budget compliance
- Experienced in funding research, foundation background research and donor development
- Development of business planning documents and non-profit Development Plans
- Handling of foundation liaisons and various foundation site visits (e.g. Carnegie, J.P. Morgan)
- Establishment and design of donor database systems (proprietary and off-the-shelf MS Access)
- Profitable launching of three membership revenue programs for non-profits
- Establishment of endowment and planned giving programs (KPMG, Deloitte Touche, Goldman Sachs)

PROJECT MANAGEMENT:

- Supervision of teaching staff and curriculum development for projects serving incarcerated women
- Establishment of four college internship programs (with Temple, Drexel, La Salle, Philadelphia University)
- Interaction and project development with Board of Directors for long range strategic planning
- Development of personnel procedures and review processes. Handled recruitment and hiring for agencies

GRANT REVIEW:

(2005 to 2006)
- At United States Department of Health and Human Services, Washington D.C. –Substance Abuse and Mental Health Services Administration: As Federal Grants Reviewer, Reviewed Applications for RFP guidelines, Compliance, Assessment Suitability, Project Planning Feasibility, Potential for Evaluation Effectiveness & Budget Justification

(2007 to 2008)
- At Rockefeller Foundation and Philadelphia Arts Commission: Assisted Panelists in Grant Reviews

SELECTED AWARD HIGHLIGHTS:

◆ $2,100,000:
U.S. Department of Defense Grant Project funded economic development of former military bases in Eastern Pennsylvania – sustaining a revolving loan fund and provision of small business technical assistance

◆ $1,320,000:
U.S. Department of Justice Chester County – Grants to Encourage Arrest and Enforcement Protection Orders

◆ $800,000: U.S. Department of Justice Chester County – Office on Violence Against Women

Related Jobs/Careers:
(Grant Reviewer, Special Events Coordinator)

WOW! RÉSUMÉS 2011-2012: Great Jobs...Extra Income...Happiness...

<u>CHAPTER 5: HEALTHCARE, EDUCATION & MISCELLANEOUS RÉSUMÉS</u>

CORE SKILLS:
- ❑ Customer Service
- ❑ Corporate Training
- ❑ Personal Growth Teaching
- ❑ Management
- ❑ Public Relations
- ❑ Public Speaking
- ❑ Photo and TV Advertising
- ❑ Research and Computers

"Cornelia is the perfect example of brains and beauty that is rare and wondrous."

"Ms. Fleiss is a great product of education, training and natural talent that makes our company proud and more valuable in countless ways."

"With hard work and the desire to improve, learn and be creative, Cornelia Fleiss has become a top-notch journalist and TV personality. She is a fine professional and a great friend to us all."

ABOVE ARE SOME WORK
EVALUATIONS &
PERSONAL REVIEWS

PORTFOLIO & REFERENCES
AVAILABLE FOR REVIEW

CORNELIA GOMEZ-FLEISS, TV Media

1000 P. Domingo Street, Carmona, Makati City**,**1207, Metro Manila
(63) 123-4567
corneliagfleiss@wowresumes.net

PROFESSIONAL EXPERIENCE:
TV PATROL, ABS-CBN Network, Manila, Philippines
2009 – 2011, *Production Manager*
- ❖ Produced shows for overseas audience, including German & English news outlets
- ❖ Assisted in production of TV mini-documentaries including women's health shows
- ❖ Performed voice-over translations for DW TV (German News) from Southeast Asia

TV MÜNCHEN, Munich, Germany
2006 – 2008, *Regional News Reporter*
- ❖ Reported on regional stories in the areas of human interest and politics
- ❖ Excelled in editing and composition (won Bavarian Editor's Award, 2007)
- ❖ Performed narration and voice-overs of own stories and did some camera work

Pro 7 Television Company, Munich, Germany
2004 - 2006, *News Assistant in Editing and Production*
- ❖ Intensive training and work in all aspects of news production and editing
- ❖ Assisted in studio administration and scheduling of broadcasts
- ❖ Worked with prominent national reporters on special features

LUFTHANSA AG, Cologne – Frankfurt, Germany
2001 - 2003, *Public Relations Assistant and Information Officer*
- ❖ Learned and applied public relations strategies in Press and Information Office
- ❖ Interacted with German and multinational public and companies to disseminate info
- ❖ Researched information and data and conducted public and commercial surveys

PHILIPPINE AIRLINES, Manila, Philippines
1998 - 2000, *Flight Attendant / International Service Trainer*
- ❖ Featured in country's flag carrier's print and TV ads for international service
- ❖ Conducted trainings in safety, security, customer service and personal growth
- ❖ Traveled and represented the company in airline conventions and travel shows

CEBU PACIFIC AIRLINES, Cebu, Philippines
1997 - 1998, *Flight Attendant*
- ❖ Performed customer service duties for the safety and comfort of air passengers
- ❖ Represented brand-new regional airline in TV and print advertisements
- ❖ Offered position in management and training including personal growth education

EDUCATION:
RWTH (Rheinisch – Westfälische Technische Hochschule), Aachen, Germany
Master of Arts Degree in Philology and Economy, 2005

University of the Philippines, Manila, Philippines
Bachelor of Arts Degree in Communications & Mass Media, 2001

Einhard – Gymnasium, Aachen, Germany
Bachelor's Degree Equivalent, 1997

PERSONAL ACHIEVEMENTS:
First Runner-Up, Miss Cebu 1997, Voted Miss Congeniality & Best Speech Presentation

Speak fluent English, German, French, Tagalog and Cebuano

Related Jobs/Careers:
(News Reporter, Flight Attendant, Beauty Contestant, TV Media, Corporate Trainer)
RÉSUMÉ #63: International Journalist – Career-Changer (2011 Retail: $299)

CHAPTER 6:

<u>GOVERNMENT-JOB RÉSUMÉS</u>

10 Model *WOW!* Résumés
(44 Job Titles)

<u>CREATE YOUR OWN RÉSUMÉ</u>:

If you are doing your own Résumé in the Occupational Category of <u>Government Jobs,</u> you can choose from among the *WOW!* Résumés in this Chapter modeling the wording, styles, formatting, bullets, borders, etc. You can also model any of the elements in the other *WOW!* Résumés in this Book.

Complete the Guides in the Appendices to fully customize and create a unique and powerful *WOW!* Résumé! As will be explained in the next page, U.S. Government Jobs have their own special application process. *WOW!* Résumés can make the process easier and the results more promising!

If you have purchased this Book (and thus become an automatic 1-year Member of wowresumes.net) you can get Free unrestricted downloads (Word or PDF Files) of up to 5 *WOW!* Résumés in addition to a Free download of the Guides in the Appendices for you to print out or edit on your computer.

<u>DISCOUNTED RÉSUMÉ SERVICE</u>:

If you need help to create a *WOW!* Résumé call 888-503-3133 or go to wowresumes.net to work with professional Résumé Writers who practice *WOW!* Résumé principles. Book purchasers have up to one year to avail of a 30% Instant Discount on any *WOW!* Résumé or other *WOW!* Résumé products such as *WOW!*-Card® Résumés, as well as other benefits including <u>Free Résumé Posting </u>on the ever-growing wowresumes.net Website and <u>Updating from Twitter, Facebook, LinkedIn & Google Profiles</u>. Members get <u>Free Updates for 1 year</u> on their Main Résumé and <u>up to 90% Discounts</u> on additional (2nd, 3rd, 4th, etc.) Customized Résumés to target Specific Jobs, Careers, Industries or Special Urgent Applications.

*See the Back Cover for *WOW!* Résumé Service & Free Membership Information*

WOW! RÉSUMÉS 2011-2012: Great Jobs...Extra Income...Happiness...

"Long" Road to Security and Success

This Chapter covers Government-Job Résumés, specifically Résumés for jobs in the United States Federal Government, one of the largest and most comprehensive employers in the world spanning most occupations at all salary levels, in all 50 States, the District of Columbia and over 100 countries around the world!

The *WOW!* Résumés in this chapter reflect the unique hiring and documentation process for U.S. Federal jobs. First of all, the Federal job application process is online (although some Federal agencies still accept a paper resume that can be mailed, e-mailed or faxed, or applicants can recreate their online Résumés on paper to refer to in interviews or as impressive reference documents in mailings and hard-copy files).

In some ways, the normal Résumé writing process will be reversed in that it would be helpful to first write a non-submitted paper Résumé that can be used as a guide for the online process or be used to facilitate the creation procedure that is required in the Federal Government's Job Application Website called USAJOBS and its USAJOBS Résumé Builder. Most Federal Agencies including jobs in the Armed Services require applicants to submit their résumés through "résumé builders" and now more than half of Federal Agencies are using the USAJOBS Résumé Builder. An applicant can use "cut and paste" from a created paper Résumé that follows the guidelines for a Federal Résumé to facilitate or augment the online process.

A Federal Résumé is usually 2 to 4 (or more!) pages in length, much longer that a typical business Résumé. The reason for the additional length is that candidates are required to fully detail and "prove" the stated skills and qualifications proclaimed in their career backgrounds. In fact, the Federal Résumé must detail "KSAs" which are point-by-point "facts" and figures that are the applicant's inventory of "Knowledge, Skills and Abilities". Specific work experience, educational/training elements and achievements must be outlined and explained to meet the stated requirements for specific job announcements that relate to the level of salary offered.

While the Federal job application process is sometimes arduous and lengthy, it is consistent in its application procedures that not just involves "building" a Résumé but can also include providing Essay answers, writing samples, transcripts, and other documents and any required follow-up to prove requirements such as Citizenship, Military or other Federal service that can lead to the sequence of qualification steps, possible interview and hoped-for job offer.

The *WOW!* Model Résumés in this Chapter represent some of the better positions available in the U.S. Federal government and cover occupations in Science, Management, Law, Healthcare, Accounting, Information Technology and Security Enforcement. Salary details commensurate with the position applied for are included in each Résumé in this Chapter.

As with all Résumés, the substance, quality of writing, composition and the aesthetics (the look) of the Résumé document are critical to grabbing and holding the attention of an interested reader (the potential decision-maker or gate-keeper). A well-crafted paper *WOW!* Résumé can be a valuable guide and final document that can lead to a more successful Federal job search whether using the comprehensive USAJOBS Website or others such as government-job-related sites as QuickHire, Avue Central and Resumix.

WOW! RÉSUMÉS 2011-2012: Great Jobs...Extra Income...Happiness...

REGINA Z. TAYLOR
290 Santa Monica Boulevard
Van Nuys, California 90063
(213) 123-4567
reginaztaylor@wowresumes.net

Target Positions:
Staff Officer / Inspector / Agent, Department of Agriculture or Appropriate Federal Agency
(2011 – 2012 Approximate Annual Salary Range: $51,630 - $115,750)

PROFILE:
❑ Over 8 years' experience in Food Safety & Food Toxicology Research in the government and private sectors
❑ Master's degree in Nutrition and Dietetics with specialty in Epidemiology
❑ Research experience in food technology focusing on oil processing technologies
❑ Supervisory and management experience in diverse work environments dealing directly with public or stakeholders
❑ Deeply committed to the Department of Agriculture's mission of protecting consumers by ensuring that the commercial supply of meat poultry and egg products moving in interstate commerce or exported to other countries is safe, wholesome and correctly labeled and packaged

WORK EXPERIENCE:

CALIFORNIA DEPARTMENT OF CONSUMER AFFAIRS — Sacramento, CA
Farm Bureau Food Safety Inspector and Agent — 2007 to Present

- Participate in the development of labeling policies and labeling compliance procedures and regulations
- Interpret policies required for meat, poultry and egg products maintenance of labeling & packaging requirement
- Provide expertise on the development of regulations pertaining to special labeling statements and claims related to new food processes, animal production, nutrient content and organic food production and irradiation
- Serve as expert in development of regulations pertaining to procedures and regulation for prior label approval
- Provide technical advice about labeling terminology for meat, poultry and egg products
- Examine meat, poultry, egg products and ingredients that are produced using new technology; Provide guidance on product identity within existing regulations and policies
- Evaluate the effectiveness of labeling procedures and programs to ensure accuracy and compliance with regulatory requirements for standards and labeling

DEPARTMENT OF VETERANS AFFAIRS — Los Angeles, CA
Supervisory Dietitian, Patient Food Service Manager — 2004 to 2007

- Provided professional and management support to Maldonado Veterans Hospital Patient Relations and Services Division
- Executed planning, implementation and management of food production and service for staff and patients
- Supported hospital mission and coordinated Food Service activities with other services and units in the facility, clinics and local community

---

WOW! RÉSUMÉS 2011-2012: Great Jobs...Extra Income...Happiness...

Regina Z. Taylor   (213) 123-4567
Page 2   reginaztaylor@wowresumes.net

WORK EXPERIENCE: (Continued)

CARGILL CORPORATION   San Diego, CA
Research Food Technologist   2001 to 2004

- Studied and examined the effects of natural antioxidants to enhance oxidative stability of oils and fried food

- Evaluated new oilseed cultivars for improved oil oxidative stability

- Investigated effect of alternative oil processing technologies on enhancing oxidative stability of frying oils

- Researched different methods/materials for developing trans fat-free crystallized fat products such as shortening, spreads and margarine

- Documented joint research results in peer reviewed journals and provided supervision to support staff

CARROWS RESTAURANT   Tempe, AZ
Shift Supervisor, Manager   1996 - 2000

- Started as wait staff with outstanding customer service while going to school at Arizona State University; Promoted to Shift Supervisor in 1998 for Weekends supervising and scheduling staff of 12

- As Manager 1998 – 2000, performed full managerial duties of planning, organizing, delegating, directing, controlling and reviewing activities of staff of 32

EDUCATION:
LOMA LINDA UNIVERSITY, Loma Linda, CA
M.S. DEGREE IN DIETETICS AND NUTRITION, 2004

RELATED COURSEWORK:
Food Selection, Preparation and Presentation
Professional Issues in Nutrition and Dietetics
Introduction to Clinical Nutrition
Quantity Food Purchasing, Production and Service
Medical Nutrition Therapy I & II
Food Systems Organization and Management
Community Nutrition
Food Systems Management Affiliation
Community Nutrition Affiliation
Advanced Medical Nutrition Therapy
Nutrition Metabolism
Nutrition Care Management
Contemporary Issues of Vegetarian Diets
Research Applications in Nutrition
Pharmacology
Principles of Epidemiology
Advanced Public Health Nutrition

WOW! RÉSUMÉS 2011-2012: Great Jobs...Extra Income...Happiness...

Regina Z. Taylor
Page 3

(213) 123-4567
reginaztaylor@wowresumes.net

EDUCATION (Continued):

ARIZONA STATE UNIVERSITY, Tempe, AZ
B.S. DEGREE CHEMISTRY, 2000; Graduated with Honors and Dean's List for 3 Semesters

COMPUTER PROFICIENCIES:

Microsoft Word, Excel, Powerpoint, Outlook
Database Software including Microsoft Access, MySQL, MS SQL 6.5/7.0

CERTIFICATIONS:
American Dietetic Association, Registered Dietetician, Current

LANGUAGES:
Fluent Spanish and conversational Portuguese

COMMUNITY SERVICE:
National City Afterschool Nutrition Symposium 2009, Panelist Speaker
Volunteer, San Diego Food Bank

**SPECIALIZED EXPERIENCE
(KNOWLEDGE, SKILLS AND ABILITIES):**

1. Knowledge of the chemical and physical properties of fat/oil-based materials and emulsions.

2. Skill in the use of advanced analytical methods including differential scanning calorimetry, GC, HPLC and/or GS/MS.

3. Ability to conceive, plan and conduct research and publish results in peer reviewed journals.

4. Knowledge of healthcare food system management.

5. Ability to manage an effective performance improvement program.

6. Ability to assess staff competence and staff training needs, create teaching material, develop lesson plans and utilize teaching techniques to meet service-staff needs

7. Knowledge of and ability to apply quality standards as specified by regulatory-accrediting organizations.

REFERENCES:
Dr. John Alvado
Professor of Dietetics and Nutrition
Loma Linda University
909-123-4567

Dr. Prash Madagartal
Vice President, Southwest Region
Cargill Corporation
480-123-4567

Related Jobs/Careers:
(Food Research, Food Technologist, Dietician)

WOW! RÉSUMÉS 2011-2012: Great Jobs...Extra Income...Happiness...

Alton Di Martini, PhD
Truman Circle #1234
Kansas City, Missouri 64130
(544) 123-4567
dradimartini@wowresumes.net

Target Position: Director of Regional Head of Government Agency or Department In the Areas of Science, Population Studies or Urban/Rural (International) Development (2011 – 2012 Approximate Annual Salary Range: $125,500 - $149,750)

AVAILABILITY: Immediate
DESIRED LOCATIONS: United States, Canada, France, French-Speaking Countries of Africa

PROFILE:

- ☑ Over 10 years' experience in Program Management and Project Analysis in the government and private sectors
- ☑ Extensive knowledge of population studies and development programs across multinational agencies/governments
- ☑ Refined abilities in strategic planning and project implementation given budget, cultural and political constraints
- ☑ Field-tested skills in resource application, program innovations and adaptations in areas of health and nutrition
- ☑ Proven leadership/communication skills developed in multicultural and multilingual urban / rural environments
- ☑ Outstanding writing skills evidenced in publications (PhD Thesis and Journals) and production of Training Manuals

WORK EXPERIENCE:

DEPARTMENT OF COMMERCE, BUREAU OF THE CENSUS | Kansas City, MO
Regional Director | Midwest, 2009 to 2010

Major Duties:
- Responsible for planning, organizing, directing, managing, and evaluating all activities of the Regional Office (RO) and its subordinate offices
- Developed and implemented local policies, within the framework of overall Bureau policy, concerning all aspects of the broad administrative and managerial functions of the Office
- Conducted and managed surveys and special censuses
- Administered and directed an information services program to disseminate information on the availability and use of Census data and products
- Directed the geographic program which evaluated Census maps for accuracy and adequacy of coverage
- Served as the Bureau's representative in appearances with the media, general public, and before key governmental bodies at the federal, state, county and local levels
- Accountable for a wide range of administrative operations to insure that Departmental, Bureau, and Division policies and procedures are strictly maintained
- Directed the phases of expansion and contraction of the organization within the Regional Office (RO) to insure that Bureau programs were initiated and completed
- Provided employment and development opportunities for a diverse workforce
- Planned for changes in the size and composition of staff and took an active role in retaining staff
- Recognized the value of cultural, ethnic, gender, and other individual differences at all levels of the organization
- Exercised judgment within regulations when selecting individuals for reassignment, detail, promotion, and other actions and took appropriate corrective or disciplinary actions with employees

---

WOW! RÉSUMÉS 2011-2012: Great Jobs...Extra Income...Happiness...

Alton Di Martini, PhD
Page 2

dradimartini@wowresumes.net
(544) 123-4567

WORK EXPERIENCE - Continued
DEPARTMENT OF COMMERCE, BUREAU OF THE CENSUS - Continued

SPECIALIZED EXPERIENCE (KSAs: KNOWLEDGE, SKILLS AND ABILITIES):

1. Knowledge of field survey data collection methods and best practices, and ability to apply them to planning and preparing complex field surveys.
2. Ability to plan and/or administer multiple phases or aspects of a program concurrently, including identification and scheduling of human and financial resources commensurate with activities, monitor progress, and take corrective actions.
3. Knowledge and ability to plan for long-term projects.
4. Knowledge of the principles and commonly applied methods of statistically based quality control as applied to field interviewer data collection activities; Ability to integrate quality control activities and tools in the larger census process.
5. Knowledge of census enumeration conditions, constraints, opportunities, and the ability to use that knowledge to identify methods and processes likely to succeed.
6. Knowledge of the application of automated tools and systems to survey and census field enumeration functions, especially the use of portable computers such as laptop and tablet computers.
7. Knowledge of administrative rules and regulations established for government employees. Knowledge of payroll, personnel, recruiting, and hiring policies and procedures; Knowledge and understanding of Excepted Service appointing authorities.

AGENCY FOR INTERNATIONAL DEVELOPMENT
Population / Health / Nutrition Program Manager

Kinshasa, Democratic Republic of Congo
2006 to 2009

Major Duties:
- As Program Manager, set the vision and led the design of health programs and projects, including long-term development projects as well as conflict or humanitarian relief issues
- Developed, managed, and evaluated policies and activities in population/health/nutrition program areas
- Set project performance benchmarks, and monitored and evaluated project implementation
- Identified and delivered solutions to management and technical problems and issues that arose during program design and implementation, in particular technical advice and support to the Health Transformation program
- Strategic Planning: For country, regional, or agency-wide programming, performed strategic analyses of health system trends, and considered future opportunities, as input to Mission strategic planning
- Developed strategic planning documents, country assistance strategies, sector strategies, project solicitations, and similar planning exercises
- Program Analysis: Performed analyses of health sector trends relating to Afghanistan, to inform senior management and program managers of relevant factors that may affect the US. assistance program
- Conducted conflict analyses and identified drivers of conflict related to health, workforce development, and youth development
- Oversaw contracted technical assistance and commodity interventions to health systems
- Ensured statistical soundness of health data
- Proposed statistical indicators of program success
- Communicated results of analysis both verbally and in writing

SPECIALIZED EXPERIENCE (KSAs: KNOWLEDGE, SKILLS AND ABILITIES):

Experience applying practices, developing reports, and making recommendations associated with population, health, and nutrition program development and management for developing countries.

WOW! RÉSUMÉS 2011-2012: Great Jobs...Extra Income...Happiness...

Alton Di Martini, PhD
Page 3

dradimartini@wowresumes.net
(544) 123-4567

WORK EXPERIENCE - Continued
AGENCY FOR INTERNATIONAL DEVELOPMENT - Continued
Specialized Experience (Skills, Knowledge & Abilities) - Continued

1. Knowledge of program/project management (design, implementation, monitoring and/or evaluation) principles, theories, concepts, methods and techniques.
2. Ability to manage international development projects in a multi-cultural team environment.
3. Ability to work in a developing country with limited modern conveniences.
4. Superior writing and verbal communication skills.
5. Knowledge of USAID programs and practices in developing countries.

AMERICAN HONDA MOTORS CORPORATION
Corporate Staff Economist

Louisville, KY
2000 to 2006

Major Duties:
- Conducted economic analysis and research on multiple economic issues
- Compiled economic information and reports of interest for the Chief Economist and other Corporate officials
- Collected/compiled information for use in economic reports and briefing books
- Wrote a variety of time sensitive economic reports concerning areas of special interest to the Chief Economist, Top Management, and Corporate Board members
- Planned and carried out projects for collecting detailed economic data which required the complete understanding of the broad research plans and goals and the principles and polices governing analysis, tabulation, and reporting; Planned and carried out complex studies and analyses including determination of data needed to complete assignments; sources, reliability, and availability of such data: method of collections; and evaluation techniques to be used in interpreting findings
- Determined techniques for data processing and analysis, and for planning the presentation of findings

EDUCATION:

UNIVERSITY OF LOUISVILLE, Louisville, Kentucky
PhD in Population Studies, 2005

WASHINGTON UNIVERSITY, St. Louis, MO
B.A. DEGREE ECONOMICS, 2000
Spent Spring Semester 1999 as Exchange Student at Oxford University, Oxford, England

LANGUAGES:
Fluent French, conversational Spanish and basic Congolese dialects of Lingala and Kingwana

COMMUNITY SERVICE:
National City Afterschool Nutrition Symposium 2009, Panelist Speaker
Greater Kansas City Food Bank, Volunteer

Related Jobs/Careers:
(Department Head, Regional Director)

WOW! RÉSUMÉS 2011-2012: Great Jobs...Extra Income...Happiness...

Maria Lee Amurao
201 Pike Street #1234
Seattle, Washington
(719) 123-4567
mlamuraopi@wowresumes.net

Target Positions:
Nurse Manager or Senior Staff Nurse at Government Hospital or Veterans Affairs Hospital
(2011 – 2012 Approximate Annual Salary Range: $92,150 - $133,775)

PROFILE:

★ Over 10 years as Licensed Registered Nurse with current certification in 2 states with specialty in Rehabilitation
★ Extensive experience in geriatric care with emphases in dementia and memory care (Alzheimer's disease)
★ Familiarity and expertise in handling veterans including those with PTSD, Neurologic and Brain dysfunctions
★ Recognized and adept in interdisciplinary healthcare teamwork in fast-paced pressure multicultural settings

PROFESSIONAL EXPERIENCE:

VIRGINIA MASON MEDICAL CENTER
Nurse Manager

Seattle, WA
2008 to Present

Major Duties:
• Plan 24-hour unit staffing based on fluctuating needs, staffing mix and maximized cost effectiveness
• Provide supervisory guidance and evaluate staff performance in collaboration with care line supervisors
• Assure current and comprehensive documentation is contained in patient charts & other pertinent medical records
• Utilize human and material resources to provide efficient and effective patient care
• Evaluate systems for care delivery and personnel management by tailoring the operating environment to the particular needs of the patient population
• Develop and support research projects directed towards improving patient care and staff development
• Provide a safe and healthful physical environment for patients and personnel and interpreting and applying organizational controls and national standards
• Assure continuing improvement of service to patients, including implementing and effective customer service program
• Understand and facilitate objectives of all student affiliation programs
• Ensure compliance with all patient rights and regulatory agency standards
• Collaborate with other health care professionals in providing continuity of services for specific health issues
• Improve continuity of professional relationships among the health care team collaborating on behalf of patients

KAISER NORTHWEST PERMANENTE
Infection Control Nurse

Portland, OR
2006 to 2008

Major Duties:
• Worked collaboratively with all levels of healthcare professionals to identify, reduce, and prevent health care related infection/colonization by identifying risks and implementing effective infection prevention and control measures based on current standards and/or recommendations
• Provided back-up clinical coverage for the facility Infection Control Nurse and assisted in identifying and eliminating exposure of patients and staff to transmittable organisms (surveillance, isolation, directives management, infection control trends and analysis)
• Prepared required reports and presentations to staff and patients
• Participated in and led clinical improvement activities related to infection control

---

WOW! RÉSUMÉS 2011-2012: Great Jobs...Extra Income...Happiness...

Maria Lee Amurao   mlamuraopi@wowresumes.net
Page 2

PROFESSIONAL EXPERIENCE (Continued):

VETERANS HOSPITAL   San Francisco, CA
Staff Nurse   2000 to 2006

Major Duties:
- Utilized the nursing process in managing, developing, implementing and evaluating each patient's individual plan of care with an interdisciplinary team to attain specific clinical outcomes
- Implemented nursing interventions as necessary for assessing patient response to surgical procedures
- Continuously monitored the environment for potential and/or actual safety hazards
- Assured adherence to strict safety procedures by all staff and guided/directed patient care delivery of support staff
- Provided input for staff evaluation to rating official(s)
- Participated in and initiated Quality Assessment/Improvement program activities as applicable to the clinical area
- Promoted collaborative practice to provide and expedite quality patient care along the health care continuum
- Acted as patient advocate to assure appropriateness and quality of care
- Assessed learning needs of patients and staff and implemented appropriate teaching plan
- Initiated and/or participated in studies pertaining to the ward assigned

HILLHAVEN CONVALESCENT   San Mateo, CA
Nurse's Aide / Nursing Home Nurse   1998 to 2000

Major Duties:
- Provided skilled nursing care for elderly residents with varying stages of dementia and Alzheimer's disease
- Performed administrative tasks, assessed residents' health conditions, developed treatment plans, supervised licensed practical nurses and nursing aides, and performed difficult procedures such as starting intravenous drips
- Worked in Hospital's long-term rehabilitation unit for patients with strokes and head injuries
- As Nursing Aide: performed routine tasks under the supervision of nursing and medical staff including: answered patients' call belts, delivered messages, served meals, made beds, helped patients eat, dress, and bathe

EDUCATION:

UNIVERSITY OF SAN FRANCISCO, San Francisco, CA
Master's Degree in Nursing, 2003

The Health Care Systems Management Masters Curriculum (All 3 Semester Credits):

NURS 0700 Theoretical Perspectives in Nursing   NURS 0704 Advanced Role Integration
NURS 0709 Legal & Ethical Issues in Health Care NURS G7 12 Financial Resources I
NURS G7 16 Managed Care Methodologies   NURS 0724 Outcomes Measurement & Data Management
NURS 0732 Disease Resource Management   NTJRS 0735 Advanced Research Methods
NURS 0740 Health Care Systems   NURS 0744 Financial Resources II
NURS 0748 Human Resource Management   NURS 0752 Practicum

UNIVERSITY OF SANTO TOMAS, Manila, Philippines
Bachelor of Science Nursing, 1997

CERTIFICATIONS:
Current Licensure:
Registered Nurse, State of California
Registered Nurse, State of Washington

Related Jobs/Careers:
(Registered Nurse, Nursing Home Nurse, Veterans Affairs Nurse)

WOW! RÉSUMÉS 2011-2012: Great Jobs...Extra Income...Happiness...

DANIEL MUSGRANGE
500 Kalupaku Road #1234
Honolulu, Hawaii
(808) 123-4567
dmusgrange@wowresumes.net

Target Position:
Security Director
At U.S. Military Base or U.S. Government or U.S. Department of State Facility
(2011 – 2012 Approximate Annual Salary Range: $68,455 - $91,750)

PROFILE:

➢ Over 8 years' progressively responsible experience in law enforcement and security in dynamic locations
➢ Skills, knowledge and abilities in the technical, tactical, strategic and public issues of security and antiterrorism
➢ Exemplary U.S. Military Service with Commendation and Achievement Medals from United States Air Force
➢ Graduate degree (Master of Arts in Criminal Justice) and continuously educated/trained in the security industry

WORK HISTORY:

HICKAM U.S. AIR FORCE BASE   Honolulu, HI
Director of Security   2008 to 2/2011

- Served as a first line supervisor to civilian and/or military police officers, planning and directing watch activities
- Assigned work, monitoring workload, analyzing the methods used and implementing changes when/where needed
- Provided technical advice and guidance to Desk /Patrol Sergeants lead police officers, and police officers in the enforcement of laws, rules and regulations
- Prepared absentee/morning reports and watch schedules/lists for the following day
- Responsible for receiving reports, maintaining desk journals, ensuring accuracy of paperwork submitted, maintaining key control for various buildings and vehicles, issuing specialized equipment, and checking detention cells
- Inspected the physical security of the areas, evaluating situations arid conditions, identifying deficiencies, and recommending or taking appropriate actions
- In charge of inspecting police activities on the installation to ensure compliance with established policies and procedures
- Responded to and investigated complaints compiling evidence, making apprehensions, preparing reports relating to criminal and security hazards, taking witness statements, and testifying as required in Military Courts Martial or Federal court proceedings
- Monitored unusual situations/conditions through personal surveillance or electronic surveillance aids
- Responded to radio calls for taking required action and requests additional support if necessary
- Responded to off-base circumstances as directed by the installation commander, in accordance with USAF regulations

DEPARTMENT OF THE AIR FORCE, MATERIEL COMMAND   Travis Air Force Base, Fairfield, CA
Police Officer   2006 to 2008

- Enforced and maintained law and order, preserving the peace, and protecting life and civil rights within the jurisdiction of the military installation
- Exercised full power of apprehension which entailed carrying a firearm, Mirandizing suspects, preserving evidence and testifying in court as it pertained to enforcing regulations on the military installation
- As Security Forces Dispatcher for Installation, dispatched police units to scenes of crimes, accidents and natural disasters
- Performed the full range of Base Entry Controller duties ensuring individuals requesting access to the installation have the proper identification credentials before entering
- Performed the full range of duties for defending protection level resources according to USAF regulations
- Served as a restricted area entry controller and immediate visual assessment sentry providing surveillance for sensitive, restricted, and limited access areas

---

WOW! RÉSUMÉS 2011-2012: Great Jobs...Extra Income...Happiness...

DANIEL MUSGRANGE
Page 2

dmusgrange@wowresumes.net

WORK HISTORY (Continued):

DEPARTMENT OF HOMELAND SECURITY, HARTSFIELD INT'L AIRPORT
Transportation Security Officer (TSO)

Atlanta, GA
2005 to 2006

- Performed a variety of duties related to providing security and protection of air travelers, international airport and aircraft including passenger screening and baggage screening
- Performed all duties in a courteous and professional manner while maximizing efficiency and vigilance
- Specific tasks involved hand-wanding (which includes the requirement to reach and wand the individual from the floor to overhead), pat-down searches, and monitoring walk-through metal detector screening equipment
- Property search techniques included operation of x-ray machines to identify dangerous objects in baggage, cargo and on passengers, and preventing those objects from being transported onto aircraft
- Controlled entry and exit points and continuously improved security screening processes and personal performance through training and development

MILITARY (SECURITY) EXPERIENCE:

UNITED STATES AIR FORCE, Dobbins AFB
Patrol Supervisor

Marietta, GA
2002 to 2004

- Conducted general law enforcement protection and security activities at one of largest airbases in Continental U.S.
- Provided first-responder action through coordination with Marietta P.D./F.D. and Fulton County Sheriff's Department
- Developed, planned and implemented security force programs in association with local authorities and Southern Command
- Promoted to 2nd-in-Command of day-to-day operations and training of staff of 15-20 personnel including supervision of 7

MILITARY SERVICE:

United States Air Force, 2001 to 2005
Joined "Operation Enduring Freedom/Noble Eagle" and served in Spain, England, Italy and Pakistan
Honorably discharged with Air Force Commendation Medal and 2 Air Force Achievement Medals

SPECIALIZED EXPERIENCE (KSAs: KNOWLEDGE, SKILLS AND ABILITIES):

1. Abilities in performing law enforcement duties that deal with apprehension and detention of individuals in cases ranging from minor incidents to felonies; performing inspections and investigative work to effect compliance of individuals with laws, rules, and regulations in the protection of life, property, and the civil rights of citizens; preparing detailed reports and citations concerning all incidents and actions taken; providing advice, guidance and instruction to police officers and conducting roll call/guard mount.
2. Skills in force protection to preserve the peace, detect and investigate crimes, arrest/apprehend violators, and assist base citizens in emergency situations.
3. Ability to enforce a wide range of federal laws and assimilate local laws for application and enforcement within federal jurisdiction.
4. Knowledge and experience to conduct preliminary and final short-term investigations of a broad range of alleged and actual crimes occurring within the military installation.
5. Ability to investigate crimes and suspected criminal activities; interview witnesses; secure crime scenes, compile and preserve evidence.

WOW! RÉSUMÉS 2011-2012: Great Jobs...Extra Income...Happiness...

DANIEL MUSGRANGE
Page 3

dmusgrange@wowresumes.net

SPECIALIZED EXPERIENCE (KSAs: KNOWLEDGE, SKILLS AND ABILITIES, Continued):

6. Skills to respond to calls for emergency assistance including traffic accidents, domestic disputes, suicides, burglary, robbery, sex offenses, unruly or truant child, missing persons, suspicious persons, neighborhood disputes, catastrophic events, scenes of crimes/natural disasters, possible murder, gang fights, and enemy attacks and make apprehensions.
7. Ability to perform specialized techniques, methods, and procedures to execute search and apprehension; detect explosives or illegal drugs; counter terrorist operations; or counter violence posing a threat to public safety.
8. Knowledge and experience to act as the on-scene commander for significant and catastrophic events as required and initiate Air Force Incident Management System (AFIMS) as needed.
9. Skills to interact with members of the public to determine their involvement in incidents to include interviewing, advising them of their rights, obtaining statements, and detaining or apprehending violators.
10. Ability to perform traffic duty to include operating radar detection devices, directing traffic, escorting dignitaries, and conducting sobriety tests.
11. Knowledge and experience to enforce weapons systems security standards, traffic rules and regulations, including those related to speed, reckless and drunken driving.
12. Ability to dispatch police units to scenes of crimes, accidents and natural disasters.
13. Abilities to receive and record telephone and personal communications of emergencies, complaints, claims violations, and accidents.
14. Knowledge in the use of computerized information systems to direct patrols, record daily blotter information, and retrieve information through the FBI's National Crime Information Center System.
15. Skills to interview witnesses and suspects to obtain and verify information.
16. Skills to receive and record radio, telephone, and personal messages and instructions involving emergencies, complaints, violations, accidents, and requests for information and assistance.
17. Skills to search prisoners and remove weapons and articles which could cause injury or be used in escape attempts.
18. Knowledge and experience to ensure individuals requesting access to the installation have the proper identification credentials before entering.
19. Skills to conduct random vehicle searches at the privately owned vehicle (POV) gates and conduct thorough searches of all vehicles at commercial gate.
20. Ability to perform random antiterrorism measures in accordance with applicable instructions.
21. Abilities to serve in visitor control center issuing base entry passes (individual and vehicle), and conduct background checks on contractors.
22. Ability to serve as a restricted area entry controller and immediate visual assessment sentry providing surveillance for sensitive, restricted, and limited access areas.
23. Skills to assess the origin and cause of intrusion detection system (IDS) alarms in the area, make required notifications, request the dispatch of response forces as required or directed, implement compensatory measures if all or part of the IDS is inoperable, and complete documentation required in accordance with IDS operational and maintenance procedures.
24. Knowledge and experience to defend installation personnel, equipment, and resources from hostile ground.

EDUCATION:

SAN FRANCISCO STATE UNIVERSITY, San Francisco, CA
Master's Degree in Criminal Justice, 2007

SONOMA STATE UNIVERSITY, Sonoma, CA
Bachelor's Degree in Business Administration, 2000

COMMUNITY SERVICE:

Toys for Tots, Honolulu, Hawaii, 2009, 2010
Neighborhood Crime Watch, Manoa Falls, Honolulu, Volunteer Captain, 2008, 2009, 2010

Related Jobs/Careers:
(Security Consultant, Antiterrorism Consultant, Police Officer)

WOW! RÉSUMÉS 2011-2012: Great Jobs...Extra Income...Happiness...

EUDORA WAHLBURG
501 Tidwell Road
Houston, Texas
(319) 123-4567
euwahlburg@wowresumes.net

Target Position: Supervisory Patent Attorney At U.S. Government Agency or Government Department or Government Branch (2011 – 2012 Approximate Salary Range: $130,000 - $168,500 / Year)

PROFILE:
- ➢ Over 8 years' experience in Patent and Copyright Law in Government and U.S. Military positions
- ➢ Broad and current knowledge of intellectual property issues and policies including international/security aspects
- ➢ Well-rounded professional experience encompassing excellent research, analytical and communications skills

WORK EXPERIENCE:

DEPARTMENT OF COMMERCE, OFFICE OF THE INSPECTOR GENERAL (OIG) Washington, D.C.
Attorney-Advisor (General) 2007 - 2010

Major Duties:
- Served as an Assistant Counsel to the Inspector General, responsible for providing legal advice and services in support of the OIG's mission to promote economy and efficiency and to prevent fraud, waste, abuse, and mismanagement in Department of Commerce programs and operations
- Provided legal counsel to the Inspector General, the Deputy Inspector General, and the various OIG operating units on a wide range of issues involving areas such as civil, criminal, and administrative procedure; fraud; appropriations; procurement; grants; federal disclosure statutes; conflicts of interest; ethics; employee standards of conduct; equal employment opportunity; discipline and other human resources matters
- Analyzed legislative issues affecting the Department and the OIG, including the review of proposed legislation, regulations, and department orders
- Provided legal advice and services to OIG staff in connection with specific audits, investigations, inspections and program evaluation, and provided legal advice and counsel to senior OIG manager in connection with internal administrative and personnel matters
- Served as the OIG's liaison with the Department's Office of General Counsel, and as the agency's liaison with the Department of Justice in connection with civil and criminal matters arising out of OIG operations and activities
- Presented the agency position before administrative or judicial bodies

DEPARTMENT OF THE ARMY Bethesda, MD
Patent Attorney 2002 - 2007

Major Duties:
- Provided expert legal advice in matters relating to the implementation of the Technology Transfer Act of 1986
- Considered all inventions for possible commercial value; Explored foreign countries for possible interest in inventions
- Provided advice and assistance to other attorneys in the area of technology transfer
- Applied intellectual property law to inventions from government and contractor employees, to technical data and computer software, and to proposals, books, technical papers, motion pictures, and technical know-how
- Coordinated activities with the Army Material Command and the Department of the Army as required
- Prepared, filed and prosecuted patent applications in the United States and in foreign countries when appropriate, on inventions of a varied and complex nature
- Represented the Government before the Patent Examiners, the Board of Patent Appeals and Interferences, and the Court of Appeals for the Federal Circuit to procure patent protection on meritorious inventions

---

WOW! RÉSUMÉS 2011-2012: Great Jobs...Extra Income...Happiness...

EUDORA WAHLBURG
Page 2

euwahlburg@wowresumes.net

BUSINESS EXPERIENCE:

OFFICE OF THE COMMISSIONER, MAJOR LEAGUE BASEBALL
Administrative Assistant/Legal Assistant

New York, New York
1999 - 2001

- Supported staff attorneys and Chief Counsel by providing a variety of legal assistance and office support services
- Processed a variety of technical legal documents which were characteristically voluminous and complex in format
- Reviewed incoming material and determined the need for assembly and preparation of a variety of legal documents, e.g. complaints, motions, orders, briefs and subpoenas
- Provided assistance to legal teams in trial preparation by performing duties such as compiling trial notebooks, assembling jury instructions, and compiling witnesses and exhibit lists
- Assembled exhibits, affidavits and other legal documents from file material
- Maintained calendar of assigned active cases and tracked filing, hearing, and trial dates
- Scheduled meetings and interviews and arranged travel by preparing itinerary and secured travel/hotel bookings
- Produced a variety of written documents and materials utilizing wide range of office software applications

SPECIALIZED EXPERIENCE (KSAs: KNOWLEDGE, SKILLS AND ABILITIES):

1) Broad-based knowledge of intellectual property laws pertaining to federal agencies, government employees and government contractors.
2) Knowledge of the technical and legal (substantive and procedural) requirements related to the protection of Government's interests in patents (including experience in the preparation and prosecution of patent applications before the US Patent and Trademark Office), copyrights and trademarks, avoidance of infringements and familiarity with the legal issues and principles related to the establishment, protection, defense and exploitation of the Government's legal rights in intellectual property.
3) Knowledge of federal acquisition laws, regulations and policy with specific knowledge of the laws and regulations applicable to rights in technical data and computer software, and the laws and regulations applicable to nontraditional contractual agreements, such as grants, cooperative agreements, other transactions (OT's) and cooperative research and development agreements (CRADAs).
4) Ability to analyze thoroughly and solve a wide variety of complex legal problems.
5) Ability to communicate effectively orally and in writing: Demonstration of communication skills in writing and in speaking so that contracting officers, scientists, engineers, patent examiners, other Government personnel and Government contractors will understand content of the communication to respond in an appropriate/desired manner.

EDUCATION:

COLUMBIA UNIVERSITY SCHOOL OF LAW, New York, New York
Juris Doctor, 2001
Law School Transcript provided, Ranked #21 out of class of 155

RELEVANT COURSEWORK AND SEMINARS/CONFERENCES
Advanced Trademark Law Seminar
Intellectual Property Law
Legal and Economic Theory of Intellectual Property
Patent Prosecution
Trade Secrets Law
Unfair Trade Practices Symposium

Copyright Law
Legal Clinic – Practical Preparation of GMU Patent Applications
Patent Law I & II
Patent and Know-How Licensing Conference
Trademark Law

RICE UNIVERSITY,
B.A. Degree in Sociology, 1996
Summa Cum Laude

Related Jobs/Careers:
(Attorney for Government, Government Agency Counsel)

WOW! RÉSUMÉS 2011-2012: Great Jobs...Extra Income...Happiness...

SANDRA JESSUP
123 Fuller Road
West Des Moines, Iowa
586-123-456
sandyjessup@wowresumes.net

Target Positions: Office Specialist / Program Coordinator / Administrative Assistant / Secretary At U.S. Government Agency or Government Department or Government Branch (2011 – 2012 Approximate Annual Salary Range: $49,500 - $76,750)

PROFILE

- ✔ 10 Years + Experience as Office Specialist, Management/Administrative Assistant and Secretary
- ✔ Outstanding skills include clerical and computer software (MS Office and proprietary government office systems)
- ✔ Well-evaluated and recognized performance at Federal Agencies providing critical public service and missions
- ✔ Bachelor's degree in English with additional courses in Business Administration, Computers and Human Resources

EMPLOYMENT HISTORY

DEPARTMENT OF TRANSPORTATION
FEDERAL AVIATION ADMINISTRATION   Urbandale, Iowa
Management and Program Assistant   10/2008 to 3/2011

- Served as a Management and Program Assistant for an En Route Facility
- Performed a combination of routine and multiple and varying assignments in support of professional, technical, and specialized occupations under the limited direction of a project/program manager and other managers
- Worked independently in preparing and analyzing work schedules considering Agency budgetary constraints
- Processed and reviewed Travel Authorization/Vouchers through the Government Trip system
- Processed time and attendance records and resolved issues
- Applied experience and advanced knowledge to perform administrative assignments for projects/programs
- Demonstrated considerable independence in planning time and coordinates only as needed with a manager
- Assisted others plan and identify resources to accomplish projects/programs tasks
- Established policies/procedures providing guidance for most assignments
- Provided recommendations to improve work processes
- Resolved most problems and work issues without the assistance of a manager
- Identified and informed managers and/or other employees of problems/issues that required attention
- Provided guidance to lower support staff members for handling routine problems and issues

DEPARTMENT OF AGRICULTURE, FOREST SERVICE   Decatur, Illinois
Grants and Agreements Specialist   2005 to 2008

- Served as a liaison and/or advisor for grant management programs and funding issues
- Provided advice and assistance regarding grant/cooperative agreement application processes and policies
- Evaluated applications before award, including the analysis of applications received in response to programs and Request for Application (RFA) requirements
- Developed and reviewed reports and correspondence in support of grant/agreement management and analysis of grant/agreement applications
- Prepared correspondence, approvals and other documentation for approved grants
- Coordinated activities related to arrangements for funding; Answered questions from grantees
- Prepared notifications of approved grants, contracts and agreements following standard procedures and guidelines
- Served as a liaison in the resolution of simple funding questions and issues

---

SANDRA JESSUP
Page 2

sandyjessup@wowresumes.net

EMPLOYMENT HISTORY (Continued)

DEPARTMENT OF AGRICULTURE, FOOD AND NUTRITION SERVICE
Secretary

Peoria, Illinois
2003 to 2005

- Served as the personal assistant to the Branch Chief
- Facilitated the clerical and administrative support work of the Branch
- Conferred with Branch Chief on decision-making for internal administrative procedures for the Branch and its subordinates
- Personally handled many requests for information, referring to Branch Chief only those calls requiring personal attention
- Assisted in implementing supervisor's intentions by explaining reporting and procedural requirements to subordinates and arranging for timely submissions to expedite the work of the Branch
- Reviewed outgoing correspondence for conformance with regulations, Branch policies, and procedural instructions, completeness of reply, clarity, proper format, grammar, typographical accuracy, and necessary attachments
- Compiled special and routine reports as requested by the Branch Chief
- Maintained the Branch Chief's calendar and scheduling appointments on own initiative based on personal knowledge of Branch Chief's workload, personal preferences and issues of importance
- Made travel arrangements for supervisor and staff, contacting travelers in route to relay information
- Established and maintained files and records, manuals, handbooks, and other related materials of the Branch
- Maintained personnel listings of all Branch employees for budgetary purposes
- Served as timekeeper for personnel in the Branch Chief's office

DEPARTMENT OF AGRICULTURE
NATURAL RESOURCES CONSERVATION SERVICE
Administrative Assistant

Spokane, Washington
2000 to 2003

- Assisted State Training Officer and other staff with a wide variety of training functions and activities including registering employees into training sessions, tracking training needs, completion and expenditures
- Assisted in the control and coordination required for processing a wide variety of personnel actions including accessions, reassignments, promotions, extensions, corrections and separations, and more
- Assisted in processing Length of Service (LOS) and other awards
- Assisted with administering Federal Benefits programs, including health benefits, life insurance, Thrift Savings Plan, flexible spending accounts, retirement coverage, leaves-of-absence, conditions of employment and more
- Provided assistance as a point of contact (POC) for EmpowHR and eAuthentication
- Helped ensure employee, partner, contractor, and volunteer access; Provided information for procedures related to investigations and other security requirements; Entered data into NEIS, E-Verify, and other systems as needed
- Performed duties in support of Integrated Acquisition System (IAS) processing activities to include entering purchase request information into the (IAS) database; file maintenance; posting and tracking procurement progress information on Excel spreadsheets and posting to the management services shared drive
- Transported government vehicles (GVs) for preventive maintenance and repairs to various servicing merchants
- Maintained and posted updated mileage information to the GSA Fleet Drive thru electronic database
- Assisted with data entry to various administrative databases, i.e. Access on-line, USDA Corporate Property Automated Information system (CPAIS)

EDUCATION

GRAND VIEW COLLEGE, Des Moines, Iowa
B.A. English, 2000

DRAKE UNIVERSITY, Des Moines, Iowa
Continuing College-Level Courses:
Accounting, Computer Databases, Human Resources, Psychology and History

---

SANDRA JESSUP   sandyjessup@wowresumes.net
Page 3

SPECIALIZED EXPERIENCE (KSAs: KNOWLEDGE, SKILLS AND ABILITIES):

- Ability to type 50+ words per minute based on a 5 minute sample with 3 or fewer errors
- Knowledge of various office automation software programs, tools and techniques used in the support of office operations and the production of a variety of documents, such as letters, reports, spreadsheets, databases, presentations and graphs
- Ability to present clear and concise information consistent with the targeted audience
- Ability to research, interpret, and apply written procedures, regulations or policies pertaining to travel, time and attendance and other administrative programs
- Ability to interpret and apply established administrative guidance for administrative and/or non-technical materials
- Receive telephone calls and visitors; ascertains nature of call and determines appropriate action
- Prepare, process and monitor all type of paperwork such as requests for the development of publications
- Process requests for publications; maintain publications inventory control; and manages bulk mailings
- Provide for the training, development and oversight of an entry level clerical helper
- Assist with correspondence and reports related to human resources functions
- Assist with filing and disposition of hard copy and electronic records
- Compose routine correspondence such as replies to inquiries concerning program questions
- Search for, assemble, and summarize information as required from files and documents

VOLUNTEER / OUTREACH / COMMUNITY SERVICE

Des Moines Art Center, Volunteer, Summers 2008, 2009, 2010
Urbandale, Iowa Flood Control District, Volunteer/Information Center, 2008
Second Harvest, Des Moines Iowa, Volunteer/Fundraiser

Related Jobs/Careers:
(Management Assistant, Administrative Assistant, Secretary)

WOW! RÉSUMÉS 2011-2012: Great Jobs...Extra Income...Happiness...

CARSON HSIEN HYUNH
1000 Sugar Creek Road #123
Charlotte, North Carolina
(244) 123-4567
carsonhhyunh@wowresumes.net

Target Positions:
Supervisory Accountant or Financial Accounts Manager-Technician
At U.S. Government Agency or Government Department or Government Branch
(2011 – 2012 Approximate Salary Range: $123,800 – 155,500 / Year)

PROFILE:

☑ 12 + Years in Accounting, Financial Accounts Management including supervisory and auditing functions
☑ Familiarity with varied Federal agencies including Dept. of Justice, Dept. of Labor and Dept. of Defense
☑ Outstanding track record of increasing responsibility and the ability to apply budgetary goals and constraints
☑ Customer service orientation with recognition that Federal Agencies are beholden to the tax-paying public

WORK EXPERIENCE:

DEPARTMENT OF JUSTICE
Accountant

Charlotte, North Carolina
2008 to 2010

- Performed or assisted in performing systematic examinations and appraisals of financial records, financial and management reports, management controls, policies and practices affecting or reflecting the financial condition and operating results of Department Of Justice activities, programs and departments
- Conducted and assisted in coordinating activities related to the detection of fraud, waste and abuse
- Provided advice and guidance when technical interpretation, opinion or decisions were solicited
- Consulted regarding legislative, regulatory and procedural interpretation and guidance
- Assessed audits with resulting findings and recommendations, audit improvements and resolutions
- Executed follow-ups on corrective actions, logistics and resource support, and personnel training
- Prepared instructions and guidance in the implementation and operation of accounting procedures
- Analyzed current and required accounting procedures to design new or improved processes
- Validated current processes with respect to regulatory requirements
- Validated a variety of accounting data that is entered into schedules and accounts
- Examined, interpreted and recorded accounting data, records and reports pertaining to multiple account within one or more accounting systems or subsystems

DEPARTMENT OF LABOR, BUREAU OF LABOR STATISTICS
Accountant

Washington, D.C.
2001 to 2007

- Provided Bureau of Labor Statistics (BLS) Division of Financial Planning and Management (DFPM) processing services including preparing allotments and allocations, tracking fixed assets and internal use software, entering miscellaneous obligations, processing reclassifications and accruals, running reports and performing routine and complex analyses
- Established and documented accounting procedures and recommended and executed changes to existing BLS accounting processes
- Served as a technical accounting authority for BLS and conducted ongoing audits of financial operations
- Provided analysis and advice regarding accounting operations, appropriation law issues, financial systems and on the effect of new laws or directives from central oversight agencies, such as Treasury, OMB, and GAO
- Responsible for the development, installation and refinement of BLS accounting applications such as Computer Cost Distribution System (CCDS), the Mail Cost Application, the Training Request Application, the Security Investigation system, and the Accounts Receivable Tracking System
- Participated in the improvement and modification of existing financial and accounting systems
- Served as a system administrator for the E2 Solutions travel system and the Citibank Procurement and Travel Card programs

---

WOW! RÉSUMÉS 2011-2012: Great Jobs...Extra Income...Happiness...

CARSON HSIEN HYUNH, Page 2   carsonhhyunh@wowresumes.net

WORK EXPERIENCE (Continued):

DEPARTMENT OF VETERANS AFFAIRS, VETERANS BENEFITS ADMINISTRATION   Baltimore, MD
Financial Accounts Technician   1998- 2001
- Performed a variety of financial services (accounts receivable, government travel, payroll technical and agent cashier as well as other support services functions in the mailroom and reproduction services)
- Served as liaison to the VA Debt Management Center (DMC)
- Monitored, controlled, validated and maintained accounting transaction and accounting records for multiple accounts
- Reconciled subsidiary ledgers to general ledgers control accounts
- Maintained control accounts and subsidiary accounts and processed accounting transactions for a variety of functions
- Maintained Government Services Agency (GSA) Fleet Automobiles

DEPARTMENT OF DEFENSE, DEFENSE LOGISTICS AGENCY   Richmond, Virginia
Cashier   1997 to 1998
- Operated a cash register; Accepted cash, personal checks, credit cards, etc.
- Prepared, verified and issued change funds as required
- Collected cash receipts, cash register tapes, checks, credit card receipts and other supporting documentation
- Compared registered tapes with Daily Activity Report and researched any discrepancies
- Prepared and maintained cash overage and shortage records for each sales cashier daily
- Maintained current dishonored check listing, verified name, mailing address and telephone numbers
- Assisted in the collection of dishonored check payments

SPECIALIZED EXPERIENCE (KSAs: KNOWLEDGE, SKILLS AND ABILITIES):

1. Ability to apply analytical methods and techniques to identify and resolve financial and/or auditing issues.
2. Ability to communicate effectively both verbally and in writing, including reports and presentations.
3. Ability to provide technical assistance and consultation or financial and /or auditing matters.
4. Ability to gather, compile and analyze financial and/or programmatic information.
5. Knowledge of accounting principles, practices and techniques.
6. Knowledge of Generally Accepted Accounting Principles (GAAP), Generally Accepted Accounting
7. Standards (GAAS) and other accounting industry regulations.
8. Ability to gather, compile and analyze financial and/or auditing information.
9. Skills in using a computer to process and analyze data, creates, edit, print or retrieve files.
10. Skills in using software to create charts, tables or graphs.
11. Skills in Customer Service balancing interests of a variety of clients, anticipating and meeting the needs of clients and achieving quality end products.
12. Knowledge and ability in Decision Making/Problem Solving using strategic and critical approaches.
13. Interpersonal Skills in showing understanding, professionalism, courtesy, tact, empathy, concern and politeness to others, including sensitivity to cultural diversity, race, gender, and disabilities.
14. Skills in Self-Management setting well-defined goals, displaying a high level of initiative, effort and commitment towards completing assignments in a timely manner.
15. Skill, Knowledge and Abilities in Accounting/Technical: Administer and manage the execution, review, and evaluation of accounting policies and programs within an organization.

EDUCATION:
NORTH CAROLINA STATE UNIVERSITY, Raleigh, North Carolina
Bachelor Of Science in Accounting, 1996; Minor in Political Science

CERTIFIED PUBLIC ACCOUNTANT, State of North Carolina

COURSEWORK:		
Financial Fraud Investigation	North Carolina Regulatory Review	Accountancy Laws
Ethical and Legal Standards for CPAs	Government Auditing Standards	Payroll Best Practices
	Taxes and Financial Reporting	Revenue Recognition

COMMUNITY SERVICE:
United Way Charlotte, Financial Advisory Board

Related Jobs/Careers:
(Accounting Manager, Government Accountant, Cashier)

WOW! RÉSUMÉS 2011-2012: Great Jobs...Extra Income...Happiness...

Robyn J. Lopez
501 Larimer Street #123
Denver, Colorado
769-123-4567
rjlopezusa@wowresumes.net

Target Position:
Mortgage Banking Industry Analyst
At U.S. Government Agency or Government Department or Government Branch
(2011 – 2012 Approximate Salary Range: $74,950 - $118,750 / Year)

PROFILE:

➢ Over 10 years in loan and mortgage industries in the private sector and at Federal Agencies serving the public
➢ Results-oriented professional with quantifiable achievements in increasing business and meeting budgets
➢ Exceptional communications in one-to-one personal contact as well as organizational teamwork and missions
➢ Knowledge, skills and abilities in the technical areas of mortgages, secondary financing & Federal loan programs

EDUCATION:

NORTHWESTERN UNIVERSITY, Evanston, Illinois
Master of Business Administration, Finance and Real Estate, 2004

UNIVERSITY OF OKLAHOMA, Norman, Oklahoma
Bachelor of Arts Degree, Communications, 1998

CERTIFICATION/LICENSURE:

Certified as Reverse Mortgage Specialist, Housing and Urban Development, FHA, 2010 to Present
Licensed as State of Colorado Mortgage Loan Broker, 2007 to Present

PROFESSIONAL EXPERIENCE:

FEDERAL DEPOSIT INSURANCE CORPORATION   Denver, Colorado
Financial Management Analyst   2007 to 2010

• Reviewed, analyzed and coordinated the completion of complex work assignments related to the administrative, financial and processing activities of assets retained from financial institutions failures
• Performed analyses and audits in accordance with the policies, procedures, goals, objectives and delegated authority specific to the FDIC's Division of Resolutions and Receiverships and the Corporation as a whole

Specialized in financial procedures and aspects of the systems utilized by the specific FDIC program areas and the financial systems utilized by external loan servicing and asset management contractors:
• The General Ledger (FIMS); the Accounts Payable System (APPO); Control Totals Module (CTM)
• National Processing System (NPS); Liability Dividend System (LDS)
• Correspondence Control Manager (CCM); Asset Information Management System (AIMS)
• Subsidiary Systems of Record which interface into the General Ledger; Loan Servicing Systems of Record
• Service Request Tracking System (STS); Automated Conversion System (ACS)
• Warranties and Representations Accounts Processing System (WRAPS)

WOW! RÉSUMÉS 2011-2012: Great Jobs...Extra Income...Happiness...

_____

Robyn J. Lopez   rjlopezusa@wowresumes.net
Page 2

DEPARTMENT OF AGRICULTURE   Faribault, Minnesota
RURAL HOUSING SERVICE   2004 to 2007
Loan Assistant (General) Area Specialist

- Served in a Loan Assistant (General) position with the U.S. Department of Agriculture, Rural Development, in Minnesota
- Performed a variety of duties related to the making and servicing of loans under delegated Rural Housing Service, Rural Business Service, and Rural Utilities Service program authorities
- Provided guidance and assistance, advising lenders, CPAs, developers, investment brokers, management firms, the general public, and others concerning eligibility and other requirements of Rural Development programs
- Gathered appropriate material, prepared correspondence, and answered inquiries as required
- Reviewed and analyzed pre-selected multi-family housing (MFH), rural utility and community facility loans and grants, including pre-applications, applications, and all supporting documents to determine eligibility
- Checked for compliance of regulatory requirements, financial position, soundness of collateral, repayment ability, and took appropriate action for orderly processing of the loan and/or grant
- Counseled borrowers regarding approved management practices such as proper use of credit, income, and other resources
- Analyzed selected annual financial statements and reports on closed MFH loans; Accompanied another specialist on visits to inspect and check progress of planned construction of rural utility, community facility, and multi-family housing projects
- Assisted in conducting triennial supervisory visits/security inspections of pre-selected MFH projects
- Assisted in conducting compliance reviews, graduation reviews, and security reviews of rural utility and community facility projects
- Received and followed up on applications for single family housing (SFH) loans in residential and rural settings
- Conducted applicant interviews to review applications of SFH loans for eligibility and financial soundness
- Reviewed plans and specifications of SFH to determine if they met building codes and Rural Development guidelines
- Made periodic visits to SFH borrower's property to inspect repairs and other property issues to determine physical condition and ensure that the property was kept in repairable condition
- Determined program suitability of inventory property and arranges for management and sale of the property
- Assisted in planning, and participated in activities, conferences, and events that marketed Rural Development programs and services
- Assisted in implementing community development principles of the Rural Development mission area; Attended trainings on community development principles and practices that was sponsored by the agency and agency partners

BUSINESS EXPERIENCE:

LAKE FRONT REAL ESTATE & LOANS   Chicago, IL
Office Manager / Broker Assistant   2001 to 2003
- Managed the main branch of start-up mortgage loan company that achieved doubling of sales and loan originations every 6 months with outstanding outreach and service to multiple ethnic and niche markets
- Instrumental in increasing business volume by 125 % year-to-year with innovative programs, seminars and promotions that resulted in doubling of revenues yearly

TOWN AND COUNTRY / AMERIQUEST MORTGAGE COMPANIES   Daly City, CA
Branch Manager / Assistant Branch Manager   1999 to 2001
- Started as telemarketer/account executive; Became consistent top producer nationally at Ameriquest
- Promoted to management; Achieved #1 regional status as Manager of Town and Country Branch in 2001
- Processed, performed pre-underwriting and packaged loan applications for submission to assigned lending institutions
- Assisted in training staff and administration of office daily activities including loan originations

_____

Robyn J. Lopez   rjlopezusa@wowresumes.net
Page 3

SPECIALIZED EXPERIENCE (KSAs: KNOWLEDGE, SKILLS AND ABILITIES):

Knowledge of the mortgage industry:
- Knowledge and Experience in the interpretation, administration or utilization of a major government business program focused on housing finance or financial sector program, including use of complex/technical guide/contract documents
- Ability to interpret and apply to complex issues the laws, regulation, policies, standards, manuals and other procedures for specific government or business programs related to securitization and mortgage housing finance
- Skills and capabilities in recommending substantive program changes and to create new approaches to program compliance and enforcement
- Knowledge of related government regulations and interfacing a very large fixed income segment of the market, with the ability to read, assess and interpret disclosure documentation, contracts and economic data for application to assessment of Ginnie Mae's program participants
- Experience in following directions in researching regulations and program parameters and the ability to work with senior staff and outside professionals to make decisions on interpretation and application of a highly technical program in the financial sector
- Ability to perform analysis related to mortgage banking financial services and regulatory requirements and to apply quantitative and narrative variables
- Capability in the use and interpretation of complex varieties of corporate, mortgage or securitization related and other financial quantitative information, including balance sheets, income statements, portfolio data, delinquency trend analyses, early payment data, servicing performance criteria, foreclosure trends, and the ability to utilize such information to handle a customer service function and to support an extensive counterparty risk analysis effort
- Experience in utilization of quantitative data including corporate financial information and mortgage portfolio data and trend analysis to determine program compliance and assess program needs in the area of mortgage banking, housing finance, and securitization; Demonstrated capability in creating spreadsheet analyses and utilizing quantitative information in a critical and creative manner with minimal supervision
- Possess training and capability in review and interpretation of the quality of performance of a mortgage portfolio or other similar financial assets, data indicative of delinquency and default trends, losses, payment obligations and financial quality of an institution; Fully capable of utilizing tools such as Excel spreadsheets to assist in data manipulation and reporting
- Direct job experience or training in reading financial statements and quantitative analyses; are fully functional in creating spreadsheets in excel and can work with professional staff to establish and apply quantitative standards to analysis of financial capability and adequacy of performance of a financial asset, such as mortgage loan servicing

Skills in oral communication:
- Ability to communicate orally with government officials, regulators, loan originators, servicers, document custodians, accountants and lawyers on complex programmatic technical issues and to organize professionals from different disciplines for problem solving
- Demonstrated experience in working with inside and outside business partners from diverse sectors including banking, financial regulatory, auditors, accountants, lawyers, operations professionals and others to support a customer service and coordination role that relies heavily on telephone conversations and conference presentations; Strong ability and track record in public speaking
- Excellent skills in handling PowerPoint presentations, acting as a participant in meetings with inside and outside parties, leading such meetings or conference calls, explaining highly technical problems and solutions to support the administration of a mortgage finance securitization program; Ability to present a technical case and respond to questions in the financial arena
- Comfortable in a lead or secondary role in partnership with senior and peer staff and outside participants in discussing a complex program of securitization, mortgage finance or other highly technical nature with a strong inclination to develop presentation skills for public speaking situations

Skills in written communication:
- Skills in written communication, documentation, record keeping, report writing and development of analytical cases relevant to financial fines, government programs in the mortgage, securitization or financial areas, including legislative, regulatory and financial or market developments and standards
- Possess the experience and demonstrated effectiveness in drafting technical communications such as program announcements, and PowerPoint presentations for public and industry groups; Ability to draft reports on business partners and market or program developments, particularly as pertinent to mortgage finance or other technical fields; Skill in establishing and maintaining excellent records of interactions in a program administration or customer service environment
- Excellent writing skills in communicating with business partners individually or as a group with ease and experience and training in drafting materials sometimes quickly and under time pressure; Ability to draft cases as an advocate for program participants in the role of a customer service professional and to defend positions before boards or meetings of peers; Excellent writing skills in drafting emails, formal letters, memoranda and presentations in financial sector customer service environment

Related Jobs/Careers:
(Loan Analyst, Financial Analyst, Mortgage Specialist, Bank Manager)

WOW! RÉSUMÉS 2011-2012: Great Jobs...Extra Income...Happiness...

Cassandra O'Dowd
100 South Emerson Avenue #123
Idaho Falls, Idaho
549-123-4567
cassodowd@wowresumes.net

> Target Positions:
> Supervisory Ecologist / Interdisciplinary Scientist
> At U.S. Government Agency or Government Department or Government Branch
> (2011 – 2012 Approximate Salary Range: $89,550 - $135,225 / Year)

PROFILE:

- ☑ 10 Years' Experience of increasing responsibility in interdisciplinary and ecological research and biodiversity
- ☑ Broad perspective on environmental protection, community economic issues and native cultural concerns
- ☑ Proven leadership skills in mentoring, supervising and reviewing research and findings of students/professionals
- ☑ Skills, knowledge and abilities in the technical and scientific aspects of natural resource research/husbandry

WORK EXPERIENCE:

ENVIRONMENTAL PROTECTION AGENCY   Idaho Falls, Idaho
Interdisciplinary Scientist   2006 to 2010

- Coordinated the planning of experimental studies of the effect of chemicals on the endocrine systems, specifically estrogen androgen and thyroid active chemicals
- Evaluated data (including histopathology data, and data from fish in vitro and biochemical measures such as vitellogenin) from bioassays utilizing wildlife and aquatic species
- Evaluated laboratory practices in avian husbandry and amphibian culture
- Solicited and integrated technical advice and comment from within EPA, from stakeholders and the general public, and other governmental agencies through established channels for validation strategy, study design, analysis and interpretation
- Evaluated information on use of reproductive assays in assessment of environmental issues confronting US EPA programs
- Developed work assignments for testing and validation of endocrine disrupting chemicals in wildlife and aquatic species, especially bioassays that utilize birds, fish, amphibians and aquatic invertebrates
- Served as Mentor and reviewed the academic research of Boise State University graduate students in toxicology

DEPARTMENT OF THE INTERIOR, NATIONAL PARK SERVICE   San Francisco County
Biologist   2004 to 2006

- Provided leadership in support of the protection and management of natural resources, while facilitating visitor access, island maintenance, and the rehabilitation of cultural resources on Alcatraz Island
- Implemented a comprehensive and proactive wildlife program of natural resource management on Alcatraz in accordance with applicable Federal laws, and NPS (National Park Service) policies and directives
- Coordinated management of the nesting western gull population of the island to protect both the colony and the safety of staff and park visitors
- Assisted with the review of proposed projects for the island and developing guidance and mitigations to minimize impacts to natural resources during project implementation
- Participated on planning teams for the island, facilitating ongoing bird monitoring efforts with cooperating agencies

DEPARTMENT OF THE INTERIOR, U.S. GEOLOGICAL SURVEY   Twisp, Washington
Biological Science Technician (Fish)   2000 to 2004

- Assisted in conducting field studies and surveys to collect fisheries data and specimens to support scientific studies
- Prepared, identified, dissected and maintained laboratory records on specimens and samples for preservation/museum use
- Performed live animal maintenance and operated and maintained a government motor vehicle and power boats
- Conducted yearly estuarine studies in Western Washington Coast and seasonal fisheries research in Lake Chelan NRA

WOW! RÉSUMÉS 2011-2012: Great Jobs...Extra Income...Happiness...

Cassandra O'Dowd
Page 2

cassodowd@wowresumes.net

SPECIALIZED EXPERIENCE (KSAs: KNOWLEDGE, SKILLS AND ABILITIES):

1. Knowledge and skills in experimental studies of the effects of chemicals on the endocrine system, specifically estrogen, androgen and thyroid active chemicals.
2. Skills and Abilities in assessing study data and other relevant scientific information and processed statistics.
3. Knowledge of wildlife monitoring and implementing project related mitigations for wildlife (especially seabirds and water birds) and related habitats.
4. Abilities working with colonially nesting seabirds and water birds, natural resource planning and NEPA work, working as a biologist and ecologist in a National Park, and working in an interdivisional and inter-agency setting.
5. Oversee and contribute to the development and validation process of assays.
6. Assess study data and other relevant scientific information and recommend modifications to the scientific approach for specific assays as necessary.
7. Develop work assignments for testing and validation of assays being conducted by the EACPD (Exposure Assessment, Coordination and Policy Division).
8. Supervise and review the compilation and summary of field and laboratory data for preparation of interim reports.
9. Provide guidance to contractors and park staff for complying with project requirements and mitigations, and where practical assists in the execution of mitigations.
10. Develop monitoring to meet program needs; Perform data management and analysis, and wrote reports.

EDUCATION:

WASHINGTON STATE UNIVERSITY, Spokane, WA
M.S. Degree in Environmental Science, Biodiversity Concentration, 2003

UNIVERSITY OF CALIFORNIA AT BERKELEY, Berkeley, CA
B.S. Degree in Zoology, 2000
Minor in Ecology, Ecosystems and Biodiversity

RELATED COURSEWORK:

Methods of Ecosystem Analysis	Biogeography, Biodiversity and Conservation
Biological Oceanography	Field Ecology
Aquatic Ecology	Wildlife Conservation
Species & Ecosystem Conservation: An Interdisciplinary Approach	Molecular Ecology
Human Dimensions in the Conservation of Biological Diversity	Molecular Ecology Seminar
Molecular Systematics laboratory	Conservation Genetics Seminar
Landscape Ecology	Ecology Seminar

TRAVEL:

Alaska National Parks including Denali National Park & Preserve, Glacier Bay National Park, Kenai Fjords National Park and Lake Clark National Park & Preserve

VOLUNTEER / OUTREACH:

Habitat for Humanity, Blackfoot, Idaho, 2007, 2009, 2010

Related Jobs/Careers:
(Interdisciplinary Scientist, Government Biologist)

WOW! RÉSUMÉS 2011-2012: Great Jobs...Extra Income...Happiness...

Fabrice Acevedo
1200 Camelback Road #123
Glendale, Arizona 85301
623-123-4567
FabAcevedo@WOWResumes.Net

Target Position:
MIS Computer Manager
At U.S. Government Agency or Government Department or Government Branch
(2011 – 2012 Approximate Salary Range: $89,700 - $119,950 / Year)

PROFILE:

✓ Specialized experience including comprehensive knowledge of IT principles, concepts, and management disciplines
✓ In-depth knowledge of hardware, computer systems and networks, proprietary software and technical support
✓ 2 Bachelor's Degrees (Computer Science and Mathematics) as well as Microsoft and CISSP (Security) Certification
✓ Wide experience in various industries and environments including Housing, Departments of Justice & Defense

FEDERAL EMPLOYMENT HISTORY:

DEPARTMENT OF HOUSING AND URBAN DEVELOPMENT
GOVERNMENT NATIONAL MORTGAGE ASSOSICATION (GINNIE MAE)   Phoenix, AZ
Management Information Specialist   2007 to Present

- Manage the efficient and effective coordination and implementation of IT projects in designing, developing, and administering major Ginnie Mae information technology projects and systems which support Ginnie Mae's program and operational requirements; Perform analysis, verification and validation, systems enhancement, and contract transitions
- Plan, coordinate, and implement major IT project initiatives
- Integrate sponsor customer requirements and participation into a comprehensive IT development and management plan according to the Department's System Development Methodology and Industry Best Practices
- Fully coordinate with all contributing organizations, including various development disciplines, management agent and owner responsibilities, for control and management of IT budget projects, and schedule, assuring that Ginnie Mae's commitments to the sponsor customer are met
- Serve as Ginnie Mae's point of contact for sponsor customers and other external agencies on assigned projects
- Perform technical reviews of IT deliverables in the Life Cycle Development of IT projects including detailed architecture design, system performance testing and test plans
- Review work-in-progress or finished work products of contractors for accuracy, adequacy, and soundness
- Provide overall implementation of major IT initiatives from requirements, through system development and implementation; Execute in accordance with federal IT laws and regulations including such as A 130, NIST, FISMA, 0MB, FISCAM, etc. with HUD's published guidelines and guidance
- Demonstrate extensive IT technical skills, expertise and experience in designing and developing major IT state-of-the-art solutions in the special areas of primary/secondary mortgage markets and financial models

CERTIFICATIONS:

Microsoft Certified Professional – Windows Server 2003/2008
CISSP (Certified Information Systems Security Professional) Certification, 2010

Fabrice Acevedo
Page 2

FabAcevedo@WOWResumes.Net

FEDERAL EMPLOYMENT HISTORY (Continued):

JUDICIAL BRANCH OF THE UNITED STATES
U.S. COURTS, SOUTHWEST DISTRICT OF ARIZONA
Computer Systems Programmer

Phoenix, AZ
2004 to 2007

- Designed, implemented and maintained computer systems that included the completion of software development project assignments involving systems analysis, computer programming, testing code, systems integration and information technology
- Gathered requirements, designed, coded, debugged and tested software written in a variety of programming languages
- Defined and executed functional and unit testing on an Agile/SCRUM development system
- Developed comprehensive test specifications, plans and walkthrough code to extract test cases
- Worked closely with District Court Clerk's Office, Probation Office and Pretrial Services Office in implementing technology solutions for the District

DEPARTMENT OF DEFENSE
DEFENSE COMMISSARY AGENCY
Supply Technician

McCllellan, CA
2001 to 2002

- Performed a variety of procurement control duties involving supplies, transfers, equipment accountability, and other general office duties according to the operational supply and equipment needs of the commissary
- Responsible for the accountability and control, procurement, issue and disposition of supplies and equipment such as cash registers, meat slicers/grinders, refrigerators, forklifts and other general equipment
- Maintained the property accounting register relating to supplies and equipment procured for the commissary
- Assisted management with cyclic accountable inventories of all supplies according to department and equipment
- Prepared, processed and reviewed various documents as required by management and Department of Defense

BUSINESS EXPERIENCE:

EDULEARN COMPUTER SCHOOL
Computer Programming Trainer and Consultant

Chatsworth, CA
2002 to 2004

- Trained, guided and consulted with students and corporate office staff in Computer Training Classes and Seminars
- Class Instructor in Visual Basic 2002 Fundamentals; Visual Basic 2002 Desktop; Visual Basic 2002Database; and C#.NET Windows Apps
- Designed 2-Day Intensive Hands-On Seminars on Database Courses such as Access 2002 Development and Visual Basic 2002 Database

SPECIALIZED EXPERIENCE (KSAs: KNOWLEDGE, SKILLS AND ABILITIES):

1) Specialized knowledge of software capabilities, telecommunications including messaging protocols, database integration schemes and Web based development in order to plan, design, develop and coordinate major organizational initiatives.
2) Knowledge and technical expertise in interpreting IT policies, procedures and strategies governing the effective and productive utilization of state of the art information technology; Provide expert technical expertise, advice, verification, guidance and recommendations to management and IT system engineers and telecommunication IT specialist.
3) Extensive technical experience and knowledge of systems integration requirements, use of case analysis techniques, development of IT network design typologies and management in order to integrate all agency IT functions as required.

_____

Fabrice Acevedo   FabAcevedo@WOWResumes.Net
Page 3

SPECIALIZED EXPERIENCE (KSAs: KNOWLEDGE, SKILLS AND ABILITIES, Continued):

4) Knowledge of system architecture disciplines and experience with integrating disparate technologies.
5) Extensive IT technical experience and skill in the application of analytical and evaluative methods and techniques to evaluate the efficiency and effectiveness of IT program operations.
6) Skill in analyzing, designing developing, implementing and maintaining state of the art computer systems, related to the primary or secondary markets or major financial systems in accordance with system development life cycle methodologies and IT Federal Laws.
7) Knowledge of and experience in developing IT systems in support of mortgage- backed securities / loan servicing and financial systems.
8) Knowledge and experience in validation and verification, guidance and recommendations to management and IT system engineers and telecommunication IT specialists.
9) Knowledge and experience in object oriented design techniques.
10) Knowledge of and experience in developing and analyzing large systems projects processing financial information.
11) Knowledge of and experience applying Federal IT and Security laws including the Clinger Cohen Act, Federal Financial Management and Improvement Act, NIST and other federal laws and regulations.
12) Ability to identify, diagnose and resolve complex problems.
13) Ability to work on a team and communicate effectively.
14) Experience writing and testing code in C/C++, C#, VB.Net, and Java.
15) Experience writing and testing code in AJAX and J2EE environment.
16) Experience with SQL databases, e.g., Informix, MS SQL, Oracle.
17) Experience writing and testing complex SQL statements.
18) Experience writing and testing code in Delphi/Pascal and Perl.
19) Experience with Agile software development.
20) Experience with bug tracking and source code management.

EDUCATION:

SAN JOSE STATE UNIVERSITY, San Jose, CA
B.S. Degree in Computer Science, 2002

ARIZONA STATE UNIVERSITY, Tempe, AZ
Bachelor's degree Mathematics, Minor in Statistics, 2000

RELATED COURSEWORK AND CONTINUING EDUCATION:

Programming Methodology	Advanced Database Systems
Software Development	Distributed Systems
Operating Systems Principles	Software Metrics and Quality Assurance
Secure Networked Systems	Data Mining
System Administration	Advanced Topic Database Design
Advanced Operating Systems	Advanced Object Oriented Design

_____

Related Jobs/Careers:
(Computer Programmer, MIS Manager)

WOW! RÉSUMÉS 2011-2012: Great Jobs...Extra Income...Happiness...

CHAPTER 7:

ENVIRONMENTAL and GREEN-JOB RÉSUMÉS

11 Model *WOW!* Résumés
(45 Job Titles)

CREATE YOUR OWN RÉSUMÉ:

If you are doing your own Résumé in the Occupational Category of Environmental and Green Jobs, you can choose from among the *WOW!* Résumés in this Chapter modeling the wording, styles, formatting, bullets, borders, etc. You can also model any of the elements in the other *WOW!* Résumés in this Book.

Complete the Guides in the Appendices including the *WOW!* Action Verbs and specific targeted Keywords (that must be researched) to fully customize and create a unique and powerful *WOW!* Résumé!

If you have purchased this Book (and thus become an automatic 1-year Member of wowresumes.net) you can get Free unrestricted downloads (Word or PDF Files) of up to 5 *WOW!* Résumés in addition to a Free download of the Guides in the Appendices for you to print out or edit on your computer.

DISCOUNTED RÉSUMÉ SERVICE:

If you need help to create a *WOW!* Résumé call 888-503-3133 or go to wowresumes.net to work with professional Résumé Writers who practice *WOW!* Résumé principles. Book purchasers have up to one year to avail of a 30% Instant Discount on any *WOW!* Résumé or other *WOW!* Résumé products such as *WOW!*-Card® Résumés, as well as other benefits including Free Résumé Posting on the ever-growing wowresumes.net Website and Updating from Twitter, Facebook, LinkedIn & Google Profiles. Members get Free Updates for 1 year on their Main Résumé and up to 90% Discounts on additional (2nd, 3rd, 4th, etc.) Customized Résumés to target Specific Jobs, Careers, Industries or Special Urgent Applications.

*See the Back Cover for *WOW!* Résumé Service & Free Membership Information*

WOW! RÉSUMÉS 2011-2012: Great Jobs...Extra Income...Happiness...

Green Millions and Green for All?!

According to a Worldwatch Report (Michael Renner, 2011, Worldwatch Institute, Washington, D.C.) "green jobs" are getting better defined and are now being better measured and tracked around the world. As of 2010, employment in renewables and supplier industries were estimated at a conservative 2.3 million worldwide. Globally, the wind power industry employs some 300,000 people (led by Spain and China). The solar photovoltaic (PV) sector employs about 170,000, and the solar thermal industry more than 600,000. There are also more than 1 million jobs in the biofuels industry growing and processing a variety of feed-stocks such as corn and sugar cane into ethanol and biodiesel (led by Brazil).

Inconsistent job definitions and lack of data gathering do not reflect the real numbers of jobs in recycling and remanufacturing jobs worldwide which are most likely in the tens of millions. For example, China is thought to have some 10 million formal and informal jobs in recycling and remanufacturing. In many countries, recycling is often done by informal networks of scavengers such as aluminum recycling in Brazil (500,000 scrap collectors) or in Cairo, Egypt where 70,000 Zabaleen recycle as much as 85% of the materials they collect. The United States has more than 1 million documented workers in recycling-remanufacturing-refurbishing.

The Bureau of Labor Statistics (BLS) of the U.S. Department of Labor received funding beginning in Fiscal Year 2010 to develop and implement the collection of new data on green jobs. The BLS will collect data that defines "green jobs" as 1) Jobs in businesses that produce goods or provide services that benefit the environment or conserve natural resources or 2) Jobs in which workers' duties involve making their establishment's production processes more environmentally friendly or use fewer natural resources.

Green Jobs will evolve from new developments and policies related to climate change, renewable energy, LEED (Leadership in Energy and Environmental Design) construction and renovation, as well as transportation-related initiatives (such as the introduction through 2010 -2011 of 6100 Compressed Natural Gas, CNG Buses in New Delhi that will have created 18,000 new jobs) and the various national movements in sustainable farming and fisheries.

The prodigious potential of green jobs will be fully realized when by choice, economics or the necessity of survival, most if not all businesses will be green and thus most jobs will by definition also be "green". There will also be countless community, national and international building and rebuilding projects if the anticipated effects of climate change come to fruition such as building flood barriers, terracing land, rehabilitating wetlands, reforestation and afforestation, and other innovative and emergency strategies to deal with other multiple environmental degenerations everywhere on the planet.

For now, outside the most progressive businesses, green jobs may also be created by entrepreneurs around the world who can secure livelihoods and profits from market niches for products and services that benefit the environment and people.

The *WOW!* Model Résumés in this Chapter include Low Carbon Deliverer; Solar Panel Installer; Carbon Markets Accountant; Eco-travel Tour Guide; Urban Farmer; Aquaculture/Sustainable Fisheries Specialist; Wind Energy Engineer/Operator; Green Building/Energy Efficiency Consultant; Biofuel Manufacturer/Distributor; Green Household Cleaning; and Green Investments Advisor.

WOW! RÉSUMÉS 2011-2012: Great Jobs...Extra Income...Happiness...

CHAPTER 7: ENVIRONMENTAL and GREEN-JOB RÉSUMÉS

Jake R. Townsend
1234 Marietta Blvd. #123
Bellingham, WA 98225
360-123-4567
jaketownsend@wowresumes.net

Solar Panel Installer (Residential and Commercial) / Insulation Specialist

PERSONAL AND PROFESSIONAL GREEN STATEMENT:
It is time to "walk the talk" personally and as a nation and society.
According to solar industry publishers & researchers at Solarbuzz, despite the recession in the U.S., solar power demand is forecast to grow "only" 25% in 2011 after a doubling (100%) growth from 2009 to 2010. While Chinese manufacturers hold the first 2 positions in world solar power cell production, Tempe, Arizona-based First Solar Inc. is 3rd in global production.

PROFILE:
- ⊙ Varied skills in Construction, Plumbing and Roofing. Warehouse forklift experience
- ⊙ Fully trained in Solar PV Installation and certified in Electronic Assembly and Fabrication
- ⊙ Dependable, organized, efficient and punctual. Mature and takes pride in quality work
- ⊙ Speak Spanish with excellent ability to communicate with co-workers, customers & management

TRAINING:
BOOTS ON THE ROOF   Seattle, WA;
6-Day Solar PV Boot Camp   September 2010
- Hands-on training covering the fundamentals of PV theory and applications, system design and estimation, and field installation of typical residential and commercial rooftop systems

PORTLAND CITY COLLEGE   Portland, OR
Certificate for Electronic Assembly and Fabrication   July 1997

EXPERIENCE:
CASCADE COMMERCIAL CONTRACTORS   Bellingham, WA
Commercial Installer   July 2008 to June 2010
- Traveled to various Retail Stores in Northern Washington, including Costco's to update and remodel the following: FRP (Fiberglass) panels, H-frame racking, gondolas, fixtures, pallet racks, cash wraps, graphics, casework, display counters, sales stations, custom mill work, slat walls and interior spaces; Operated forklift to pull orders and restock pallets

U.S. SHOWER DOOR, INC.   Tacoma, WA
Residential and Commercial Installer   Jan. 2002 to Feb. 2008
- Installed a variety of Swanston tub-surrounds, shower doors, heavy glass, various size mirrors, accessories (TP holders, grab bars, medicine cabinets, towel bars, fire extinguishers), sliding closet mirror doors, wire shelving and closet organizers
- Worked with homeowners and supervisors of major job sites: University of Washington, Willamette University & Tacoma General Hospital

COAST PLUMBERS   Spokane, WA
Plumber (Residential and Commercial)   Dec. 1999 to Jan. 2002
- Plumbed everything from under-slab plumbing to trim-out for commercial and residential job sites; Assisted Contractors in Habitat for Humanity Project in Seattle, WA

ANDERSON CONSTRUCTORS   Portland, OR
Construction Framer and Roofer   Nov. 1997 to Nov. 1999
- Framed houses from small to big projects (Pulte Homes) and remodels; Assisted in residential roofing projects

EDUCATION: PORTLAND CITY COLLEGE, Portland, OR, AA, Humanities; 1995

COMMUNITY: Community Volunteer including Bellingham Habitat for Humanity and Northern Washington Food Bank

---

Related Jobs/Careers:
(Green Energy Worker, Photovoltaic Panel Installer, Insulation Specialist)
RÉSUMÉ #74: Solar Panel Installer (2011 U.S. Retail: $299)

DIANA J. AGUIRRE, CPA
51 Carteret Street
Trenton, NJ 08601
(609) 123-4567
dianajaguirre@wowresumes.net

Carbon Markets Accountant and Carbon Trader

CERTIFIED PUBLIC ACCOUNTANT, States of New Jersey and New York

PERSONAL AND PROFESSIONAL GREEN STATEMENT:

Beyond the economic and financial, Accounting can make a profound difference in the lives of people and the planet. Whatever the fate of "cap and trade" in North America in 2011 and thereafter, it has already been established that monetary metrics have now to be applied to what has traditionally been ignored or neglected, the value and pricing of nature and Earth "services". I am excited to be able to apply my past learning and experience to contribute to the merging fields of environment, finance and public policy.

SUMMARY OF QUALIFICATIONS:

❑ Broad knowledge of industries and some 20 years' experience in mid-sized to large companies
❑ Directed accounting, financial analysis and reporting to management and regulatory agencies
❑ Coordinated and monitored budgeting and forecasting processes; Developed strategies and plans
❑ Managed employee medical, workers compensation, property/general liability insurance programs
❑ Performed treasury functions of cash management, loan compliance and banking relations
❑ Proven decision-making and analytical skills. Strong interpersonal skills committed to excellence

PROFESSIONAL EXPERIENCE:

Diana J. Aguirre Professional Corporation, Trenton, NJ   Jan. 2006 - Present
Self-Employed; Provide financial, accounting and property management services to clients including:
The Tolson Group, White Horse, NJ   Feb. 2007 - Oct. 2009
Sales of $250M Food Manufacturing, Contract Assembly and Packaging
Corporate Controller; Responsible for the accounting and reporting of finance and operations

■ Reported to the President on Corporate and Divisional operations
■ Interacted with Divisional Officers regarding financial and operational activities, government contracts, insurance, intercompany transactions, accounting, tax and cash flow matters
■ Responsible for accounting systems and the development of Company policies and procedures
■ Directed the Annual Year-End Certified Audit by independent accountants
■ Managed employee medical, workers' compensation, property and general liability insurance programs
■ Monitored cash balances and invested funds to obtain high yield while maintaining safety and liquidity

WOW! RÉSUMÉS 2011-2012: Great Jobs...Extra Income...Happiness...

DIANA J. AGUIRRE, CPA, dianajaguirre@wowresumes.net
(Page 2)

PROFESSIONAL EXPERIENCE (Continued):

Amway Global, Miami, FL   April 2000 - Jan. 2006
Sales of $3.5Billion International Direct Sales and Catalog Sales
Financial Reporting and Budgets Manager; Responsible for corporate financial reporting and coordination of the financial planning process

- Directed the preparation of consolidated financial statements for management, SEC filings and other stockholder reports
- Directed public reporting process to ensure legal, regulatory and public disclosure compliance
- Designed and monitored budgeting and forecasting processes to include development of the Corporate Annual Budget

Quality Management Administrator; Responsible for the education of employees in Quality Management and for the administration of a Quality Improvement Process

A & W Restaurants of New Jersey, Trenton, NJ   June 1991 - Aug. 1999
Sales of $150M National Restaurant Chain
Senior Accounting Manager; Responsible for corporate accounting and financial reporting

- Directed accounting functions of general ledger, payroll, accounts payable and sales through four managers and a clerical staff of 40
- Ensured general ledger and annual report accurately reflected the financial and operational activities of 102 restaurants
- Designed and implemented new accounting systems which included conversion from manual batch to a computerized point of sale entry system
- Supervised preparation of financial statements, annual budgets/special cost studies for management

EDUCATION:

Fordham University, Bronx, NY; B. S. Accounting Degree, 1990

TRAINING:

Professional Seminars on Carbon Markets, 2009 – 2010, in London, U.K. and International Conferences:
1. Cap-and Trade
2. The United Nations Framework Convention on Climate Change and the Kyoto Protocol
3. Offsetting Principles and Clean Development Mechanism (CDM) Basics
4. The European Union emission Trading Scheme
5. Towards a Global Emission Trading Architecture
6. The Regional Greenhouse Gas Initiative
7. North American Regional Emission Trading Schemes
8. US Federal Cap-and-Trade program
9. Post-2012 and Global Negotiations
10. Voluntary Markets

Related Jobs/Careers:
(Cap and Trade Specialist, Environmental Accountant)

WOW! RÉSUMÉS 2011-2012: Great Jobs...Extra Income...Happiness...

Hans Schuman
1234 South 10th Street #123
Tucumcari, New Mexico 88401
(575) 123-4567
hansschuman5@wowresumes.net

Wind Turbine Engineering and Operations

PROFILE:

- Educated and experienced as Electrical Engineer with updated practical knowledge in wind technologies
- Knowledge in the areas of hardware development, firmware programming, control systems, and system design
- Computer Proficiencies include C/C++ Programming, Verilog, Matlab, AutoCAD, MS Project & MS Office Programs
- Special Training (Post-Graduate) in Wind Energy Technology (see **SPECIAL TRAINING** below)

EDUCATION:

NORTHWESTERN UNIVERSITY, Evanston, Illinois
B.S. Electrical Engineering, — Computer Design (2006), Certified Engineer in Training by PELS Board, Illinois, July 2006

SPECIAL TRAINING:

MESALANDS COMMUNITY COLLEGE, Tucumcari, New Mexico
Associate of Applied Science Degree, Wind Energy Technology, 2010
Courses included: Introduction to Wind Energy, Field Safety and Experience, Wind Turbine Climbing and Safety (I, II, & III), Introduction to Environmental Science, Introduction to Hydraulics, Wind Turbine Mechanical Systems, Wind Turbine Operations and Maintenance, Power Generation and Distribution, Wind Turbine Siting and Construction, Wind Turbine Diagnosis & Repair.

TECHNICAL (ENGINEERING) EXPERIENCE:

HYDRONOVATION WATER TREATMENT SYSTEMS, INC.   Santa Rosa, New Mexico
Contracted Electrical Engineer   October 2008 to December 2010
- Debugged microprocessor control logic and sequence flow, updated and added features
- Designed hatter backup system with emergency valve control
- Redesigned electrical layout of prototype system

FUJIFILM DIMATIX PIEZOELECTRIC PRINTHEADS   Northbrook, Illinois
Engineering Intern   January 2008 to March 2008
- Wrote invention disclosure describing a vision system (or print head module alignment
- Assisted senior engineer with hardware testing on fluid level sensor prototype
- Updated wetted components of ink jetting stand to meet customer's solvent specifications
- Assisted Director at Engineering with maintaining action item database
- Produced/maintained technical documentation for senior engineering team and customer
- Performed and documented chemical compatibility tests; gained experience with class 100 clean room

FLUID SERVER TECHNOLOGIES PROTOCOL TRANSLATION DEVICES   Chicago, Illinois
Engineering Intern   June 2007 to September 2007
- Designed and constructed custom display panel for customer: Cisco 5 Systems
- Produced and maintained custom build order documentation including product refinement
- Assisted senior engineer with project management using Microsoft Project

SIERRA MONITOR CORPORATION HAZARDOUS GAS DETECTION SYSTEMS   Gary, Indiana
Engineering Intern   September 2006 to December 2006
- Performed hardware and firmware testing on infrared gas detector
- Produced documentation on failure analysis resulting from hardware firmware testing
- Assisted development team with documentation at infrared gas detector research

---

Related Jobs/Careers:
(Green Energy Worker, Wind Turbine Operator, Wind Technology Specialist)
RÉSUMÉ #76: Wind Energy Engineer (2011 U.S. Retail: $299)

WOW! RÉSUMÉS 2011-2012: Great Jobs...Extra Income...Happiness...

Alvin Jiles
1234 Cambie Street #123
Vancouver, BC, Canada V6T IL4
604-123-4567
alvinjiles@wowresumes.net

Low Carbon Deliveries of Groceries, Take-Out Food & Merchandise

GREEN STATEMENT:

The "greenest" food and consumer products are a function of how they are produced and the environmental impact of their journey from factory or farm to local market and ultimately to the consumer. The average produce from a national supermarket chain in the U.S. can travel an average 1100 miles from farm to plate. Even the local pizza parlor or take-out restaurant delivers neighborhood pizza or take-out in old polluting vehicles traveling short distances. Locally sourced products are most often the "greenest" choice. Low or "Zero" Carbon delivery such as motorcycles or human-powered cargo-trailer bicycles are potentially viable options for local customers.

WORK EXPERIENCE:

GREEN TRIKES   Vancouver, BC, Canada
Local Delivery Service employing tricycles and mountain bicycles with cargo trailers
Personal Shopper – Deliverer   2010 to Present
➲ As Co-Owner of local "Green" Business, perform services in Burnaby and West Vancouver neighborhoods
➲ Deliver merchandise, groceries and take-out food to office workers during lunch hours and in-bound residents daily
➲ Promote, encourage and practice green living with community businesses, local residents for transport & shopping

HUNGRY MIKE'S PIZZA   Portland, Oregon
Non-franchised pizza restaurant that practices local sourcing, full composting and green packaging
Restaurant Manager / Pizza Delivery   2007-2009
➲ As Co-Owner delivered pizza and performed restaurant management and operations in North Portland district
➲ Instituted bike and motorcycle deliveries when possible to minimize carbon footprint, save fuel and encourage exercise

MASENGALE DOCUMENT DELIVERY   Portland, Oregon
Delivery Service founded by college associates and 2 Portland/Salem bike clubs
Bike Messenger   2003 to 2007
➲ Made document pickups/deliveries (including court summons) for law firm and corporate clients in downtown Portland

EDUCATION:

University of Oregon, Eugene, Oregon
Bachelor of Arts, English Literature, 2003

GOALS:

To work for, venture with or start (and model or expand) a green local business that practices "low carbon" strategies while promoting economic and employment sustainably in small communities in urban environments.

Related Jobs/Careers:
(Green Personal Shopper, Local Products Deliverer, Local Foods Distribution)

RÉSUMÉ #77: Low Carbon Deliverer - Groceries (2011 U.S. Retail: $299)

Olga Shiminsky
1234 Figueroa Street #123
Los Angeles, CA 90012
(213) 123-4567
olgashiminksy@wowresumes.net

Green Building /Energy-Lighting Efficiency Consultant

PROFILE:

☑ Third generation lighting industry professional, also experienced in Green Building materials & systems
☑ Creative and multitalented, with extensive experience in consultative sales, marketing, and design
☑ Superb collaborative and interpersonal skills with well-developed written/verbal communication abilities
☑ Highly skilled in customer and vendor relations; talented at building "win-win" partnerships/relationships
☑ Passionate and inventive creator of innovative marketing strategies/campaigns with bottom-line results
☑ Keenly interested in emerging technologies; Professionally and personally committed to sustainability
☑ Documented results and top-sales performance in the fields of green building lighting systems and products

KEY STRENGTHS AND COMPETENCIES:

Strategic Sales and Customer Development
Needs Assessment and Product Education
Strategic Market Positioning and Sales Expansion
Organizational Design and Operations Management
High-impact Sales Presentations
Display, Collateral, and Website Design
Website Editing and Maintenance
Tradeshow Representation & Management

PROFESSIONAL EXPERIENCE:

National Account Sales (contract position), 2008 to Present
LEDEXICA LIGHTING, Sherman Oaks, CA
A young and dynamic green tech startup has "cracked the code" to attractive and functional, general illumination via environmentally friendly LED technology. Offered and accepted a contract sales role.
✓ Research and engage specialized markets in office lighting and building energy use
✓ Perform valuable introductions to prospective key strategic national accounts based on online leads
✓ Collaborate with engineering department for product enhancements bases on customer surveys
✓ Synchronize promotional programs with accounting, engineering and research and development
✓ Work closely with website developers for refinements and updates to website offerings and promotions
✓ Achieved #1 Sales Position in entire Southern California region for 2 consecutive years: 2009 & 2010

WOW! RÉSUMÉS 2011-2012: Great Jobs...Extra Income...Happiness...

Olga Shiminsky   olgashiminsky@wowresumes.net
Page 2

PROFESSIONAL EXPERIENCE (Continued):

Principal / Freelance Consultant, 2003 - 2007
OLGA SHIMINSKY CONSULTANCY, Fullerton, CA
Self-employed consultant in the areas of Lighting and Green Building Techniques.
✓ Successful completion of individual design projects totaling 450+K annually
✓ Provided sales and marketing support to varied companies
✓ Conceived, designed and produced Open House & Green Fair events
✓ Managed & edited company websites
✓ Green building specialist for Mayor's initiative on sustainability & climate change
✓ Reconceived and managed retail lighting department
✓ Designed showrooms' advertising collateral
✓ Sourced manufacturer's OEM supply chain
✓ Curatorial Committee, ecoLOGIC exhibition, Los Angeles Design Museum

National Showroom Sales Manager, 1997 - 2002
WESTERN LIGHTS, San Diego, CA
On behalf of leading architectural product manufacturer, delivered successful sales presentations to existing and potential clients, nationwide. Developed and maintained professional relationships with 100+ key commercial and residential accounts, including retail showrooms, architects and designers. Provided technical support, and proven client satisfaction.
✓ Serviced and managed $1M in customer accounts
✓ Coordinated with, and helped train and manage a network of (50) independent sales agencies nationwide
✓ Designed and executed rep sample kits, end products, and national advertising campaigns
✓ Designed, marketed and managed Master Dealer and QuickShip programs
✓ Designed, managed, and staffed wholesale market showroom
✓ Managed tradeshow attendance, and represented firm to multiple national audiences

Western Region National Account Manager, 1994 - 1996
AMLICO (AMERICAN LIGHTING COMPANY), Torrance, CA
✓ Performed blueprint takeoffs; successfully created commercial interior and exterior product specifications
✓ Assembled product schedules, made internal purchasing recommendations, tracked product shipment & delivery, and provided post-delivery service
✓ Consistent and reliable delivery of complete product packages to the nation's largest specialty retailers
✓ Personally managed Supercuts and $3.5M Old Navy accounts. Worked regularly on Gap and Banana Republic outlets, as well as occasional Chevy's FreshMex and Border's Bookstores

EDUCATION:

CALIFORNIA STATE UNIVERSITY AT SAN DIEGO, San Diego, CA
B.A. Degree in Cinema / Communications, 2000

Professional Development:
US Green Building Council, LEED AP, April 2005
Pacific Energy Center, SoCal Institute of Architecture and Green Building and Energy Efficiency Seminars
American Institute of Architects, ADPSR, IESNA Classes, Current Continuing Education

---

Related Jobs/Careers:
(LEED Building Consultant, Energy Efficiency Specialist)
RÉSUMÉ #78: Green Building Consultant (Page 2 of 2) (2011 U.S. Retail: $349)

WOW! RÉSUMÉS 2011-2012: Great Jobs...Extra Income...Happiness...

Dante J. Lujano
123 Lincoln Avenue, #A
Springfield, MO 65721
Tel. (417) 123-4567
dantejlujano@wowresumes.net

Biofuel Manufacturing-Distribution for a Regional Environmental Services Company

PERSONAL AND PROFESSIONAL GREEN STATEMENT

I was born in Chicago, IL of Mexican immigrants. Most of my family has worked in the restaurant industry, including myself when going to school. I thought I would become a chef until I realized that I could create a greater impact for my family with a business that is related to food but is all about taking care of the environment and waste (vegetable oil and grease from restaurants) that turns out to be valuable. Biodiesel reduces particulate matter emitted by diesel engines by as much as 80 to 90%, reduces carbon dioxide when used in place of petroleum diesel with the added benefit of eliminating exhaust smell. Cooking, eating, breathing and (making a living) are all related!

GOALS

To start or join a model green company in the Midwest (preferably in Missouri or Kansas) that promotes environmental practices, as well as engage in progressive labor and business practices to benefit the company, customers, employees and the community.

ACCOMPLISHMENTS

Obtaining a Bachelor's degree in a technical field and being able to craft a green career path that is a source of inspiration and personal commitment.

RELEVANT EXPERIENCE

STATE OF MISSOURI FARM BUREAU   Springfield, MO
Staff Researcher   2008 – 2010 (December)
⊙ Conducted research and field studies in the Southern Missouri region on soil fertility and pesticide use

ATASCO OIL COLLECTION SERVICE   Joplin, MO
Truck Driver and Account Executive   2005 – 2008
⊙ Provided regular collection services ("55 gallon" accounts) at restaurants and hotels in Southwest Missouri region

STONE HILL WINERY BISTRO   Branson, MO
Sous Chef   2001 - 2005
⊙ Started as Cook's Assistant and progressed to Line Cook and Sous Chef

EDUCATION

SOUTHWEST MISSOURI UNIVERSITY, Springfield MO
B.S. Degree in Food Science, 2008

INSPIRATION & REFERENCES

Alcohol Can Be A Gas! Fueling An Ethanol Revolution For the 21st Century (2008) by David Blume: a 596 encyclopedic book that presents an alternative system for countries (Brazil sources 18% of its total transport energy from ethanol from sugarcane while over 40% of ALL its vehicles are flex-fuel) and local communities that offers sustainable economic stimulation including benefits in life quality and technical (alcohol fuel is clean, cool-burning 105 octane) and environmental performance (useable for clean, smoke free heating, cooking and commercial applications).

Related Jobs/Careers:
(Biodiesel Collector, Green Energy Worker, Vegetable Oil Recycler)
RÉSUMÉ #79: Biomass Manufacturer / Biofuel Distributor (2011 U.S. Retail: $299)

WOW! RÉSUMÉS 2011-2012: Great Jobs...Extra Income...Happiness...

<u>CHAPTER 7: ENVIRONMENTAL and GREEN-JOB RÉSUMÉS</u>

Alice Mai Chan
1234 East 70th Street #123
New York, NY 10001
212.123.4567
chanalicemai@wowresumes.net

Green Investments Advisor

PERSONAL AND PROFESSIONAL GREEN STATEMENT

The "Green Economy" (which includes renewable energy, restoration and sustainable construction) is already worth in the multiple trillions, not even counting "nature services" such as clean air, water, pollination and biodiversity benefits. Green investment advising will develop standards that evolve from traditional finance and accounting toward specialized fields that are multi-disciplinary and multi-faceted. Just as important as picking the right green company winners and losers will be the realization that environmental performance is a powerful indication of overall management excellence.

PROFILE

❑ Over 10 years of successful professional experience in the financial industry culminating in green investments analysis/advising
❑ Results-oriented with recognized and rewarded performance in sales, business development and outstanding client relations
❑ Highly skilled in creating sound investment solutions, developing high-levels of market growth, and facilitating effective financial management strategies to increase portfolio value
❑ Proven ability to effectively handle multi-task levels of management responsibility with minimal direction from superiors while supervising personnel, providing team leadership, motivation, and development
❑ Solid communication, interpersonal, time management, analytical, organizational, and leadership skills with a go-getter attitude
❑ Experienced in forecasting, account performance analysis, investor relations, market research, financial planning, and networking
❑ Passion for balanced management, social responsibility and the increasing competitive advantage of sustainable business practices

AREAS OF EXPERTISE

• Investment Strategies	• Client/Investor Relations	Financial Planning
• Market Growth & Expansion	• Portfolio Management	Business Analysis
• Relationship Building	• Strategic Business Planning	Ecosystem Valuation
• Asset Management	• Cross-selling	Cap and Trade Analysis
• Market Analysis & Penetration	• New Business Development	Sustainable Management

RELEVANT PROFESSIONAL EXPERIENCE

Investment Banker, JP MORGAN BANK New York, NY 2001 to 2004 and 2006 to 2010
Assumed full responsibility for overseeing trust and investment management accounts valued at over 1360M in market value while continuously identifying, evaluating and advising investors and management.
<u>Key Accomplishments</u>:
★ Received Service Star Award in 5Quarters of 2002/2004 and Outstanding Performance Valuation throughout tenure
★ Secured over $85M in business relationships with focus on performance and customer service

EDUCATION & TRAINING

UNIVERSITY OF PENNSYLVANIA, WHARTON SCHOOL OF BUSINESS, Philadelphia, PA
MBA in Finance, 2006

UNIVERSITY OF CALIFORNIA AT BERKELEY, Berkeley, CA
B.S. in PENR (Political Economy of Natural Resources), 2000

Licensed Series 66 and Series 7 Stockbroker, Current 2011

INSPIRATION & MOTIVATION

Presidio School of Sustainable Management, San Francisco, CA, Seminars in Sustainable Management/Ecosystem Valuation, Summer 2010
Resolution Fund LLC, Washington D.C., Workshops in Redevelopment and the Restoration Economy, 2008

Related Jobs/Careers:
(Sustainable Businesses Analyst, Sustainable Management Specialist)

RÉSUMÉ #80: Green Investments Advisor (2011 U.S. Retail: $299)

WOW! RÉSUMÉS 2011-2012: Great Jobs...Extra Income...Happiness...

Sandra Rodriguez Collins
1234 Market Street #123
San Diego, CA 92103
(619) 123-4567
sandrarcollins@wowresumes.net

Green Household Cleaning / Green Cleaning Products / Sustainable Janitorial Services

PERSONAL AND PROFESSIONAL GREEN STATEMENT:
As homes and commercial buildings become greener and more sustainable in construction, energy efficiency and water use, the cleaning of the indoors is a major consumer and business issue. According to the U.S. EPA, Americans spend on average 90% of their time indoors where pollution can be as much as 100 x higher than outdoors. Cleaning services are at least a $50 billion industry with 68,000 businesses (according to the University of Missouri). The use of cleaning chemicals and processes affect health and environment. Green cleaning services can positively benefit the health of workers and capture environmentally and health-conscious customers by utilizing green cleaning agents that are certified and by offering extra household green products such as bio plastics and organic linens and beddings.

SUMMARY OF QUALIFICATIONS:
☑ Over 23 years' experience in janitorial/housekeeping in hotels and residences
☑ Received 5 outstanding employee awards from Hilton Hotels and Marriott International
☑ Punctual, dependable, well organized, efficient and hard-working and honest
☑ Ability to multitask and work effectively under pressure and meet deadlines
☑ Work well independently and as an innovative team member or large crew
☑ Professional with excellent communication skills with co-workers and the public
☑ Committed to green cleaning principles and practices for health and environment

CORE SKILLS:
• Can promptly and accurately report incidents and avoid potential safety hazards
• Able to clean various surfaces, such as windows, woodwork, counters, and walls
• Experience in sweeping, mopping, stripping, waxing, and buffing all types of floors
• Extensive experience cleaning bathroom, showers, mirrors, sinks, toilets, and floors
• Able to remove trash from all floors to maintain cleanliness and safety of facility
• Operate cleaning equipment, including: Floor Scrubbers, Buffers, Rug Shampooers & Wax Machines

CUSTOMER SERVICE:
• Able to listen effectively to clients, resolve their problems, and maintain excellent customer relations
• Can direct clients and provide them with accurate information about the company and all of its services
• Able to perform my cleaning duties around many clients discreetly, safely, and effectively

RELEVANT EXPERIENCE:
GREEN LEAF HOUSEKEEPING, San Diego, CA, **Housekeeper On Call**, 2007 to Present
HILTON HOTEL RESORT, San Diego, CA, **Senior Housekeeper**, 2004 to 2007
AZALEA GARDENS, Chula Vista, CA, **Gardener/Cleaner**, 2002 to 2004
MARRIOTT INTERNATIONAL, San Diego, CA, **Housekeeper**, 1997 to 2002
GENERAL SERVICES ADMINISTRATION, San Diego, CA, **Kitchen Helper**, 1995 to 1997

OTHER EXPERIENCE:
FATHER ALFRED MEMORIAL CENTER, San Diego, CA, **Cook**, 1994 to 1995
RAY KROC FOUNDATION, San Diego, CA, **Dishwasher/Laundry**, 1993 to 1994
NEW BRIDGE FOUNDATION, National City, CA, **Prep Cook**, 1992 to 1993
HARBOR LIGHTS MISSION, San Diego, CA, **Cook**, 1991 to 1992

TRAINING:
GCCC (Green Cleaning Company Certified Cleaner), International Janitorial Cleaning Services Association, 2010
IBP (Introduction to Blood borne Pathogens), Occupational Safety and Health Agency, California, 2007

EDUCATION:
Institute for Global Ethics Completed Ethical Fitness Seminar San Diego, CA 2007
C.H.E.F.S Program Vocational Diploma San Diego, CA 1990
Chula Vista High School, High School Diploma, Chula Vista, CA, 1985

Related Jobs/Careers:
(Green Cleaning Services, Environmentally-Friendly Products)

Alvin Manfredy
1234 Union Street #123
Manchester, New Hampshire 03102
603-123-4567
alvinmanfredy@wowresumes.net

Urban Organic Farmer / Local Produce-Sales / Farm Educator

GREEN FACTS REGARDING URBAN FARMING:

❖ 800 million people are involved in urban agriculture contributing to feeding cities around the world
❖ Urban agriculture can contribute to the necessity, practicality and acceptance of organic farming globally
❖ Low income city dwellers who spend 50% of income on food can be assisted economically and nutritionally
❖ There are some 3,500 CSAs (Community Supported Agriculture) Organizations in the United States (2010)

GOALS:

❖ To help create a successful urban farming infrastructure (Community Supported Agriculture) in a community of need
❖ To advance the cause of organic farming and organic food consumption in urban settings
❖ To encourage youth and minority community groups to promote their own "ethnically-flavored" CSAs

RELEVANT EXPERIENCE:

MANCHESTER CSA (COMMUNITY SUPPORTED AGRICULTURE)   Manchester, New Hampshire
Assistant Director, Farm Operations   Mar 2005 to Dec 2010
⊙ Started as Farm Hand and Truck Driver in 2 sister farms in Manchester and South Hooksett, New Hampshire
⊙ Mastered the seeding, cultivating and harvesting of heir-loom fruits and vegetables utilizing organic methods in soil preparation, natural pest control and seasonal propagation of native species of community-desired produce
⊙ Promoted to Community Relations and eventually to present position of Assistant Director
⊙ Employed community programs that solicited and gained the acceptance of the Manchester Restaurant Association to foster the relations between the restaurant industry and organic agriculture
⊙ Implemented the CSAs operational budget and in-house training programs for Manchester at-risk youth
⊙ As Assistant Director, implemented outreach to regional CSAs to share technical and program information for the overall enhancement of organic horticulture
⊙ Upon departure for "greener pastures" with the support and encouragement of the MCSA board and membership, assisted in making Manchester operation a model of efficiency, innovation and community service for urban agriculture in the Northeast United States and beyond

WHOLE FOODS   Boston, Massachusetts
Stock Clerk / Cashier   2001 to 2005
⊙ Worked in busy Boston grocery store; Prepared fresh produce and sold high-quality merchandise to community customer base; Learned the food business and introduced to organic products

TRAININGS CONDUCTED:

At Manchester Community Center Springs & Summers (2008 to 2012):
Urban Farming Business Topics including Urban Faming Business Planning; Finance/Lending Programs; Direct & Wholesale Marketing; Packaging and Retailing; Labor Issues; Local Regulations, Zoning and Licensing.
Hands-On Farming Classes including Composting; Worm Farming; Soil Testing; Horticulture, Non-Chemical Farming; Aquaculture; Bee-keeping; Small farm equipment and tools; Food Processing; Water Usage; Renewable Energy.

EDUCATION:

DANIEL WEBSTER COLLEGE; Nashua, New Hampshire
B.S. Horticultural Science, 2004

Related Jobs/Careers:
(Organic Farmer, Community Supported Agriculture, Commercial Urban Agriculture)
RÉSUMÉ #82: Urban Farmer / Local Produce-Sales / Farm Educator (2011 U.S. Retail: $299)

Cassandra Treblehorn
1234 Pimsley Circle #123
Cumberland, MD 21501
301-123-45667
casstreblehorn@wowresumes.net

Eco Travel Tour Guide / Ecotourism Specialist

GREEN STATEMENT:

Ecology and Tourism have not been traditionally compatible. Ecotourism is no longer a niche but is becoming mainstream out of necessity and is exploding in interest from the general public. As a growing segment of a multi-trillion dollar world industry, eco travel provides opportunities to preserve biodiversity, lands, water ecosystems, historical and archeological sites while promoting the economic and cultural sustainability of local communities.

GOALS:
- To be a worthy representative of ecotourism in professional, personal and community pursuits
- To combine travel, leisure, history, culture and business in a career that provides value and meaning
- To work for an organization that focuses on authentic customer service and great products/services

CORE SKILLS & APTITUDES:
- Enthusiasm and passion for travel, history and environmentalism
- Commitment to learning about localities, cultures and travel destinations
- Immensely self-motivated with great ability to work on own initiative
- Excellent confidence and ability to speak in public and in dealing with people
- Refined communication skills from work in the U.S. Natural Park Service and hospitality
- Exceptional team player with ability to function in diverse cultures (Speak Spanish fluently)

RELEVANT EXPERIENCE:

UNITED STATES PARK SERVICE   Berkley Springs, MD
Park Ranger, Chesapeake & Ohio Canal National Historical Park   2008 to Present
- Perform full ranger duties including interpretation and education
- Provide park interpretive programs to visitors intended to foster stewardship of natural resources
- Execute law enforcement and education by applying special park regulations to visitors and educating the public of the park and region's natural and cultural history
- Complete administrative duties related to maintenance schedules, policy reviews and emergency checklists

OCEANIA CRUISE LINES (NAUTICA)   Miami, Florida
Spanish and English Tour Guide   2005 - 2008
- Guided ship passengers on excursions on historical, historical and archaeological sites
- Played an active role in the welcoming, enjoyment and safekeeping of all visitors to the ship
- Liaised regularly with other members of the Tour team and provided input daily meetings
- Carried out daily duties such as litter picking, light cleaning, and stocking of sanitary supplies
- Organized and implemented displays, activities, trails and quizzes for port of call excursions
- Proactively promoted the on-board tour destination programs including special expeditions

WOW! RÉSUMÉS 2011-2012: Great Jobs...Extra Income...Happiness...

CHAPTER 7: ENVIRONMENTAL and GREEN-JOB RÉSUMÉS

Cassandra Treblehorn
Page Two

casstreblehorn@wowresumes.net

RELEVANT EXPERIENCE (Continued):

DELTA AIRLINES

Atlanta, GA

Flight Attendant

1998 to 2005

- Excelled in customer service to ensure the safety and comfort of airline passengers
- Applied principles and techniques acquired in professional/continuous airline training

TRAINING:

THE NATURE CONSERVANCY, Denver, Colorado
Community-based Ecotourism, Certification, 2010

DELTA AIRLINES FLIGHT ATTENDANT TRAINING, Atlanta, Georgia
Curriculum Included:

Passenger Handling and Safety	Sanitation / Food-borne Illnesses
Regulations and Accident Review	Unusual Situations and Security
Unarmed Assault / Armed Assault	Emergency Evacuations-Land/Water
Security Mindset / Risk Assessment	Human Factors and Decision-Making

EDUCATION:

UNIVERSITY OF NEVADA AT LAS VEGAS, Las Vegas, Nevada
B.A. Degree in Hospitality, 2005

LEARNIT! COMPUTER TRAINING, Miami, Florida
MS Office Software and Basic Internet Classes, 2008

CERTIFICATIONS:

Basic Cardiac Life Support
Adult/Child CPR & First Aid

Member, American Heart Association

Related Jobs/Careers:
(Sustainable Tourism, Flight Attendant)

RÉSUMÉ #83: Eco Travel Tour Guide / Ecotourism Specialist (Page 2 of 2) (2011 U.S. Retail: $329)

WOW! RÉSUMÉS 2011-2012: Great Jobs...Extra Income...Happiness...

Calvin Krostner
1234 Dale Avenue
Tampa, Florida 33603
(813) 123-4567
calvkrostner@wowresumes.net

Aquaculture / Sustainable Fisheries Specialist

(GREEN) FACTS/ISSUES REGARDING AQUACULTURE & SUSTAINABLE FISHERIES:

- World fish stocks are near full exploitation levels at the beginning of the 21st century with ¼ of food species depleted
- Global production from fishing and aquaculture is about 150 million tons yearly (33% and growing from aquaculture)
- The U.S. has a $9 billion annual (2010) trade deficit for seafood; Imported seafood is 80% of seafood consumed in U.S.
- 40% of imported seafood in U.S. is from aquaculture; There is room for enormous growth potential in U.S. aquaculture
- Ecosystem Approach to fisheries called for to protect/conserve ecosystems while providing food, income, and livelihoods
- Sustainability is a worldwide challenge; U.S. must grow aquaculture that meets environmental and food safety standards

PROFILE & SPECIAL SKILLS:

☑ Academic (Bachelor's degree and post-graduate studies) background in Fisheries Science and Aquaculture Research
☑ Hands-on and "Dive-in" Orientation to produce results and positive outcomes for company, community and planet
☑ Advisor to Tampa Bay Restoration LLC with mandate to balance development, coastal protection and local livelihoods
☑ Expertise in Tropical Fish Ecology: How Species & Habitats Affect Each Other, & Assessing Bycatch & Habitat Damage
☑ Skilled in presenting and promoting practices in sustainable fisheries including the local viability of commercial fish farms

RELEVANT EXPERIENCE:

WEEDON ISLAND AQUAFOODS — Tampa, Florida — 2007 to Present
Aquaculture Specialist / Fisheries Scientist
- Managed 2-year restoration of historical fishponds in Weedon Island State Fisheries District
- Conducted and supervised research into upgrade of RAS (Recirculating Aquaculture System)
- Co-managed the production of freshwater/saltwater species of fish, mollusks & crustaceans
- Assisted with budgets and costs, transportation of production to wholesale and direct buyers

MASINGALE FISHERIES — Gloucester, MA — 1999 to 2005
Fisherman/Supervisor
- Selected fishing grounds, plotted courses and computed navigational positions
- Operated fishing gear, directed fishing operations and supervised fishing crew members
- Recorded fishing activities, weather and sea conditions
- Maintained engine, fishing gear and other on-board equipment

EDUCATION & TRAINING:

AUBURN UNIVERSITY, DEPARTMENT OF FISHERIES & ALLIED AQUACULTURES, Auburn, Alabama
Bachelor of Science in Fisheries Science, 2007
Core Courses Included:

Principles of Aquaculture	Hatchery Management	Fish Health
Genetics	Aquaculture Production	Environmental Law
Marine Ecology	Watershed Management	Internship in Fisheries

Related Jobs/Careers:
(Fish Farm Worker, Fisheries Consultant, Aquaculture Scientist)

RÉSUMÉ #84: Aquaculture / Sustainable Fisheries Specialist (2011 U.S. Retail: $299)

WOW! RÉSUMÉS 2011-2012: Great Jobs...Extra Income...Happiness...

CHAPTER 8:

<u>NETWORK MARKETING RÉSUMÉS</u>

10 Model *WOW!* Résumés
(32 Job Titles)

<u>CREATE YOUR OWN RÉSUMÉ</u>:

If you are doing your own Résumé in the Occupational Category of <u>Network Marketing</u>, you can choose from among the *WOW!* Résumés in this Chapter modeling the wording, styles, formatting, bullets, borders, etc. You can also model any of the elements in the other *WOW!* Résumés in this Book.

Complete the Guides in the Appendices to fully customize and create a unique and powerful *WOW!* Résumé! Remember that the factual details of the network marketing company itself and your company colleagues are just as important as your own qualifications, especially leaders' credentials.

If you have purchased this Book (and thus become an automatic 1-year Member of wowresumes.net) you can get Free unrestricted downloads (Word or PDF Files) of up to 5 *WOW!* Résumés in addition to a Free download of the Guides in the Appendices for you to print out or edit on your computer.

<u>DISCOUNTED RÉSUMÉ SERVICE</u>:

If you need help to create a *WOW!* Résumé call 888-503-3133 or go to wowresumes.net to work with professional Résumé Writers who practice *WOW!* Résumé principles. Book purchasers have up to one year to avail of a 30% Instant Discount on any *WOW!* Résumé or other *WOW!* Résumé products such as *WOW!*-Card® Résumés, as well as other benefits including <u>Free Résumé Posting</u> on the ever-growing wowresumes.net Website and <u>Updating from Twitter, Facebook, LinkedIn & Google Profiles</u>. Members get <u>Free Updates for 1 year</u> on their Main Résumé and <u>up to 90% Discounts</u> on additional (2nd, 3rd, 4th, etc.) Customized Résumés to target Specific Jobs, Careers, Industries or Special Urgent Applications.

*See the Back Cover for *WOW!* Résumé Service & Free Membership Information*

WOW! RÉSUMÉS 2011-2012: Great Jobs...Extra Income...Happiness...

CHAPTER 8: NETWORK MARKETING RÉSUMÉS

Buyer and Opportunity Networker Beware?

According to prolific writers/researchers in network marketing, Rod Nichols and Sue Seward (Entrepreneur Magazine, January 2007 & Home Business Magazine, December 2010), the network marketing industry now has over 3,000 companies, 50 million representatives and sales of over $100 billion worldwide with a 91% growth in the last 10 years. Starting in the 1940s when a California vitamin company decided to sell its products through independent representatives (eliminating advertising costs) who introduced the products and the company to family and friends (making small product overrides of personal sales and the sales of those they introduced to the company), network marketing has become a proven business and marketing/distribution model.

Despite problems from public misunderstanding and a few fraudulent companies, today's networking companies feature legitimate products and services that offer income opportunities for the right person who decides to seriously and systematically pursue a business through hard work, patience and perseverance. Millions of individuals around the world have achieved success in otherwise limited economic opportunities, especially women.

Even if network marketing is easy to enter and start, the business is not for everyone. Problems in the past (and present) have arisen because of personal misconceptions as well as company deficiencies. Sometimes products, the company and the concept of network marketing are overhyped resulting in unreal expectations, disappointment and failures. Network marketing success is slow in building (like most careers) that takes perhaps 5 years to build. While a company may have thousands or tens of thousands (as in the larger network marketing companies) of successful practitioners, there is a high turnover rate of those joining and quitting the business.

Lack of success in network marketing stems from lack of work and effort by individual representatives and is worsened by a company's lack of training and support. Furthermore, new representatives are first very excited by compensation plans that are eventually difficult to attain or are too complex to understand. When a company's compensation is very lucrative for the big producers at the expense of the average or new representative, motivation to continue and work at the business wanes and leads to failure.

Still, network marketing is booming and finding the right company with the right products and/or services may be the answer in the tough economic times in industrialized countries and may still be one of the few opportunities for women in the developing world. Laid-off workers are familiar with network marketing as a home-based business that can supplement or replace lost income. Many companies are household names with their own famous brands. Even the billionaire Warren Buffet is involved in network marketing (his Berkshire Hathaway currently owns the Pampered Chef, and once owned World Book and Kirby Vacuum).

Network Marketing is especially suited to the Internet age with the ability for a representative to market products anywhere and anytime with the company's representative-customized website. Requiring no technical skills or special knowledge, just about anyone can join a company with a relatively small investment (although new Representative must be aware of the pressure or risk of buying too many products initially).

The *WOW!* Model Résumés in this Chapter include ones for Representatives who represent these companies: Zrii, Amway Global, World Ventures Travel, Avon, Amsoil, Pampered Chef, Organo Gold Coffee, Mary Kay, Tupperware and a fictional company (NoSuperStars.Com). *WOW!* Résumés does not endorse any network marketing company and advises anyone interested in network marketing to perform due diligence on any potential company and be aware of the issues and requirements for individual business and personal success.

WOW! RÉSUMÉS 2011-2012: Great Jobs...Extra Income...Happiness...

CHAPTER 8: NETWORK MARKETING RÉSUMÉS

NETWORK MARKETING SALES RÉSUMÉ FORMAT

THE "5 Ps"

(ALL IN IDEALLY IN ONE PAGE with Links or References to Further Information)

Basic Contact Info including Name, Phone Number(s), Email and your Networking Marketing Personal Website or Company Website.

****For Privacy and Security Purposes, do NOT include any address info except for City****

PROPOSITION

What is your company all about in terms of product, mission and history (in summary), including valid testimonials and honest reviews of company? What makes your company unique or special?

PRODUCT or SERVICE

What are your company's specific products or services with its unique or special benefits, values or "ingredients"? Where are your products made and who makes them?

PEOPLE

Who are the members and leaders up and down in your organization and who are You and how do You fit in? Share your personal story that would attract recruits and customers, including any hardships or challenges or exciting accomplishments.

PRICING (and Promotions)

What are prices of products (and services) and what are special promotions and pricing advantages for members and "leaders"?

PROFIT

What are your company's "compensation" plans? Summarize programs and include honest and real figures for specific (but unnamed) members including your own profits or gains. Tell about outstanding performers and earners, including those with "normal" income. People want honesty! Some are just looking for part-time opportunities or decent money!

Basic Profile Information including single lines for education, employment and community:

Can Condense and Summarize Years and Groups of Jobs in 1 industry

---

WOW! RÉSUMÉS 2011-2012: Great Jobs...Extra Income...Happiness...

Maria Perez Sandoval
Urión 100, Col. Atlatilco
02860 MEXICO, D.F., MEXICO
(52) (55) 1234-1234
mperezsandoval@wowresumes.net

Zrii Ayurveda Nutrition & Weight Loss
Nutritional Products Based on Amalaki Fruit and Synergistic Botanicals
"Beyond the Body: Ayurveda and Optimal Health with Zrii"

PROPOSITION:

Become an Independent Executive using and selling Zrii Nutritional Products that promote health and natural weight loss. Market products to health-conscious individuals including members of gyms, health clubs, as well as to health professionals such as chiropractors.

PRODUCTS:

All drinks and powders are patented and exclusive all-natural formulas of amalaki fruit, 7 botanicals & 22 premium vitamins/minerals:
NutriiVeda Mixed Powders (22 ounces)
Accell Berry Drinks & Powders
Original Amalaki Drinks (25 ounce/750 ml Large Bottles)
NutriiVeda Drinks & Powders (Vanilla & Chocolate)

PEOPLE:

Headed by CEO & Founder Bill Farley (purchased Northwest Industries in 1985 for $1.4 Billion and completed initial $565 million public offering of Fruit of the Loom, Inc.), Zrii is the first third-party product to receive an endorsement for the Chopra Center for Wellbeing (founded by Dr. Deepak Chopra and Dr. David Simon). Zrii is one of the fastest growing MLM companies since its startup in 2007.

As of 2011, Zrii has over 75,000 Independent Executives in the U.S., Canada & Mexico. Zrii is managed and marketed by network marketing veterans who have gained successful reputations and records of success at other networking marketing companies/start-ups.

My personal upline Independent Executives are Silvia Fung and Priscilla Jong who are supportive on a regular (often daily) basis in the education, marketing, promotion and sales of Zrii products and the building of a business minded and health conscious team.

PRICING (and Promotions):

(Go to my website at myzrii.com or: http://sfung.myzrii.com for latest info)

✓ Initial one-time membership is regularly $39.00 and there are frequent promotions of only $29.00 to join.
✓ Independent Executives (those who agree to an "Auto shipment of products to use and sell) earn "7 ways" (see below)
✓ Zrii Independent Executives and Preferred Customers (those who get auto-shipments but are not members) get wholesale prices

PROFIT (Compensation Plan(s):

(Got to my website at myzrii.com or: http://sfung.myzrii.com for more info)

The Zrii "Prosperity Plan" for Independent Executives has 7 components:

• Fast Start Training Bonus Paid Weekly
• Unilevel Royalty Bonus Paid Monthly
• Matching Bonus Paid Monthly
• Fast Start Bonus Pool Paid Monthly
• Infinity Bonus Paid Monthly
• All-Star Bonus Paid Quarterly
• Founders Bonus (Share 2% of commissionable sales for each new market opened and continue to share 1% in subsequent years)

PERSONAL PROFILE & BUSINESS BACKGROUND:
Lifelong native and resident of Mexico City
Mother of 2 boys and 1 girl
Languages and Literature Teacher at Santa Teresa School for Girls, Mexico City
Active in Colonia Atlatilco Neighborhood: Beautification, Holiday Parades and Community Events
Business Goal: Develop health food business with Zrii and local products
Learning Computers for Business and for Education
Monthly Income goal for 2011: 6,000 MXN (Mexican Pesos) = $500 U.S. Dollars/Month

---

Related Jobs/Careers:
(Independent Distributor, Home-Based Businesses, Alternative Medicine)
RÉSUMÉ #85: Network Marketing / MLM Distributor: Zrii Ayurveda Nutrition/Weight Loss (2011 U.S. Retail: $249)

WOW! RÉSUMÉS 2011-2012: Great Jobs...Extra Income...Happiness...

Luciana Vieira
Rua Visconde de Porto Seguro 1234
Sao Paulo-SP 04642-000, BRAZIL
(11) 3285-1234
lalavieira@wowresumes.net

Amway Global
International Direct Selling Company Marketing Consumer Products in over 80 Countries
"Culturally Sensitive, Environmentally Conscious with 50 Years of Entrepreneurial Experience"

PROPOSITION

Provide direct selling and business opportunities for entrepreneurs in your neighborhood or around the world offering well-known brands; Build a network of support locally, regionally and from the entire global corporation to foster growth, success and community.

PRODUCTS and SERVICES

Major Product Categories include:
- Vitamins, Minerals and Dietary Supplements (Nutrilite Brand #1 worldwide in 2008 retail sales)
- Skin Care and Cosmetics (Artistry Brand)
- Cleaning Products (since 1959)
- Oral/Dental Care (Glister Brand)
- Cooking/Kitchen (Queen/iCook Brands)
- Water and Air Purifications (eSpring and Atmosphere Brands)

PEOPLE

Founded in 1959 by Rich DeVos and the late Jay Van Andel, Amway developed into the most recognizable and successful direct marketing company that now has more than 3 million IBOs (Independent Business Owners) in over 80 markets worldwide. Amway "adapts it business model to the cultural and economic needs and standards of the markets in which it operates...business model varies slightly from market to market".

PRICING (and Promotions)

Nominal amount to join to become an IBP (independent Business Owner): approximately $50 in U.S. markets.
Sample Retail Prices:

Nutrilite 450 g Protein Powder: $30.75	Artistry Time Defiance Skin Care System: $166.95
See Spray Cleaner (1 liter): $7.80	Magic Foam Carpet Cleaner (21 oz.): $8.40
Atmosphere Air Purifier: $859.99	eSpring Water Purifier System: $922.79

PROFIT and Compensation Plans

- Retail Profit on product sales to customers: 29% average when sold at Suggested Retail Prices
- Monthly performance bonuses ranging from 3% to 25% of business volume depending on monthly productivity
- Monthly and annual leadership bonuses and other cash awards and business incentives based on group performance

---

PERSONAL PROFILE & BUSINESS BACKGROUND

Recent College Graduate from Pontificia Universidade Catolica de Sao Paulo in Accounting
Accounting Manager in Family Clothing Business in Sao Paulo
Enjoy travel and fashion shows
Passionate about Amway Global's Artistry Cosmetic Products
Monthly supplemental income goal for 2011: 1000 BRL (Brazilian Reales) = 600 US Dollars/Month

---

Related Jobs/Careers:
(Independent Distributor, Home-Based Businesses, Household Products, Cleaning Products)

RÉSUMÉ #86: Network Marketing / MLM Distributor: Amway Global (2011 U.S. Retail: $249)

WOW! RÉSUMÉS 2011-2012: Great Jobs...Extra Income...Happiness...

Ellen Magpantay
1234 Broadway #123
San Diego, CA 92107
(619) 123-4567
ellenmagpantay@wowresumes.net

World Ventures Travel
Industry Certified Travel Company Offering Business and Leisure Opportunities
"Become a Leisure Travel Consultant (LTC) with 'Business in a Box' Online Travel"

PROPOSITION
Provide passionate individuals with training and business infrastructure to enjoy and book "dream trips" that are "unmatchable" in price, uniqueness and excitement. Membership includes an online retail travel website, online travel tutorials and exam, as well as the ability to obtain higher level travel industry training.

Members pay $199.95 up front and $24.99 per month: "taking the bulk buying concept of Costco and applying it to travel". Thus for a one-time registration charge & monthly fee, members have access to sell and enjoy deeply discounted vacations.

PRODUCTS and SERVICES
The "Rovia" Search Engine is used to power the retail websites of LTCs (Leisure Travel Consultants). Airfare search is comprehensive including Southwest Airlines. There is a "Match or Beat" price guarantee for online bookings against Expedia, Orbitz, Priceline and Travelocity. The WorldVentures Rovia system also includes a cruise vacation search. At any one time (currently) there are some 70 "Dream Trip" Vacations available.

PEOPLE
Founded in 2006 by network marketing veterans Wayne Nugent and Mike Azcue, WorldVentures LLC has been certified with standard industry organizations including IATA, ASTA & CLIA for its entire existence. America West Co-Founder Michael Conway is a member of the WorldVentures corporate staff and ex U.S. Senator Mike Rose serves as legal counsel.

PRICING (and Promotions)
Sample "Dream Trip" prices:
✓ Jamaica vacation at the Grand Lido Braco (1 week for 2 adults) = $890 vs. Travelocity price of $1050
✓ Cabo San Lucas trip to Riu Palace (5 days for 2 adults) = $758 vs. Travelocity price of $950

PROFIT (and Compensation Plans)
Binary Compensation Plan plus Unique Bonuses:
- Every sale generates $50 direct commission and team building bonuses of $100 earned every 6 sales with 3 on each side
- When agents (LTCs) make 3 or more sales in a week, every cycle for that week is doubled to $200 (for team building
- Every 6th cycle WorldVentures gives awards of "Travel Dollars" instead of the normal cash payout
- Residual income of $20 for every sales earned when individuals achieve "Director" rank (90 agents on each binary team)
- Monthly product fees are waived once agent (LTC) achieves 4 retail sales and waiver continued if agent has 4 active sales

---

PERSONAL PROFILE & BUSINESS BACKGROUND:
15-Year Resident of Southern California, originally from Philippines (Travel Agent)
Mother of 3 and part-time Customer Service Representative for Wells Fargo Bank
Enjoy travel to Europe, China, Philippines, Southeast Asia, South America, and Caribbean Cruising
Member of Lyon's Club and San Diego Chamber of Commerce
Graduate of University of Santo Tomas (Philippines) in Business Administration
AA Degree in Banking from San Diego City College
GOAL: Supplemental Income in 2011 from WorldVentures Travel of $1,000 per Month

---

Related Jobs/Careers:
(Independent Distributor, Home-Based Businesses, Travel Agent)

WOW! RÉSUMÉS 2011-2012: Great Jobs...Extra Income...Happiness...

Yoko Fujiwara
1-10-5 Akasaka
Minato-ku, Tokyo 107-8420, JAPAN
03-3224-1234
yokoujiwara@wowresumes.net

Avon Beauty Products
Promoting beauty, success and critical issues for women worldwide
"The Company for Women"

PROPOSITION

"Avon Ladies" are part of global popular culture: Independent Sales Representative who use direct selling (network marketing) to market and sell desirable cosmetic and fashion products. Avon empowers women's causes such as Breast Cancer Health Care, Domestic Violence Prevention and Women's Training and Literacy, the Environmental Movement, and Global Disaster Relief through the Avon Foundation and through special product sales. (By the way there are also thousands of "Avon Gentlemen".)

PRODUCTS and SERVICES

Products include perfumes, powder and rouge compacts, lipsticks, other toiletry products (including for men), children's products (such as shampoos and toys), jewelry and clothing. Worldwide brands include Avon Color, Anew, Skin so Soft, and affiliated product introductions through celebrities such as Reese Witherspoon (Avon's Global Ambassador), Derek Jeter and Salma Hayek.

PEOPLE

Founded in 1886 by a 28-year old American David H. McConnell who sold books door-to-door and found that the perfume he gave out proved to be much more popular to women than his books, Avon took its name in 1939 and is now in over 100 countries with 41,000 employees and over 5 million Independent Sales Representatives generating over $10.5 Billion in sales.

Chairman & CEO Andrea Jung is the longest tenured female CEO among Fortune 500 Companies. Avon's stable of celebrity Salespeople and Spokespersons include Gemma Arterton, Courteney Cox, Patrick Dempsey, Fergie, Jennifer Hudson, Serena Williams & Venus Williams. Avon was the first major cosmetic company to end animal testing on all its manufactured products.

PRICING (and Promotions)

Sample Prices:
Anew Ultimate Age Defying System: $28.00
Avon Enhanced Renewing Lotion, 6.8 oz.: $19.50

Reese in Bloom Fragrance: $34.00
MagiX Finish Liquid Foundations SPF 10: $11.00

PROFIT (and Compensation Plans)

Avon has a nominal membership fee of between $10 to $20. On the first 4 orders, Independent Sales Reps get 50% commission, and 20% thereafter. Recruiting a new Independent Sales Rep results in $20 per recruit and when one becomes a Unit Leader, one can also earn from the recruited down line's sales. To become a Unit Leader, ones has to sell $250 products directly and the recruited Independent Sales Reps sell $1200 in products in total. A Unit Leader earns up to 7% of the down line's dales if they sell products over $100.

PERSONAL PROFILE & BUSINESS BACKGROUND:
Two-Year College Student (Graduation 2012) at Tama Art University, Tokyo, Japan
Volunteer at Tsukishima Senior Center, Tokyo, Japan
Desire to travel and learn foreign languages such as English and French
Passion to sell Avon Skin Care Products, Avon designer clothing and accessories
GOAL: 2011 Supplemental Avon Income of 75,000 JPY Japanese Yen = 900 U.S. Dollars

---

Related Jobs/Careers:
(Independent Distributor, Home-Based Businesses, Cosmetics, Beauty Consultant, Sales Representative)
RÉSUMÉ #88: Network Marketing / MLM Distributor: Avon Products (2011 U.S. Retail: $249)

WOW! RÉSUMÉS 2011-2012: Great Jobs...Extra Income...Happiness...

Lawrence Wickerman
1234 Eglinton Ave West #123
Toronto, ON, Canada M7A 3E5
(416) 123-4567
larryackerman@wowresumes.net

AMSOIL Synthetic Lubricants & Chemicals
API (American Petroleum Institute) Certified Synthetic Motor Oil and Organic Fertilizers
"The First in Synthetics"

PROPOSITION

Aiming at enthusiastic motor vehicle owners and knowledgeable customers, formulate clean and high performance synthetic motor oils that need to be replaced up to only once a year or up to 25,000 miles and create a hybrid retail and network marketing opportunity for "Dealers", Preferred & Catalog Customers, and Commercial Accounts in North America and beyond.

PRODUCTS (and Services)

For all types of engines for motor vehicles including cars, motorcycles, (diesel) trucks, snowmobiles, boats: synthetic motor oils, synthetic grease, oil filters and air filters. AMSOIL "Dealers" (through AMSOIL's ownership of AgGrand Organic Liquid Natural Fertilizers) can also sell Certified Organic Fertilizers to farmers, golf courses, gardeners and ranchers.

PEOPLE (and Policies)

Founded in 1972 by Albert J. Amatuzio, a retired jet fighter pilot for the U.S. Air Force, AMSOIL became the first synthetic motor oil to meet American Petroleum Institute (API) requirements.

Founder Amatuzio states: "Our policy has always been to promote AMSOIL products with facts, not wild claims...straightforward way we promote our products...very important to maintain a good reputation, both personally and professionally..."

PRICING (and Promotions)

Sample Retail Prices in U.S. Dollars:
Signature Series 0W-30 100 Synthetic Motor Oil (1 Quart): $10.50
SAE 10W-30 100% Synthetic Motor Oil (1 Quart): $9.15

AMSOIL Ea Synthetic Nano-fiber Oil Filter: $14.35
AMSOIL SDF88 Oil Filter (Power Stroke Diesel): $23.60

PROFIT (and Compensation Plans)

$30 (U.S. Dollars) Per Year Dealer Fee (To get products at wholesale and to sell AMSOIL products):
INDEPENDENT DEALER: must be sponsored by another dealer, can sell products and receive commission from sponsored Dealers/Accounts
PREFERRED CUSTOMER; can purchase AMSOIL products at Dealer price but not interested in reselling (can upgrade at future time)
RETAIL ACCOUNTS: Physical Retail Outlets that can carry & retail AMSOIL products – Must be sponsored by Dealer who gets a commission
COMMERCIAL ACCOUNTS: Businesses who wish to be end-users of AMSOIL products: Get wholesale discount but cannot resell products
-There are no territories to restrict Independent Dealers; AMSOIL online customers are assigned to Dealer closest to customer-

---

PERSONAL PROFILE & BUSINESS BACKGROUND:

Engineer Supervisor for Ontario Park Authority, Toronto, Canada
Bachelor's degree in Chemical Engineering, 2000, Queen's University, Kingston, Ontario
Abiding interest in Organic (Urban) Farming; Live in extended family of 8
Dealer in AMSOIL Products since 2005 with specialty in organic liquid fertilizer sales
GOAL: Supplemental Income in 2011 of 1000 CAD (Canadian Dollars) = 1000 U.S. Dollars/Month

---

Related Jobs/Careers:
(Independent Distributor, Home-Based Businesses, Automotive Care, Organic Fertilizers, Synthetic Oil)
RÉSUMÉ #89: Network Marketing/MLM Distributor: AMSOIL Synthetic Oil Products (2011 U.S. Retail: $249)

WOW! RÉSUMÉS 2011-2012: Great Jobs...Extra Income...Happiness...

Ashton C. Major
100 Featherstone Street
LONDON, EC1Y 8SY, UNITED KINGDOM
(44) 071-123-4567
ashtonmajor@wowresumes.net

Pampered Chef Kitchen & Food Products
Direct Selling of Kitchen Tool, Food Products and Cookbooks with the "Party Plan" System

PROPOSITION

Offer business and social opportunities for the cooking aficionado (the talented or enthusiastic cook or cook-to-be) and those who love food (who doesn't?) to sell desirable products and the concept of preparing delicious quality meals economically and quickly.

The Pampered Chef "Party Plan" is a time-tested direct selling approach (proven successful by Tupperware, etc.): using the products, a Pampered Chef Consultant (Independent Distributor) does a Cooking Show demonstration at a home. The Consultant cooks food and guests get to eat during the show!

PRODUCTS and SERVICES

Various quality kitchen and cooking tools, cookbooks and various food products such as kitchen utensils, cookware, pantry items and various innovative and useful products for kitchen and dining table. The gamut of items include Nylon tool sets, thermometers, roasting pans, skillets, sauté pans, griddles, stock pots, quality Stainless Steel, whisks, can and jar openers and juicers. Available are bamboo products & stoneware products such as pie plates, deep dish bakers, and muffin/loaf pans, etc.

PEOPLE (and Policies)

Founded in 1980 by Doris Christopher who implemented the Tupperware party plan system with kitchen and food products. Marla Gottschalk is the current CEO. Since 2002, Pampered Chef has been owned by Warren Buffet's Berkshire Hathaway.

Pampered Chef holds regular promotions of various products where partial sales proceeds are contributed to "Feed America".

PRICING (and Promotions)

Sample Retail Prices in U.S. Dollars:
Roasting Pan with Rack & Meat Lifters: $153.00
Reversible Bamboo Carving Board & Carving Set: $184.50
Stoneware Plates and Pans: $16 to $70

11" Square Grill Pan & Grill Press: $299.00
Large 18" x 15" Bamboo Platter: $31.95
Dining Table Pieces: $12 to $160 (16-piece set)

PROFIT (and Compensation Plans in U.S. Dollars)

✓ To sign up as Consultant: Mini Starter Kit ($65) or Full Consultant ($155: ½ refunded if $1,250 in sales in 30 days)
✓ 8 Consultant Career levels from Consultant to National Executive Director: Commissions of group sales up to 31%
✓ Targeted Retail Sales Scenario based on average (2009) Cooking Show Sales Average of $450 per Show:
  2 Cooking Shows/Week = $850/month; 3 Cooking Shows/Week = $1,300/Month; 4 Cooking Shows/Week = $1,800/Month

---

PERSONAL PROFILE & BUSINESS BACKGROUND:
2 ½ Years as Pampered Chef Consultant
Weekly Cook/Volunteer at East London Homeless Center
Unemployed (since 2008) Barrister (Barclays Bank)
Education: LLD, 1998, King's College School of Law, London, U.K.
Married with 2 adopted children
Enjoy football, gardening and sailing
GOAL: 2011 Supplemental Income from Pampered Chef of 1,000 GBP (Pounds)=$1,550 U.S. Dollars/Month

---

Related Jobs/Careers:
(Independent Distributor, Home-Based Businesses, Kitchen Consultant, Cooking Advisor, Culinary Sales)
RÉSUMÉ #90: Network Marketing / MLM Distributor: Pampered Chef Products (2011 U.S. Retail: $249)

WOW! RÉSUMÉS 2011-2012: Great Jobs...Extra Income...Happiness...

Rubia Wulandari
Jl. Medan Merdeka Selatan, No. 123
Jakarta 10110, Indonesia
(62) (21) 3435-1234
rubiawulandari@wowresumes.net

Organo Gold Coffee
"Full Health and Wealth Potential"
Coffee and Tea Products Blended with Ganoderma (Ling Zhi) Herb/Mushroom

PROPOSITION (and Principles)

Build direct selling (network marketing) opportunities with coffee (and tea) products based on 100% Certified Organic Ganoderma Lucidum ("perhaps the most amazing botanical on Earth"). Position the Independent Distributor "in front of five powerful industries": 1) Health & Wellness; 2) Weight Loss; 3) Home Based Business; 4) The Internet; 5) Coffee (the second largest traded commodity in the world).

"Since people drink so much coffee anyway, people won't have to change their habits if they also want to be healthy."

PRODUCTS (and Services)

Gourmet Black Coffee	Gourmet Mocha Coffee	Gourmet Latte Coffee
Gourmet Hot Chocolate	Gourmet Organic Green Tea	Premium Beauty Soap (w/Ganoderma, & Grapeseed)

PEOPLE (and Policies)

Founded in 2008 (starting in September 2008) by Direct Marketing Legend Bernie Chua (built a 500,000 Member Direct Sales organization in the Philippines and Prior Company Won Direct Sales Company of the Year for 3 years in a row), Organo Gold has an exclusive "strategic alliance" agreement with one of the largest Certified Organic Ganoderma producers in the world.

Shane Morand is Vice President of Sales and Marketing charged with introducing Organo Gold in North America.

Jay Noland is Director of Training and Personal Growth (13 years in MLM; built Member base of 55,000+ in 20+ countries).

PRICING (and Promotions)

Sample Prices of 4 Packets in U.S. Dollars:

Gourmet Black Coffee: $4.95	Gourmet Mocha Coffee: $8.95	Gourmet Latte Coffee: $5.95
Gourmet Hot Chocolate: $8.95	Gourmet Organic Green Tea: $6.95	King of Coffee: $9.95

PROFIT (and Compensation Plans)

✓ Membership Levels from Market Associate to Supervisor to Consultant and up with various Packs (products at wholesale)
✓ Retail profit: Paid cash each day for personal sales & weekly for internet sales
✓ Fast Start Bonus: Paid on a weekly basis as Sponsors earning $20, $30 or $80 per Pack
✓ Other Bonuses include: Dual Group Bonus; Uni-Level Bonus (team development); Generational and Universal Bonus Pools

---

PERSONAL PROFILE & BUSINESS BACKGROUND:
Small Shopkeeper in Jakarta Selatan, Jakarta, Indonesia
Graduate of Universitas Padjadjaran, Bandung, Jawa, Barat, Indonesia, International Business, 2003
Member of Jakarta Selatan Jawa Ethnic Arts & Crafts Community Affairs
Member of Jakarta – Singapore Travel Society
Market Associate Level with Organo Gold since March 2010
GOAL: 2011 Supplemental Income of 3 Million IDR (Indonesian Rupiah) = 333 U.S. Dollars/Month

---

Related Jobs/Careers:
(Independent Distributor, Home-Based Businesses, Beverage Sales, Marketing Associate, Herbal Coffees & Teas)
RÉSUMÉ #91: Network Marketing / MLM Distributor: Organo Gold Coffee (2011 U.S. Retail: $249)

WOW! RÉSUMÉS 2011-2012: Great Jobs...Extra Income...Happiness...

Vidya M. Shivpuri, M.D.
100 Bhulabhai Desai Road #123
Mumbai, India 400 026
(22) 2363-1234
vidyamshivpuri@wowresumes.net

Mary Kay Personal Care Products:
Cosmetics, Fragrances and Toiletries
"Empowering Women to be Independent Entrepreneurs and Forces of Good in their Community"

PROPOSITION (and Principles)

From the entrepreneurial and visionary legacy of its legendary founder, Mary Kay Ash, build a direct selling (network marketing) business based on great products that meet the highest standards of quality, safety and performance.

Mary Kay Ash: "The success of Mary Kay Inc. is much, much deeper than just dollars and cents and buildings and assets. The real success of our Company is measured to me in the lives that have been touched and given hope."

PRODUCTS (and Services)

In the U.S., there are roughly 200 Mary Kay products available. In other countries, fewer products are available due to reformulations to meet local laws or consumer preferences. Some products are created for a specific country (India for example was opened as a market in 2006). In the early 1990s many products were introduced for the growing market of women of color.

PEOPLE (and Policies)

- After being in direct selling for already 25 years and facing the limits of being a woman entrepreneur, Mary Kay Ash founded Beauty by Mary Kay in 1963 with $5,000 in savings and the help of her then 20-year old son, Richard
- Mary Kay Ash became an icon in American business and now Mary Kay Inc., a privately held company has revenues of $2.4 Billion (2007 figures) with an Independent Sales force of 1.8 million worldwide (as of 2008) in over 35 countries
- Richard Rogers, Mary Kay's son is the Executive Chairman; David Holl is president and named CEO in 2006
- Mary Kay scientists consult with independent dermatologists and medical experts and conduct over 300,000 tests annually in Dallas, USA and Hangzhou, China; Mary Kay Inc. does not conduct animal testing for its products and is a PETA pledge member

PRICING (and Promotions)

Sample Prices in U.S. Dollars:

TimeWise Age-Fighting Moisturizer: $22
Satin Lips Set: $18
TimeWise 3-in-1 Cleanser: $18

Mary Kay Ultimate Mascara (Black): $15
Oil-Free Eye Makeup Remover: $15
Satin Hands Pampering Set: $34 per set

PROFIT (and Compensation Plans)

✓ $100 Starter Kit for all Consultants: Registration, Seller's ID, Online Storefront, Catalogs and Sales Tools
✓ Reps/Consultants can purchase products at 50% discount after reaching order minimums; Up to 30% gross profit on sales
✓ Leadership Compensation, Bonuses and Rewards for Individual and Group Performance
✓ Independent Sales Directors (14,000 in U.S. & 33,000 worldwide) & Independent National Sales Directors (500 worldwide)

PERSONAL PROFILE & BUSINESS BACKGROUND:
Medical Doctor (Family Medicine) in Mumbai, Educated in USA (Johns Hopkins University, 2003)
Purchaser of Mary Kay products since college days and new Consultant in 2008
Mother of 1-year old infant boy & Volunteer at Dharavi Pediatric Center
GOAL: 2011 Supplemental Income from Mary Kay of 15,000 INR Indian Rupees = 333 U.S. Dollars/Month

---

Related Jobs/Careers:
(Independent Distributor, Home-Based Businesses, Personal Care, Beauty Consultant, Cosmetics)

RÉSUMÉ #92: Network Marketing / MLM Distributor: Mary Kay Personal Care Products (2011 U.S. Retail: $249)

WOW! RÉSUMÉS 2011-2012: Great Jobs...Extra Income...Happiness...

Mai kuh Zhang
123 BAOSHAN JIUCUN, BAOSHAN DISTRICT
201900 SHANGHAI, P.R. CHINA
(21) 1234-1234
zhangmaikuh@wowresumes.net

Tupperware Brands Home Products
Multi-Brand, Multi-Category, Multinational Company
"Featuring Preparation, Storage and Serving Products for the Kitchen and Home"

PROPOSITION (and Principles)
As the pioneer of the "party plan" (invite friends and neighbors to a home to see product and business demonstrations), offer entrepreneurial opportunities to women and the new global middle class with excellent, functional and innovative products.

Note: In China due to laws enacted in 1998 that limits "pyramid selling", Tupperware products are sold through franchised "entrepreneurial shopfronts". There are approximately 5000 "shopfronts" in China with the Tupperware brand in Chinese characters translated as "hundred benefits".

PRODUCTS (and Services)
Some of the most popular & innovative branded products (among hundreds) include:
"Eleganzia" and "Illusions": a "glasslike" range of serving dishes
"Flatout" & "MiniMax" & "Go flex: Bowls that flatten for storage and can be expanded when needed
"Stuffables" & "Bungee": Refrigerator storage with flexible lids for overfilling
"UltraPro" & "UltraPlus": plastic casseroles that are safe when used in microwave or conventional ovens

PEOPLE (and Policies)
Tupperware was founded in 1946 by Earl Silas Tupper in Orlando, Florida who developed plastic containers used to contain food and keep it airtight (formerly patented "burping seal"). Tupperware introduced the party plan as a direct marketing strategy. Tupperware Brands Corporation operates a family of 8 brands in nearly 100 countries with sales revenues of $2.1 Billion with 2.4 million salespeople. In May 2007, Tupperware announced Brooke Shields as the celebrity spokesperson for its "Chain of Confidence" campaign in the U.S. to celebrate the strong bonds and self-confidence developed from female friendships.

PRICING (and Promotions)
Retail Prices of Sample Products in U.S. Dollars:

"Go-anywhere serving & storage collection" (9-Pc): $30.00   Medium Eco Water Bottles (4 bottles): $34.00
Floresta Serving Dishes: $29.50   Complete Kitchen Prep Set: $99.00
Tupperware Revolutionary Microwave SmartSteamer: $139.00   Quick Shake (Mixer) Container: $13.00

PROFIT (and Compensation Plans)
Initial Membership Kits:
✔ $79.00: Business Kit with Support Materials and Selection of Products with retail value of $355.00
✔ $119.00: Executive Business Kit with Support Materials and Selection of Products with retail value of $525.00
✔ Tiered Structure: Consultants to Managers to Star Managers/Directors and to the top level of Legacy Executive Directors

---

PERSONAL PROFILE & BUSINESS BACKGROUND:
Born in Hubei Province with Accounting Degree (2005) from Huazhong Normal University, Wuhan, PRC
Entrepreneurial Shopfront Owner with 3 friends in Shanghai, PRC
Desire to triple Tupperware franchises in 2 years
GOAL: 2011 Personal Full-time income from Tupperware of 15,000 CNY (Chinese Yuan) = 2,260 U.S. Dollars/Month

---

Related Jobs/Careers:
(Independent Distributor, Home-Based Businesses, Plastic Products, Household Products, Food Storage)
RÉSUMÉ #93: Network Marketing / MLM Distributor: Tupperware Consumer Products (2011 U.S. Retail: $249)

WOW! RÉSUMÉS 2011-2012: Great Jobs...Extra Income...Happiness...

Jonathan Lee Soo
100 Napier Road
Singapore 258508, Republic of Singapore
(65) 0000-1234
jleesoo@wowresumes.net

NonSuperstarsMLM.Com:
World's First Distributor-Owned Profit-Sharing MLM Company
"Credible Extra Income, Ordinary People's Dreams, Better World"

PROPOSITION
The World's First Distributor-Owned Profit-Sharing MLM Company only 3 layers deep!
No one is "filthy rich" so everyone is enriched with monthly distributions of community income pool from 30% of company profits! Share of monthly distributions based on activity and time spent assisting others.

PRODUCTS and SERVICES
The company only markets and sells products and services that are "Green", "Fair Trade", and "Sustainable" featuring village crafts and fabrics, natural products such as botanicals, foods and rapidly renewable materials from sustainably managed jungles, fisheries, organic farms and orchards. Solar, biomass, mini-wind power are emphasized in production/shipping.

PEOPLE
Distributors/Reps/Members are people from all over the world (nominal membership fees as low as $1/month) that are from unique cultures and backgrounds looking to supplement their monthly family income. The "recruitment" structure is only 3 layers deep with emphasis on community pooling of resources, expertise and financing. 30% of Profits are redistributed monthly.

PRICING (and Promotions)
Unique products and services are competitively priced in their industry categories. Markups are never exorbitant, with the objective of returning a fair profit for distributor income and 30% allocation of total profits back to all distributors monthly. (Distributors get 20 to 40% off retail prices for their own consumption or for resale.)

PROFIT
Very transparent compensation plans with immediate full income to new distributors / members. Emphasis is on product development, sales, marketing and distribution. Monthly income levels range from $30 to $3,000 including profit sharing.

PERSONAL PROFILE & BUSINESS BACKGROUND:

Born in Malaysia and raised in Singapore (Citizen): Married with 2 children
Senior Engineer at Singapore Transit Authority (Changi International Airport)
Enjoy travel, rock music, museums, holidays, ethnic Malay, Indian, Chinese and Japanese Foods
Bachelor's Degree in Electrical Engineering at Nanyang Technological University, 1998
Independent Distributor for NonSuperstars.Com for 12 months
Business Goals: Earn 1300 Singapore Dollars ($1000 US)/month & 10 new Distributors in 2011

Related Jobs/Careers:
(Independent Distributor, Home-Based Businesses, Social Businesses, Community Entrepreneurship, Profit-sharing Enterprises)
RÉSUMÉ #94: Network Marketing / MLM Distributor: Non Superstars Network (2011 U.S. Retail: $249)

BLANK PAGE

-FOR NOTES-

CHAPTER 9:

UNIQUE STORY RÉSUMÉS

10 Model *WOW!* Résumés
(46 Job Titles)

CREATE YOUR OWN "UNIQUE STORY RÉSUMÉ":

If you are doing your own "Unique Story Résumé", you can choose from among the *WOW!* Résumés in this Chapter modeling the wording, styles, formatting, bullets, borders, etc. You can also model any of the elements in the other *WOW!* Résumés in this Book.

Complete the Guides in the Appendices to fully customize and create a unique and powerful *WOW!* Résumé! You can both have a "regular" *WOW!* Résumé and an accompanying "Unique Story Résumé" which can be used in lieu of the usual Cover Letter for either a specific target or multiple applications.

If you have purchased this Book (and thus become an automatic 1-year Member of wowresumes.net) you can get Free unrestricted downloads (Word or PDF Files) of up to 5 *WOW!* Résumés (including "Unique Story Résumés") in addition to a Free download of the Guides and Keyword-Lists in the Appendices for you to print out or edit on your computer.

DISCOUNTED RÉSUMÉ SERVICE:

If you need help to create a *WOW!* Résumé call 888-503-3133 or go to wowresumes.net to work with professional Résumé Writers who practice *WOW!* Résumé principles. Book purchasers have up to one year to avail of a 30% Instant Discount on any *WOW!* Résumé or other *WOW!* Résumé products such as *WOW!*-Card® Résumés, as well as other benefits including Free Résumé Posting on the ever-growing wowresumes.net Website and Updating from Twitter, Facebook, LinkedIn & Google Profiles. Members get Free Updates for 1 year on their Main Résumé and up to 90% Discounts on additional (2nd, 3rd, 4th, etc.) Customized Résumés to target Specific Jobs, Careers, Industries or Special Urgent Applications.

*See the Back Cover for *WOW!* Résumé Service & Free Membership Information*

WOW! RÉSUMÉS 2011-2012: Great Jobs...Extra Income...Happiness...

A New Kind of "Cover Letter"

When seekers for jobs or employment prospects get the chance to tell their unique stories, people pay attention and often give these "special" individuals extra consideration or even explicit offers for positions or career opportunities. Many moving stories in bad economic times that reach the media result in multiple offers of jobs and in some instances direct help such as money and donations.

The unique story that is true, real and humanistic can be used in general to create a special résumé that can stand out from the rest. The résumés in this chapter will use a potent formula that can create a powerful and authentic "story resume" using the "5 Cs" including one element which turns the concept of "offer" around to the advantage of the opportunity-hunter and job-seeker: the "applicant" offers a "Coupon" which is a tool to make a decision-maker interested in getting tremendous value for the enterprise or organization by way of, for example, temporary salary reduction, extra hours or a <u>contractual</u> pledge for certain commitments such as punctuality, cheerfulness or other tangible or intangible behaviors and acts.

The other "Cs" of Character, Color, Commitment and Capabilities are woven together to create a work and life story that are a narrative summation and a declaration of who the individual person is. How the story is told will make the substance of a person's essence interesting, poignant and compelling as would a short news article or feature. Any life is and can be presented as unique.

In the context of looking for a job or career, the person's story is as much for the person himself or herself as it is for those who would assess the person's qualifications. To know oneself and how to portray personal uniqueness make for a more focused and confident person. Additionally, because there are many qualified and deserving people in the marketplace, crafting and depicting a unique story in the most moving way would give someone the advantage of attention. Added to the emotional and humanistic aspects of the story, the final C of "Coupon" or offer is a call to action or determination for the decision-maker to give immediate and serious consideration to the job-seeker.

The various points in each "C" category on the next page are a good guide in what to include in a "Unique Story Résumé". The "Cs" need not be in the order shown but each "C" can be a short paragraph that ties in with the rest and all together to portray a story that will move the reader (evaluator for a potential job) emotionally, intellectually and finally practically.

A well written story with humor, visceral insights and striking imagery or feeling will serve as a connection between the job-seeker and the decision-maker. All things being equal, a good person that someone can care about might just win an immediate interview and the job itself. The job-seeker's highlights of his or her unique "Capabilities" and the climatic "Coupon" or unique offer in the areas of salary, hours, clients, assets, tools, etc. might be the clincher to win the position subject to a face-to-face meeting to finalize the "deal".

The Unique Story Résumé can be used in lieu of the traditional Cover Letter. While the customary cover letter can pinpoint selling points for an applicant that are tailored for a researched company or prospective employer, the Unique Story Résumé can accomplish the same objectives with the added plus of being unique in the marketplace, especially in its Unique Offer ("Coupon") that is a way to close or clinch the job or at least the job interview!

WOW! RÉSUMÉS 2011-2012: Great Jobs...Extra Income...Happiness...

"UNIQUE STORY" RÉSUMÉ FORMAT

THE "5 Cs"

ALL IDEALLY IN ONE PAGE with References to Your Other Résumé(s)

[with CAPTION or "Headline"]

CHARACTER

Career or Family History as applicable; Community background;
Example of Character and Personality:
Industriousness, Honesty, Authenticity, Dignity, Humility, Persistence, and other Intangible Traits

COLOR

Unique Back Story Backgrounds; Interesting Events and Persons; Unusual Circumstances; Humor; Moving Testimonials; Graphic Details as appropriate; Etc.

COMMITMENT

Work Ethic, Pledges, Vows, and Bigger-Than-Self Goals

CAPABILITIES

Specific Skills, Accomplishments, Hints at Heroism, "Personal Bests";
Strengths, Knowledge, Abilities, Certifications, Education (Formal and *Informal*)

"COUPON" OR UNIQUE OFFER

Contractual Offer to work for a certain amount for a certain time period;
Trial (probationary) period that includes unique conditions;
Assets to the table: such as appropriate and legitimate client base, tools, equipment, influence circles, unique social networks;
Calculate real and specific figures in dollars, hours, output, production, etc.
Research Info and Interesting Facts and Statistics

Basic Profile Information including single lines for education, employment and community:

Can Condense and Summarize Years and Groups of Jobs in 1 industry

---

Patrick Mulford
1000 Forest Hill Blvd. #123
West Palm Beach, Florida 33401
561-123-4567
patrickmulford@wowresumes.net

"Seeking Full-Time Work for over 18 Months, Financial Manager, Father of 3 Still Upbeat and Trying"

My name is Patrick Mulford. I have been an Analyst and a Manager in the Financial Industry. These jobs were my identities and still are, but now I know that who I really am is a proud father of 2 boys (Matt and Gerald) and 1 girl (Rebecca), ages from 15 to 6. Matt is the mature young man of 15 while Becky is the 6-year old wonder-child.

I lost my job at Portico Financial in West Palm Beach in June 2009 and I have been looking for full-time work ever since. I thought myself a victim at first, like many others in the U.S. recession that has hit Florida particularly hard. But we're all in the "same boat" and we cannot think or act like victims. There have in fact been blessings because of these bad times. We get to know what is important and most valuable: family, friends and community, as well as health and reputation.

I am upbeat because I have upgraded my skills and knowledge even as I have tried to apply for just about anything resembling financial and accounting work. I have found time to volunteer in the community (the United Way) to help those who are worse off than me and also to help people like me with programs such as Clothing Banks, Job Fairs and Job Search Networking. My next employer will get someone very valuable and full of energy, motivation and flexibility. I take the best from my past and offer even greater potential.

The financial industry will come back here in Florida because banking, lending and financial services are the backbone of our community. Everywhere I have worked in finance, I have produced. From my early days at First National Bank in Atlanta to my several years as Financial Manager at Auto Nation to my last position at Portico Financial I have contributed greatly to the bottom-line. I increased business and expanded customer bases with my technical and financial aptitudes, as well as my management and interpersonal skills. And now I have been certified as a Reverse Mortgage Specialist that will be projected to be a huge consumer-oriented market, especially here in the South. The local and regional economies have been devastated but there are still great untapped assets in our state and region that will bring back our communities in terms of jobs, capital and sustainable growth.

As an additional advantage for a hiring organization, I can work at home since I possess expert computer capabilities. I can save my next employer a lot of overhead and offer great productivity with my flexibility and relentless work ethic that nonetheless is balanced with family and community activities. I can discuss any amenable contractual arrangements and will sign on to my offer of "Bottom-Line Production" that will surpass your industry average by 100% guaranteed or "Money-Back"! I can be reached anytime while I serve family and community!

EMPLOYMENT:
FIRST NATIONAL BANK, Atlanta, GA: Personal Banker, Assistant Branch Manager, 1998 to 2003
AUTO NATION, Orlando, FL: Financial Manager, Consumer & Fleet Sales, 2003 to 2006
PORTICO FINANCIAL, West Palm Beach, FL: Regional Financial Manager, 2006 to 2009

SKILLS:
Financial Analysis; Capital Budgeting; Portfolio Management; Supply Chain Management; Real Estate Appraisal/Valuations; Computer Proficiency includes Microsoft Forecaster and SYSPRO 6.0

EDUCATION:
SPELMAN COLLEGE, Atlanta, Georgia: Bachelor of Science in Accounting (Minor in Finance), 1998
HOUSING & URBAN DEVELOPMENT: Certified National (and Florida) Reverse Mortgage Specialist, 2/2011

WOW! RÉSUMÉS 2011-2012: Great Jobs...Extra Income...Happiness...

Svetlana Kasparov, MD
1000 Friars Road #123
San Diego, CA 92101
619-123-4567
lanakasparov@wowresumes.net

"New" American with World-Class Skills/Education in Pharmacy and Biology

My name is Svetlana Kasparov. Everyone calls me "Lana". I was born in Tula, Russia just south of Moscow and have studied in Moscow University in the field of Pharmacy. I worked for only 1 year in Pharmacy before my family and I immigrated to New York in the United States when I was 22.

I lived and worked in New York for almost 10 years before I pursued my long-time dream of studying medicine. I immigrated from my immigrant family by going to California whereupon I started my medical studies at U.C. San Diego Medical School at the age of 34. Now I have reached my goal of becoming a doctor before age 40. At age 39!

As an immigrant among many and then a "new" American I want to relate my feelings about my family, my old and new country and my chosen fields of Pharmacy and Medicine. First I must tell about my parents and my one brother and one sister, both younger. My parents were teachers in Tula, Russia who always had lofty dreams for their children. Our father passed on us his intellect and discipline, while my mother her courage and determination to find a good life for our whole family. When we first struggled in New York as my parents and myself searched for jobs and careers, our family always held together. My younger brother and younger sister are now in college and since they came to America as young teenagers, they are as American and New York as can be, complete with accent and confident ambition. My brother wants to become a banker while my sister wants to become a professor in the field of law. I know they will make it.

As for me, I want to give my all to a life of purpose. I feel I already have all my material needs met. I am even lucky to have a small house that is already paid for. I look lovingly at my 10-year old Honda every day. It is because I did not splurge and because I received a scholarship that I was able to get a decent townhouse when prices were still reasonable 8 years ago. I am lucky to be able to earn a good income for the rest of my life. Now I want to find a position that will give me the feeling that every day I am making someone's life better, especially those who are now what my family and I were once: new to the country or just not lucky enough to access all the necessary social and health services that all citizens should get in any country.

My career goal is to work as a pediatrician in a small town or rural community in the Southwest United States or else in an HMO that has services in less-affluent communities in such areas as military or border towns. Since the end of my residency in Pediatrics, I actually have more time than when I was in Med School or when I worked over 60 hours a week as a Pharmacist. I am playing a little piano again, running daily and studying advanced Spanish. I know that I will find a HMO or a group practice where I will enjoy work every day!

EMPLOYMENT: 1995 - 2002 Pharmacist at various New York and New Jersey pharmacies incl CVS and Spieglers.
2003 – 2010 Part-time Administrator at Skaggs School of Pharmaceutical Sciences

SKILLS AND EXPERIENCE:
Pharmacological Knowledge and Applications; Internship and Residency in Pediatric Medicine including immunological research, prenatal care and childhood development

EDUCATION:
Moscow University, Doctor of Pharmacy, 1994
University of California San Diego, Doctor of Medicine, 2008, Passed California Boards, 2009

Related Jobs/Careers:
(Physician, Medical Doctor, Foreign Pharmacist)

RÉSUMÉ #96: Own Unique Story: Immigrant Pharmacist Becomes MD (2011 U.S. Retail: $249)

WOW! RÉSUMÉS 2011-2012: Great Jobs...Extra Income...Happiness...

Maurice L. Faber
1000 Hot Wells Blvd. #123
San Antonio, TX 78223
(210) 123-4567
mauricefaber@wowresumes.net

YOUNG SENIOR CITIZEN, OLD-SCHOOL SAVVY AND HIGH-TECH SMARTS:

"New Age Math: 70 is the New 50 and Over 55 is Better than Ever"

I admit I am 69 almost 70. I also admit that I am quite scared to be seeking employment at my "age" but I am enCOURAGEd by my courage. I know I can not only find a job but I know I will do a great job. The statistics show it and my record shows it.

The Bureau of Labor Statistics knows all about us. In countless studies we who are over age 55 are more productive, have better attendance, more loyal, more work-place safe and easier to instruct, and we are even less ill or acutely sick than all age groups! One powerful concrete example from the U.S. Department of Labor is that even though workers over age 55 make up 14% of the labor force, they account for less than 10% of all workplace injuries. And you can definitely teach an old dog new tricks! I just started Facebook and Twitter last month!

As for my own unique career background, summarized only briefly below, I have many skills, capabilities and experiences that have added to my formal and informal education. I was one of the best business services salespeople in the 70s and 80s. There was already a large computer industry back then!. Main frames and large data centers that offered large and mid-size companies computing and technical capacities that may now be company "in-house". Imagine selling million-dollar systems and 3-year plans to senior management in the days of punch cards and typewriters. I did extremely well and eventually started my own consulting company.

What can I offer an employer today? How about someone who can work like a horse for the next 10 years (I am certified healthy as such by my physician). How about a salesperson who will stand out in the room or meeting because the rest are in fact young "whipper snappers" who have less life experience than the "old guy" who knows just as much (through extra study if necessary) and who came in not just on on-time but early! How about an achiever who strives to beat his old "records" that were quite legendary already? How about a worker who doesn't count company time but rather production time?!

To summarize, my work and career motivations are for giving value to companies and their customers beyond just the monetary and the temporary. I am in it for the long-term because a good name and goodwill are priceless!

PAST EMPLOYMENT:
IBM; TRW; Texas Instruments; Compaq Computer; Allied Business Systems; American Express; Motorola; Texas Chamber of Commerce; Tandem Consulting Services

SKILLS:
Customer Relationship Management; SWOT (Strengths, Weaknesses, Opportunities, Threats) Analysis; Telemarketing; Direct Sales; Sales and Product Presentations; Motivation and Training

EDUCATION:
NORWICH UNIVERSITY, Northfield, Vermont: Bachelor of Science in Mathematics
RICE UNIVERSITY, Houston, TX: Master's Degree in Business Administration

PERSONAL BESTS: Met the legendary CEO Jack Welch in 1991 at a Leadership Breakfast in Los Angeles and also met then-candidate for U.S. President Al Gore in a 2000 AARP fundraiser in Florida (I was "only" 59 then).

Related Jobs/Careers:
(Semi-Retired Worker, Old-School Salesperson)

WOW! RÉSUMÉS 2011-2012: Great Jobs...Extra Income...Happiness...

Elipidia Maria Salcido
1000 Glen Oaks Boulevard
San Fernando, CA 91340
818-123-4567
emsalcido@wowresumes.net

"Student Immigrant Caregiver: From South of South to North of Good and Values"

I am California-born and a legal and proud citizen of the United States. But my family came from south of where most of my community comes from, that is we immigrated from south of Mexico, from Honduras in Central America. I am about to graduate from college at California State University at Fullerton, but I am still working in the community not by necessity but by choice. I am working as a caregiver in my parent's Residential Care Home for the Elderly (RCFE). By happenstance, my own grandmother is now one of the Care Home residents.

I am studying to complete my Public Administration Degree from California State because I want to work in a large facility as an Administrator or Activities Director. Nonetheless I know what the most important position is in home-care for the elderly, however large or small. It is the daily care given by hardworking caregivers and assistants (CNAs or Certified Nurse Assistants) and the working staff that make the most difference in the lives of residents. When someone comes from the ranks of daily caregivers and attendants of residents, that person understands what it takes to make people happy and sane. When people give genuine care from the heart and from persistent effort, lives are enriched and given value.

When I give care it is with the literal idea that my charges are family and friends. My grandmother is as challenging as any person in a convalescent home or assisted living facility. She now has dementia with some signs of Alzheimer's, but she is still my grandma "Lola" and she will always be special and valuable. If we treat all residents this way, our own lives are made meaningful and in fact easier. Elderly residents intuitively know that they challenge the patience and stamina of workers and staff. When they get genuine attention and love, everyone is happier and less stressed.

As for running the "business" of elderly care or any residential facility, I come from the administration side with my academic background and my family history as well. My parents have had their care-home for 15 years. I grew up in the business. My mother was the do-everything person while my Dad did the paperwork. What I learned about administration is to have perfect documentation that comes from diligence and ultimately from caring about people, from workers to outside service people to the licensing authorities and of course the residents and their families. It is just as difficult to find a great administrator as it to find a kind and hard-working caregiver. My Dad says, "When your heart and papers are straight, things go great!"

I offer myself as a *volunteer* intern-caregiver for a full month in a facility that I am applying to be an Administrator or Assistant Administrator. In our field and discipline it is hard to fake goodness and values!

EMPLOYMENT: 2007 – 2010, Salcido Care Home of San Fernando, Caregiver and Assistant Administrator; Before 2007: Summer and Seasonal Jobs at the Rose Bowl and at the Valley Flea Market

SKILLS: Administration; Writing and situational analysis; Caregiving including medical-related activities such as medications, charting and assessments; Budget analysis and supplies procurement; Fluent in Spanish

EDUCATION:
California State University at Fullerton; B.A. Degree in Public Administration, 2011
California Department of Social Services, Certified RCFE Administrator Expires August 2012

Related Jobs/Careers:
(RCFE Administrator, Bilingual Caregiver)
RÉSUMÉ #98: Own Unique Story: First Generation Citizen-New Graduate-Caregiver (2011 U.S. Retail: $249)

Julius B. Jones
1000 Hill Avenue
Toledo, OH 43602
419-123-4567
juliusjones@wowresumes.net

"Bankruptcy 'Expert' Seeking Job and Consulting Opportunities"

Let's get the first thing out of the way. I declared personal bankruptcy in February 2010 after fighting to keep my business afloat for as long as possible for the 12 to 15 people I employed. I had a business for 17 years that was a business equipment leasing company that was obviously reliant on the health of local businesses and capital lending from local and regional banks here in Northern Ohio.

The economic downturn starting in late 2008 accelerated very quickly for us because we rely on bank financing for our 2,500 customers to upgrade or acquire leased equipment. In a matter of 4 months, business went down 90%. We still had to operate our owned business building and other overhead including health care for my employees some of whom had been with me for 10 years or more. I honored write-offs from my long-time customers. My operations went down to 5 employees including me. I tried to hang on for as long as possible for the sake of my employees and my remaining customers. The personal guarantees on my business credit led to my personal bankruptcy. Now I am looking for work!

I have always considered myself successful in my business career, even "upper middle class" not from attitude or culture but because we were blessed with assets and income. I lost my commercial building and business assets. I am hanging on to my house and a good paid-off vehicle. But with no steady income and a bankruptcy to my name, I may now be considered "poor", at least temporarily.

The question is what to do now? Even as my company was winding down and business was drying up, I have been proactive in the job-search process, starting with my own employees! I started community workshops and networking fairs for the out-of-work and new college graduates who have come back to Akron because of the tight job market everywhere. We have a lot of unused human assets that can turn our local economies around!

Speaking of a human asset, I can do work in many areas of business, management and consulting. I of course know business equipment and organizational management. I have developed skills and abilities in starting, growing and sustaining a business. And yes I have knowledge about losses and insolvency and if within the control of the business owner, how to avoid bankruptcy in financial and people assets.

Hire me as a manager or supervisor or foreman and I can be compensated by how I IMPROVE the bottom line of my division, department or small team. I am a hands-on manager in how I deal with personnel and transactions as well as how I work side-by-side with my co-workers at all levels. Let's get the job done for the company and the community!

EMPLOYMENT: (Before 1993 and the start of my own Company J. Jones Leasing a $3.5 Million Revenues Company)
Xerox Corporation (1982 -1985): Field Technician and Sales Representative; IBM (1986 – 1990): Copier Sales; Coleco Office Systems (1990- 1991): District Manager); AKA Leasing (1991-1993): (Leasing Manager and Consultant

SKILLS: Sales, Mechanical Aptitude (including car and engine restoration); Negotiations, Financial Analysis; Workplace Diversity Management; Workshop and Communications Leader (Community Job Bank); Writing

EDUCATION:
Case Western Reserve University, Cleveland, Ohio, B.S. in Business Administration
University of Akron, Computer, Organizational and Finance Courses

---

WOW! RÉSUMÉS 2011-2012: Great Jobs...Extra Income...Happiness...

Alexander Werth
1000 Marquette Road #123
Chicago, IL 60601
312-123-4567
alexwerth@wowresumes.net

"Let's Put Youth Back to Work and Rebuild the Economy with Confidence and Capital"

I don't like it! I don't like moving back home but I have no choice since my graduation last month from Northwestern. I can have part-time jobs here in Chicago and develop my career search here. My parents can afford to have me back in my old bedroom in their 4 bedroom house in the suburbs but they have been affected by the economic crisis too. Their retirement nest egg is cut by more than half. They still have their jobs and careers but their outlook on the future is less confident.

I have a sense of disappointment since I know I have a solid education from a great school in a field (Economics) that I love. My disappointment is a call to action to find a company or organization that will benefit from my focused motivation to thrive in a community and in the world economy.

I have had many jobs and am working part-time now. Jobs are not necessarily the problem; it's the type of job both in pay and satisfaction that is the challenge. Some of my friends with college degrees or some college education can mostly find low-paying jobs right now. The truism that a college degree will equate to higher earnings does not apply if many jobs that are available don't require college degrees in the first place. As for job satisfaction, that is a more personal issue. One can be happy digging ditches or unhappy in a glamour position. The connection between what is important in someone's life is often missing from the work they find or end up getting.

The research from my course studies is no longer academic. The deep recession with its lagging job recovery means that my age group (16 to 24) will be affected for the next 2 or 3 decades! Youth unemployment among college graduates is stuck at 9% from the usual 5% while unemployed high school graduates are *double* their traditional 12%. Nearly one quarter of young high school graduates are unemployed! I know many of these people in the Chicago area! These young people aren't even thinking of using the opportunity of "free time" to go to school at any level to improve themselves as they had done in the past.

The youth are discouraged but not defeated. Certainly not me! I know the easy answer is to provide social "safety nets" for unemployed youth who are in financial hardship and debt through no fault of their own. The average debt for students graduating with an undergraduate degree from a public college is $19,535 and for those graduates from a private institution $25,350, 33% and 55% more respectively than 10 years ago! Just to make ends meet! I know that I am paying down my own debt and only making small inroads thus far.

What I can do about things? A lot locally! By example and by a career in community banking that takes advantage of my skills, knowledge and abilities. I desire to work at a community bank that has programs to provide youth with consumer loans, entrepreneurial capital and debt-counseling leading to savings. I have a wide social network from school/neighborhood and on-line. I have tremendous research skills and energy! I have an in-depth knowledge of capital markets and their impacts locally. I can be an intern or trainee until I can prove my "Werth" (Alex)!

EMPLOYMENT: Present: Southside Café: Part-time Manger and Barista
2007 - 2010: Part-time Teller at First National, Delivery, Title Company Clerk, Waiter, Caterer

SKILLS: Econometric Research, Marketing Field Studies, Financial and Portfolio Analysis, Data Mining

EDUCATION: Northwestern University, B.A. Degree in Economics, 2010

Related Jobs/Careers:
(Bank Economist, Financial Researcher, Data Mining)

RÉSUMÉ #100: Own Unique Story: Motivated Youth Intern-Trainee (2011 U.S. Retail: $249)

WOW! RÉSUMÉS 2011-2012: Great Jobs...Extra Income...Happiness...

Augustine Sundenberg
1000 Rudgear Rd #123
Walnut Creek, CA 94596
(925) 123-4567
augiesundenberg@wowresumes.net

"Job-Sharing Human Resource Experts Will Create A Profitable 'Power of Two'"

There are three parts to my story: the first is about job-sharing in general, the second is my background, the third is about my potential partners or job-sharers whom I introduce briefly and who have their own stories.

Basically, job-sharing is just like it sounds. Two people share a full-time job by dividing up the full-time hours, responsibilities, duties and compensation. Typically job-sharers are motivated by getting more time to balance their lives and attend to personal and family responsibilities. The ultimate reasons for sharing job include health, caring for parents or children, to pursue leisure or vocational activities or to just slow down or find career equilibrium.

My rationales are to care for my ailing mother, to pursue my art and enterprise of pottery, and to direct my career in human resources and employee benefits to the point where I can give fewer clients or employees more focused attention. Since I will be more centered and less-stressed at the workplace, I will be an even greater human resource asset for a mid-size to large company who can profit from getting two highly skilled professional and motivated employees or consultants in me and the potential partners (3 prime candidates) I now introduce.

Gabriela (Gabby) Sanchez is a Professional Benefits Specialist who has had over 20 years in Human Resources including having been a successful Manager for 5 years at Wells Fargo Bank. Gabby is a professional friend who is also interested in helping take care of his ailing husband and is interested in volunteering.

Janet Wilkinson is also a Human Resource Professional who is pursuing a graduate degree for the next 2 or 3 years and would like to contribute her 10 + years of benefits and personnel experience in retail.

Melissa Block is a recent graduate in Business Administration with a focus on Human Resources Management and is looking to enter the field of human resources in a technical (benefits) or administrative capacity. Having waited to have her first child in Samuel (now 18 months old) has motivated Melissa to explore the world of job-sharing.

We as potential job-sharers, especially in the human resources field, are fully cognizant of the questions employers have about job-sharing. At the option of the potential employer any pair among the 4 of us is ready, willing and able to create a proposal that addresses issues and concerns with regard to responsibilities, duties, time scheduling, communication, supervision and yes compensation and benefits for the hiring company. What the employer will get will be a set of skills, abilities, experience and knowledge that is unique, highly competitive and bottom-line and results-oriented. The "power of 2" will make profits true!

EMPLOYMENT: 1998 - 2010 Charles Schwab, Human Resource Manager and Benefits Specialist;
Before 1998: Librarian and Head Librarian and various branches at the San Francisco Public Library

SKILLS: Administration of Employee Benefits including 401ks, Group and Individual Health Insurance; Budgeting, Management of Personnel; Knowledge of Federal Laws including ERISA and Health Care Act of 2010

EDUCATION:
Fordham University, Sociology and English Majors
University of California Berkeley, Master of Science in Library Science

---

FULL RESUMES & SETS OF REFERENCES AVAILBLE UPON REQUEST OR AT INTERVIEW(S)

Related Jobs/Careers:
(Human Resources Specialist, Employee Benefits Administrator)

RÉSUMÉ #101: Own Unique Story: Job Sharer / Manager Part-Time (2011 U.S. Retail: $249)

WOW! RÉSUMÉS 2011-2012: Great Jobs...Extra Income...Happiness...

Ramon Fontaine
1000 Tropicana Avenue #123
Las, Vegas, NV 89127
702-123-4567
ramonfontaine@wowresumes.net

"Housing-Challenged but Fully Functional and Valuable Worker/Handyman"

I can fix just about anything and do any necessary work with my hands, own tools or with my pickup truck. I've chosen not to participate in the housing market as a buyer or renter and actually now it seems like I've been wise to do so.

I am here in Las Vegas for the last 7 years, the last 5 living in my truck and the occasional weekly hotel when I do long projects or big jobs. I am a veteran of the Bush I Gulf War and left the lakes of Minnesota by way of Kuwait and Fort Hood, Texas. I went through my rough years of alcohol and disillusionment before I decided to go sunnier climates. Las Vegas is probably not the best place to land as an addict. The fact that I have survived in "Sin City" and developed friends, "family" and community is a testament to my recovery. I like my lifestyle and believe it or not I am growing a humble but decent retirement fund because I don't speculate (in housing) or gamble (against the house or anybody).

We are actually blessed in America, recession or not, Democratic or Republican. We can make our own opportunities despite any economic or external factors. Once we decide to become resourceful, practice discipline and work really hard, we can make it!

I know that most of my homeless friends are in their predicament because of things that they feel are beyond their "control". I am trying to set an example but not be judging of them. As a community we are like any other. There are the good, the bad and definitely the ugly. When people get to know me I teach them survival skills and share with them "secrets" such as where to get free meals, where to stash valuable items from the elements and theft, how to earn some quick legal money without gambling and how to use the local system of resources and giveaways if in real need.

What are some of my job skills and abilities that will benefit an employer or owner or company or project? I can lay down foundations, frame and drywall buildings, install plumbing, heating, ventilation, air conditioning, insulation and electricity, do flooring, tiling, fencing, masonry and swimming pools, painting, landscaping and clean up. I have references and testimonials from local homeowners, contractors and companies. Honesty, competence, meeting deadlines and quality work are my calling cards.

I can do the smallest of jobs at the shortest of notification and at the best value. If there is a need for a construction team from short-term to long-term, I can beat any bid by at least 30% with a team of professionals who are licensed, legal and loyal workers who may not have roofs over their heads but can create any structure or building that is quality and built in America by Americans.

EMPLOYMENT: (1990 – 1999): United States Army, Construction Specialist with tours in Kuwait, Iraq & Texas; 2000 – 2003: Odd jobs in roofing and landscaping; 2003 – Present: Self-employed

SKILLS: Carpentry, Electrical Wiring, Galvanizing, Blueprints, Stone Work and Brick Work; Fencing and Posting; Xeriscaping and Water Sprinkler Systems; Construction of Pontoons and Sanitary Facilities

EDUCATION: High School Diploma, Mankato, Minnesota, U.S. Army Electrical Certification; Workshops in Solar Panel Installation and Water Conservation Techniques in Construction

---

FULL RESUME OR REFERENCES AVAILBLE UPON REQUEST OR AT INTERVIEW

Related Jobs/Careers:
(Handyman, Home Repair, Construction Worker)

RÉSUMÉ #102: Own Unique Story: Homeless Contractor / Laborer (2011 U.S. Retail: $249)

WOW! RÉSUMÉS 2011-2012: Great Jobs...Extra Income...Happiness...

Catarina Jackson-Pelitz
1000 Jewell Avenue #123
Denver, CO 80202
303-123-4567
cjackson-pelitz@wowresumes.net

"'Socialist Socialite'? Maybe, But a Real Patron of the Arts and the Cultivation of Hidden Talent."

The wealthy and the under-privileged need each other more during hard times. Most of the really wealthy in fact get wealthier during bad economic times because of their built-in advantages: guilt and cash war chests grow. And the poor, well the poor don't have those systemic advantages. So I am valuable when society is running normal and invaluable when everything is disintegrating or seemingly so.

To examine my lifestyle and background will be only partly revealing to what I represent. I was born into "society" in Sacramento where everything might be considered not as lofty as a San Francisco or New York or Chicago or even Los Angeles or Dallas. But remember Sacramento produced or developed some major captains of industry from its center as the eventual capital of California: from Wells and Crocker and Stanford and Huntington and Strauss. Perhaps mostly 18th Century, but now long- established and storied.

After only an upper-middle class upbringing because of family circumstances I got my schooling at Columbia University. I did reside in the major epicenters of society mentioned above including the seat of national power in Washington D.C. Then when I turned to my own creative pursuits in writing books, I became more professional in my career as fundraiser and steward of small institutions and charities including organizations in "off-site" locales such as Kansas City and Omaha. It turns out that money is everywhere and so are talent, needs and art.

I have the requisite skills of Grant Writing and Proposal Development; Research Data Collection and Analysis; Gift/Donor Identification for Fundraising and Strategic Partnerships; Leads & Prospecting.

And I do know people. Not just in whatever degree of separation or through channels of connection. I know people eyeball to eyeball, cell phone to cell phone unblocked and caller identified. I know people because people wanted to or want to know me. I like to think it is because of my own accessibility when I gained my own notoriety with some of my books and side accomplishments and because I truly relish in the success of talented personalities and the development of passion-inspiring causes. "Let's hear what Catarina Pelitz says about this". Any plea or please will be genuine if not immediate.

So then, hire me for my charm and talents because I get money from the hard and easy sources and from places that I have cultivated just for these economic times. I hypothesized from my writing research and academic studies that speculation would most likely result in some economic disaster. It was theory and conjecture on my part that will now pay dividends for an organization or entity that needs funds and resources.

EMPLOYMENT: 1993 – 2010: United Way; Make a Wish Foundation; Friends of the New York Public Library; Kansas City Chamber of Commerce; Crocker Museum; Getty Center for the Arts

SKILLS/ABILITIES: Presentations and Public Speaking; Government, Foundation and Corporate Grants; Management and Leadership of Multicultural Staff; Speak German and some Japanese

EDUCATION:
Columbia University, English and Psychology
BOOKS: Grant Us Your Graces; Memoirs Of An American Geisha; Where Not To Find Yourself;
Zeitgeist Of The Lost Decade Of The 1990s; After Columbia

FULL RESUME OR REFERENCES AVAILBLE UPON REQUEST OR AT INTERVIEW

Related Jobs/Careers:
(Corporate Grants, Foundation Grants, Non-Profit)
RÉSUMÉ #103: Own Unique Story: Published Author / Charity Fundraiser (2011 U.S. Retail: $249)

WOW! RÉSUMÉS 2011-2012: Great Jobs...Extra Income...Happiness...

Orlando Thomas Marker
1000 Bellfort Street #123
Houston, TX 77001
(713) 123-4567
otmarker@wowresumes.net

"Laborer with Values and a Contractor's License to Serve the Community"

Yes I'm black or African-American in polite circles. And circle the "American". I do have some European lineage as many of my people do and I also have Indian (as in Cherokee) blood in my veins. I was born in Oklahoma, raised in Texas and labored throughout the West from New Mexico, Oklahoma, Texan and California. I say "labored" because that is what I have done all my life, despite of or maybe because I did get a college degree from Oklahoma State.

I eventually worked for Conoco Oil which became Occidental which eventually became Enron. Yes that Enron – although I was long gone before the headlines. I have worked on oil fields and in cotton fields. I have managed materials-recycling and recycled my own materials. I have worked odd jobs and jobs managing engineers and "technical" laborers sometimes without the formal title and recognition. I can discuss these jobs in person in detail with humility and wisdom and without resentment.

I have dealt with all sorts of folks from CEOs and owners to the lowest illiterate farm hands. They have taught me all my technical, management, work and "people" skills.

After my many company and organizational jobs that also included being a school teacher, I eventually struck out on my own. I came back to Texas after several years in California. In 5 months, starting from scratch, I obtained my Texas General Contractor (B) License and have worked on varied projects for the last 5 years in the Houston area with an excellent record of customer satisfaction and community volunteering that I hope have brought good to some and satisfaction to many.

What I can do for you Mr. or Ms. Employer? I am physically and emotionally fit to work very long hours with enjoyment! I look for a job well-done, regardless of time and effort on my part while at the same time recognizing deadlines, budgets and schedules. You will see bottom-line value and concrete profits. One quick example: I managed as a general contractor a fire-sprinkler renovation of a large residence that made the property a valuable commercial property in Northern California. What would usually be an $80,000 to $100,000 job I did for $15,000 (!) and that was with only $6,500 cost to me. How? Through persistent research, hands- on management, and honest "look-in-the-eye" interactions with subcontractors on their "spare time" using their expertise and specific licenses and certifications, as well as showing the owner/employer everything about the job. I can do the same for you!

QUICK SUMMARY:
Straight forward, "no bull" legal contracting work that is on average 20 cents to 30 cents on the dollar with top quality and on schedule or before deadline.

COMPANIES/ORGANIZATIONS WORKED FOR: Occidental Oil; LiquiFactor Recyclers, Tulsa, Oklahoma School District; Zuni Pueblo Casino & Resort; Hillhaven Convalescent Hospital, D.R. Horton; Pulte Homes, etc.

JOBS HELD & ACCOMPLISHMENTS:
Farm Hand; Oil Derrick Inspector; Laboratory Technician; Recycling Supervisor; Construction Foreman, Tiler, High School Math Teacher; Casino Maintenance Specialist; Laborer; Contractor: All with satisfied Employers!

EDUCATION & CERTIFICATION:
New Mexico State University, Chemical Engineering, 1991; Licensed General Contractor, State of Texas, Current

---

Related Jobs/Careers:
(Laborer, Recycler, Low-Cost Repair, Professional Renovations)
RÉSUMÉ #104: Own Unique Story: Licensed Contractor w/Degree & Community Roots (2011 Retail: $249)

WOW! RÉSUMÉS 2011-2012: Great Jobs...Extra Income...Happiness...

Suresh, Li Xiuxiu, Sofia, Ikeoluwa, Nour, Sergey, Indahwati, Carlos, World Citizen
Country's Largest City, Top 15 World Urban Metropolis
India, China, Brazil, Nigeria, Egypt, Russia, Indonesia, Mexico

Ordinary World Citizen with Extraordinary Motivation, Transformation and Courage

I am new to our country's largest city (with a population of over 15 million people: Mumbai, Shanghai, São Paulo, Lagos, Cairo, Moscow, Jakarta, Mexico City)... I am young, educated with a college degree, the first in my family to go to a university and the first to leave my village for more than 1 year. I graduated with a degree in (Business Administration...) with courses in (English and Internet Marketing...).

I have been working part-time in the City as I establish my residence and business and social networks. I know it is very competitive for new and recent graduates to enter the best companies and organizations, but I am here to stay and pursue my goals and objectives of improving myself and helping my family as I contribute to the progress and growth of our national economy.

Today is a new world and a new era for our nation. We belong to the global village. We are the digital and information generation who are aware of our age's problems, issues and opportunities. We are proud of our history and culture. We celebrate our ethnicity and regional differences; we are secure in our identities even if there will be struggles and challenges ahead.

I personally care about our natural environment. Our village, even though remote has been affected by degradations in the air, soil and water. Our idyllic life is a part of a romantic past that now must face the realities of climate change, water shortages, loss of biodiversity and contamination of food and drinking water. We know there are better approaches to solving problems in rural communities that are also social and political problems.

You may be surprised to hear about politics from someone young, inexperienced and someone from a country like mine that has some legacy of repression and lack of overall freedom. There I mentioned the "r" word and the "f" word. I think if people are honest and allowed to express their feelings, the country itself will be more stable and prosperous. Don't misunderstand me. I am proud to be a citizen of my country. I respect authority just I respect my elders and my parents. But the leaders need to know what their citizens think and feel. I want to make my country a better place to work play and live! Our leaders can be great and visionary!

What can I actually offer a company or organization? In addition to my education and training, I offer my world-renowned work ethic that I inherited from my father and mother. I work extremely hard and also work very smart. I am flexible and trainable and willing to travel or relocate. Like many from our region of the country, I possess the culture of down-to-earth values and the ability to learn and apply new skills quickly. Let's create and develop the new great products and services for the global economy! I am the new 21st Century citizen-worker!

The most important event in my life happened.....

EMPLOYMENT: 2007 – 2010, Office Intern, Sales Representative, Advertising Clerk, Computer Tech Support...
Before 2007: Seasonal Jobs/Internships at International Companies and Government Agencies...

SKILLS: Marketing, Sales, Financial Analysis, Office Administration, Accounting, Computer Programming, Web Development, Public Relations, Statistical Analysis, Laboratory Work, Internet Research...

EDUCATION:
University (in Mumbai, Shanghai, São Paulo, Lagos, Cairo, Moscow, Jakarta, Mexico City), 2008/2009/2010/2011
Bachelor's Degree in (Business Administration), (Computer Science), (English), (Environmental Science)...

Related Jobs/Careers:
(Laborer, Clerk, Office Worker, Salesperson, Tech Support, Translator, Intern)

RÉSUMÉ #105: Own Unique Story: Ordinary World Citizen, Extraordinary Character (2011 U.S. Retail: $249)

WOW! RÉSUMÉS 2011-2012: Great Jobs...Extra Income...Happiness...

CHAPTER 10:

WOW!-Card® RÉSUMÉS

10 Model *WOW!*-Card® Résumés
(20 Job Titles)

CREATE YOUR OWN *WOW!*-Card® RÉSUMÉ:

You can convert any Résumé to a *WOW!*-Card® Résumé. You can follow the examples in any of the *WOW!*-Card® Résumés in this Chapter. You can manually create your own *WOW!*-Card® Résumés by buying blank white or color 4" x 6" index cards at a stationary store and print out your Résumé information on a good home or business printer. Or check on line for websites that print out "Post-Cards" of the right size (for direct mailing) once you have your information completed and formatted.

Complete the Guides in the Appendices including the *WOW!* Action Verbs and specific targeted Keywords (that must be researched) to fully customize and create a unique and powerful *WOW!* Résumé!

If you have purchased this Book (and thus become an automatic 1-year Member of wowresumes.net) you can get Free unrestricted downloads (Word/PDF Files) of up to 5 *WOW!* Résumés (including *WOW!*-Card® Résumés) in addition to the Guides/Keyword-Lists in the Appendices for you to edit and print out.

DISCOUNTED RÉSUMÉ SERVICE:

If you need help to create a *WOW!* Résumé call 888-503-3133 or go to wowresumes.net to work with professional Résumé Writers who practice *WOW!* Résumé principles. Book purchasers have up to one year to avail of a 30% Instant Discount on any *WOW!* Résumé or other *WOW!* Résumé products such as *WOW!*-Card® Résumés, as well as other benefits including Free Résumé Posting on the ever-growing wowresumes.net Website and Updating from Twitter, Facebook, LinkedIn & Google Profiles. Members get Free Updates for 1 year on their Main Résumé and up to 90% Discounts on additional (2nd, 3rd, 4th, etc.) Customized Résumés to target Specific Jobs, Careers, Industries or Special Urgent Applications.

*See the Back Cover for *WOW!* Résumé Service & Free Membership Information*

WOW! RÉSUMÉS 2011-2012: Great Jobs...Extra Income...Happiness...

Ever Ready to Grab Attention!

The last chapter of this book introduces what I have contemplated for the last 20 years as a simple but revolutionary development in the art and science of résumé writing-presentation: the "*WOW!*-Card Résumé". The *WOW!*-Card® Résumé is created on a card that is 4 inches by 6 inches, dimensions that are regulation-size for U.S. Postal Service mailing of postcards that can be mailed (as of 2011) at a first class cost of 28 cents per mailing instead of the first class mailing cost of 44 cents. The *WOW!*-Card® Résumé is versatile and easy to use!

The *WOW!*-Card® Résumé, however, is not just or even primarily for mailing purposes, but would function as a résumé in its own right. The difference between a job-holder or business owner and a job-applicant or student is the difference represented by a business card versus a traditional résumé on a full-page of paper. Now the *WOW!*-Card® Résumé is something in between, useful for a job-seeker as well as someone employed or someone marketing themselves or products/services. A business card evokes an image of a person already employed and associated with a position or a business while a traditional résumé is from someone still seeking a position or identity. The *WOW!*-Card® Résumé can be used by a job-holder (business person) or job-seeker. The *WOW!*-Card® can be a bold statement by either a job-seeker or a job-holder (or business owner). The job applicant and decision-maker (regarding the available job) will create a new relationship with the use of this new presentation/marketing tool. The *WOW!*-Card® Résumé is a quick ad and a creative message that can supplement a traditional résumé and may be the door opener to an interview and eventually a position or a "sale"!

The *WOW!*-Card® Résumé as will be illustrated in the rest of this chapter will be 2-sided with the "Front Side" consisting of a powerful "ad" or compelling Résumé information. The "ad" can be catchy, concise and despite its limited space as full of substance as possible. The "Back Side" can be used for mailing purposes, with a return address (with full contact details) on the upper left corner, and the middle of the card being the addressee (the company or organization applied to) just below a catchy phrase that may be a motto or the job-seeker's objective. The upper right corner of the "Back Side" will allow space for a 28 cent stamp (as of 2011).

If the *WOW!*-Card® Résumé is not to be mailed out (i.e. is handed out instead), then the "Back Side" can be quite creative. A brief narrative can be placed on this entire Back Side or it can just focus on an "Offer" or "Coupon" that would get the decision-maker or reader's attention. This chapter will feature *WOW!*-Card® Résumés that are condensed from the main *WOW!* Resumes that have been fully detailed elsewhere in the book. As you will see, many possibilities are available. Use imagination and creativity!

How about personal photos that you may use in lieu of graphics? There are pluses and minuses to a photograph. Some companies may not be interested in accepting them for reasons of being potentially exposed to claims of discrimination. That is, an applicant may in the end claim that based on the photo he or she was not hired because of race, ethnicity or other characteristic that is not related to the job. However, photos and creative graphics are potentially very positive and attention-grabbing, and would distinguish the applicant from the competition, especially if the applicant can achieve the effect of "a picture is worth a thousand words".

Notes: With basic software and a good printer, you can do your own *WOW!*-Card® Résumés with blank 4x6 index cards (color or white) or you can go to websites that have full card printing services. wowresumes.net offers *WOW!*-Card® Résumés that can be mailed to customers or picked up at participating retail outlets. A *WOW!*-Card® Résumé can supplement a traditional Résumé or can be used as an introduction that can quickly lead to interviews and requests for more information.

WOW! RÉSUMÉS 2011-2012: Great Jobs...Extra Income...Happiness...

WOW!-Card® Résumé #1
Based on Résumé #23, **International Investment Banker / Bond Trader / Currency Trader**

ACTUAL SIZE OF 4" x 6"

Front ("Main") Side of *WOW!*-Card® Résumé

Katarina V. Wilsmeier

123 Burroughs Road, Tarzana, CA 91702 ♦ 818.123.4567 ♦ katarinavw@wowresumes.net

BANKER / TRADER: BONDS – CURRENCY – INVESTMENT PORTFOLIOS
Licensed Series 7 and 63

Problem-Solver, "Idea Person" with Outstanding Communications
Experienced in International Markets
Fluent in English and German

Employment History:

Union Bank Capital Management, Los Angeles, CA; 3/2010 to Present	*Trader, Fixed Income Settlements*
Lincoln Financial, Phoenix, AZ, 2008 to 2010	*Benefits Counselor, Pension Funds*
Charles Schwab, San Francisco, CA, 2007 to 2008	*Investments Specialist/Broker*
Wells Fargo Advisors, Los Angeles, CA 2006 to 2007	*Trader, Interest Rate Derivatives*
Citigroup Private Bank, Baltimore, Maryland, 2004 to 2005	*Relationship Officer*
Hypo-Bank, Munich, Germany; 2001 to 2002	*International Money Transfer Clerk*
Gwinner & Ulrich Publishers, Munich, Germany; 2000 to 2001	*Student Apprentice*

Education:
UNIVERSITY OF MARYLAND, College Park, Maryland
Bachelor of Arts degree in Finance 2005
ELLY-HEUSE REALSCHULE (HIGH SCHOOL), Munich, Germany, Diploma 2000
COMPUTER PROFICIENCIES: Microsoft Word and PowerPoint;
Bloomberg, SEI, PORTIA, TPG, AXYS, Advanced Excel including financial modeling forward rates and duration

Selected Achievements:
Developed business in banking, mortgages & investments including hedge funds, growing departmental revenue 21% year over year
Managed $200 million in client assets, establishing portfolio rebalancing strategies & making recommendations to meet client goals
Placed daily equity and mutual fund trades for clients up to $11 million with portfolio analyses, asset allocations and S&P ratings
Sold municipal bonds, advised clients on asset allocations & the construction of portfolios generating commission in top 10%
Presented retirement solutions to San Fernando Unified School district (Southern California) helping company win 1 of 3 contracts

---

(2011 U.S. Retail $199 for 100 2-Sided *WOW!*-Card® Résumés, 2 Versions: "Mailing" & "Hand-Out Ad")

This *WOW!*-Card® Résumé condensed information from a main Résumé. This example shows no graphics that can be included as will be shown in the other *WOW!*- Card® Résumés in this chapter.

WOW!-Card® Résumé Tip:
Keep Fonts consistent from a main Résumé to present a unified "marketing look".

WOW! RÉSUMÉS 2011-2012: Great Jobs...Extra Income...Happiness...

WOW!-Card® Résumé #1
Based on Résumé #23, **International Investment Banker / Bond Trader / Currency Trader**

ACTUAL SIZE of 4" x 6"

Back (Mailing or "Advertisement") Side of *WOW!*-Card® Résumé

Katarina V. Wilsmeier
123 Burroughs Road
Tarzana, CA 91702

-Place
28 Cents of
Stamps Here-

Mr. Robert Jaworski, Senior Vice President
China Agricultural and Commerce Bank
1500 Wilshire Boulevard, 18th Floor
Los Angeles, CA 90013

(ABOVE DESTINATION ADDRESS
LEFT BLANK FOR MAILOUTS)

2011 Retail Price of $199
for 100 *WOW* Résumé Cards
with FREE Setup Fee ($50)
for wowresumes.net Members
(Details at www.wowresumes.net
and Description at Back of Book)

(2011 U.S. Retail $199 for 100 2-Sided *WOW!*-Card® Résumés, 2 Versions: "Mailing" & "Hand-Out Ad")

This *WOW!*-Card® Résumé can be mailed out (first class) in the U.S. A mostly blank Back-side with the same Front (Main) Side can also be used as interview time confirmations, an informal (handwritten) "thank you" note with the front Résumé info as reinforcement, etc. The rest of the *WOW!*-Card® Résumés in this chapter will be examples for handing out or for use as inserts and complementary marketing for various activities and presentations.

WOW! RÉSUMÉS 2011-2012: Great Jobs...Extra Income...Happiness...

WOW!-Card® Résumé #2
Based on Résumé #62, **Non-Profit & Grants - Fundraiser**

ACTUAL SIZE of 4" x 6"

Front ("Main") Side of *WOW!*-Card® Résumé

Janice Marsalas

1234 Chestnut St. #123; Philadelphia, PA 19093
(215) 123-4567
janmarsalas@wowresumes.net

Published Author (7 Books) / Expert Fundraiser

CAREER PROFILE:

◆ Organizational and consultative experience with successful record in securing grants and funding
◆ Extensive background in the non-profit sectors combined with expert familiarity in corporate operations
◆ Exceptional in communications skills honed by training in Multi/Cross-Cultural Conflict Resolution
◆ Developed proficiencies in Fundraising, Grant Reviews, Fund Development, Project Management & Events

Institutions & Organizations Served Successfully:

■ Temple University	■ The City of Camden, New Jersey	■ Martin Luther King March
■ Chester County, PA	■ Northern Philadelphia Public Trust	■ Morrison Baptist Church
■ PA Healthcare Consortium	■ Camden Emergency Women's Services	■ DynaMight Community Group
■ Philadelphia Mayor's Office	■ La Salle University	■ Frankford Hospital

---

(2011 U.S. Retail $199 for 100 2-Sided *WOW!*-Card® Résumés, 2 Versions: "Mailing" & "Hand-Out Ad")

WOW!-Card® Résumé Tip:
Add catchy and powerful Captions or Highlights (with figures, facts and specifics).

WOW! RÉSUMÉS 2011-2012: Great Jobs...Extra Income...Happiness...

CHAPTER 10: *WOW!*-CARD® RÉSUMÉS

WOW!-Card® Résumé #2
Based on Résumé #62, **Non-Profit & Grants -Fundraiser**

ACTUAL SIZE of 4" x 6"

Back (Mailing or "Advertisement") Side of *WOW!*-Card® Résumé

Janice Marsalas, Author/Fundraiser: Philadelphia, PA, USA

CRITICAL SUBSTANTIAL FUNDS ACQUIRED IN TOUGH TIMES!

SELECTED AWARD HIGHLIGHTS:

$2,100,000:
U.S. Department of Defense Grant Project funded economic development of former military bases in Eastern Pennsylvania – sustaining a revolving loan fund and provision of small business technical assistance

$1,320,000:
U.S. Department of Justice Chester County – Grants to Encourage Arrest and Enforcement Protection Orders

$800,000:
U.S. Department of Justice Chester County – Office on Violence Against Women

Direct Contacts in 35 States & 30+ Countries!

*UCLA Educated (Bachelor's Degree in International & Area Studies, 2000)
& Law Courses from Temple University*

Call:
(215) 123-4567
or
Email:
janmarsalas@wowresumes.net

(2011 U.S. Retail $199 for 100 2-Sided *WOW!*-Card® Résumés, 2 Versions: "Mailing" & "Hand-Out Ad")

Note:
This 2-sided *WOW!*-Card® Résumé can be handed out at Job-Fairs, Networking Meetings, with Employment Applications, and at Interviews upon entering or exiting, or used as inserts / enclosures with mailed out "thank you" notes or cover letters (or Unique Story Résumés) or used as ready creative substitutes for business cards and full Résumés. (See *WOW!*-Card® Résumé #1, page 180, for mail-out example.)

WOW! RÉSUMÉS 2011-2012: Great Jobs...Extra Income...Happiness...

CHAPTER 10: *WOW!*-CARD® RÉSUMÉS

WOW!-Card® Résumé #3
Based on Résumé #9, **Public Relations / Non-Profit Administration**

ACTUAL SIZE of 4" x 6"

Front ("Main") Side of *WOW!*-Card® Résumé

JOSEPHINE V. DeMORAY
12345 Broussard Street #123 Baton Rouge, LA 70601
305-123-4567
jvdemoray@wowresumes.net

Seeking a challenging career in the field of public relations or non-profits

"Some are born great, some achieve greatness, and some hire public relations officers."
Daniel J. Boorstin (American social historian and educator)

P R EXPERIENCE
KYTL FM, Baton Rouge, LA
Programs Coordinator / PR Director, 2007 to Present
Created and implemented award-winning public relations for KYTL FM and sister station 710 AM

LOUISIANA STATE CAPITAL PRESERVATION SOCIETY, Baton, Rouge, Louisiana
Docent and Assistant PR Director, Fundraiser Seasons 2005 to 2011
Created and implemented Public Relations Plan for Private Foundations Campaign 2010

EDUCATION:
McNeese State University Baton Rouge, LA
Bachelor of Arts in Public Relations 2007
Minor in Broadcast Journalism; Academic Scholarship Recipient; Grade Point Average: 3.75 in major

---

(2011 U.S. Retail $199 for 100 2-Sided *WOW!*-Card® Résumés, 2 Versions: "Mailing" & "Hand-Out Ad")

WOW!-Card® Résumé Tip:
Use a witty or thought-provoking quote about an industry or occupation to stimulate attention and interest, and to show knowledge.

WOW! RÉSUMÉS 2011-2012: Great Jobs...Extra Income...Happiness...

WOW!-Card® Résumé #3
Based on Résumé #9, **Public Relations / Non-Profit Administration**

ACTUAL SIZE of 4" x 6"

Back (Mailing or "Advertisement") Side of *WOW!*-Card® Résumé

JOSEPHINE V. DEMORAY
305-123-4567
jvdemoray@wowresumes.net

PR SPECIALIST / NON-PROFITS ADMINISTRATOR

OTHER EXPERIENCE
MCNEESE STATE UNIVERSITY, Baton Rouge, LA
Information Desk Manager, 2005 to 2007
Disseminated information about the University and city of Baton Rouge to callers/visitors

CAMP TWIN PINES, Lafayette, LA
Youth Counselor, Summers 2001 to 2005
Aided mentally and/or physically challenged individuals in day-to-day endeavors in summer camps

TESTIMONIALS/EVALUATIONS

"Ms. DeMoray has fulfilled potential and abilities in public relations and promotions with the requisite personality to succeed and make a name for herself and the organization with whom she affiliates."

[De Moray] "is an excellent worker with outstanding character and the ability to adapt, learn and apply."

"Josephine is a talent and a godsend who knows about creativity, hard work and a can-do attitude."

(2011 U.S. Retail $199 for 100 2-Sided *WOW!*-Card® Résumés, 2 Versions: "Mailing" & "Hand-Out Ad")

Note:
This 2-sided *WOW!*-Card® Résumé can be handed out at Job-Fairs, Networking Meetings, with Employment Applications, and at Interviews upon entering or exiting, or used as inserts / enclosures with mailed out "thank you" notes or cover letters (or Unique Story Résumés) or used as ready creative substitutes for business cards and full Résumés. (See *WOW!*-Card® Résumé #1, page 180, for mail-out example.)

WOW! RÉSUMÉS 2011-2012: Great Jobs...Extra Income...Happiness...

WOW!-Card® Résumé #4
Based on Résumé #61, **Architect / International Designer / Urban Planner**

ACTUAL SIZE of 4" x 6"

<u>Front</u> ("Main") <u>Side</u> of *WOW!*-Card® Résumé

INTERNATIONAL ARCHITECT DESIGNER

V. R. Varaja

DrVaraja.vtkintldesign@wowresumes.net

1234 Rue Airlie #1000 ■ Montréal, QC, Canada H5C 2W6 ■ (877) 123-4500

PROFILE:

⊙ Expert at fusing advanced technologies and the human scale for beautiful, healthy and functional built environments

⊙ Head of a firm that operates as a distributed office by forming project-based teams and collaborations worldwide

⊙ Utilize state-of-the-art 3D software tools from outside the field of architecture in order to create new realities

⊙ Conduct own research to evolve firm's design tools to foster creations that are both unexpected and thought-provoking

⊙ Master of Architecture and PhD in Urban Planning; Fluent in English and Hindi; Conversant/literate in French & Spanish

EDUCATION

McGill University, Montréal, Quebec, Canada, PhD in Urban Planning, 2003
Columbia University, New York, New York, M.A. in Architecture, 1998
Indian Institute of Technology Delhi Hauz Khas, New Delhi, India, B.S. in Computer Science, 1995

(2011 U.S. Retail $199 for <u>100</u> 2-Sided *WOW!*-Card® Résumés, 2 Versions: "Mailing" & "Hand-Out Ad")

WOW!-Card® Résumé Tip:
Use simple but effective <u>graphics</u> (in this case just a simple shape that contains text from the main Résumé) that keeps a unified "marketing look" including consistent fonts across all documents and presentation materials from any business cards to letters to potential future brochures.

WOW! RÉSUMÉS 2011-2012: Great Jobs...Extra Income...Happiness...

WOW!-Card® Résumé #4
Based on Résumé #61, **Architect / International Designer / Urban Planner**

ACTUAL SIZE of 4" x 6"

<u>Back</u> (Mailing or "Advertisement") <u>Side</u> of *WOW!*-Card® Résumé

V. R. Varaja

DrVaraja.vtkintldesign@wowresumes.net
(877) 123-4500

REPRESENTATIVE PROJECTS
<u>Varaja, Targot & Kohl International Design (vtkintldesign.com), Montreal, New York, New Delhi</u>

ARCHITECTURE
2007 – 2010: Designed and managed 2 projects in Quebec, Canada & New York, New York: >100k sq. m. / >USD200M
2009: Won nation-wide competition to design and manage new 1000 acre Jawaharail Nehru University Campus, New Delhi
2006 – 2009: Assisted Indian State of Madhya Pradesh to create and redesign 3 large contiguous townships & public sites

DESIGN
2009 – 2011 Commissioned to design proposals for display and furniture lines for La Maison Ogilvy, Montréal, Canada
2010: Designed LEED AP Certified Components for Temperate Zone Buildings: TEMPAbrane Invertible Building Membrane
2009: Designed Project Template for use by urban and village "architects" in India for township planning, design & build-out

ACCOMPLISHMENTS/INNOVATIONS/AWARDS

★ Lectures and Shows in U.S., Europe, China, India & Middle East
★ 2008, 2009, 2010: Named as #1 Design Firm in India
★ 2009 - 2011: Firm's "Retro-Avant-Garde" Design Show included in Museum of Modern Art (New York)
★ 2005: Firm's Display purchased for permanent collection by Board of Directors of Pompidou Museum (Paris, France)
★ 2000: Along with Partner, Hans Kohl 2 of Forty (Best US architects) under Forty (years old) by AIA
★ Add value to <u>every</u> client's goals, investments and desires by designing with excellence and being attuned to the technical, situational and socio-economic conditions of <u>each</u> project

HIRE THE BEST & BRIGHTEST!

(2011 U.S. Retail $199 for <u>100</u> 2-Sided *WOW!*-Card® Résumés, 2 Versions: "Mailing" & "Hand-Out Ad")

Note:
This <u>2-sided</u> *WOW!*-Card® Résumé can be handed out at Job-Fairs, Networking Meetings, with Employment Applications, and at Interviews upon entering or exiting, or used as inserts / enclosures with mailed out "thank you" notes or cover letters (or Unique Story Résumés) or used as ready creative substitutes for business cards and full Résumés. (See *WOW!*-Card® Résumé #1, page 180, for mail-out example.)

WOW! RÉSUMÉS 2011-2012: Great Jobs...Extra Income...Happiness...

CHAPTER 10: *WOW!*-CARD® RÉSUMÉS

WOW!-Card® Résumé #5
Based on Résumé #54, **Massage Therapist / Physical Therapist / Life Coach**

ACTUAL SIZE of 4" x 6"

Front ("Main") Side of *WOW!*-Card® Résumé

Zara

Saito

1234 Kapiolani Blvd. #123
Honolulu, HI 96813
(808) 123-4567
zarasaitomassage@wowresumes.net

CREDO/MODALITIES
"Body Heart and Soul in all Great Traditions of East and West"
Yoga
Meditation
Hypnotherapy
Biofeedback
Raw Foods Nutrition

EDUCATION

University of New Mexico, Albuquerque , New Mexico
Bachelor of Science in Physical Therapy, 2000

Santa Fe School of Massage, Santa Fe, New Mexico, Certificate, 1998
Acupuncture School of New Mexico, Santa Fe, NM, Certificate, 1993

(2011 U.S. Retail $199 for <u>100</u> 2-Sided *WOW!*-Card® Résumés, 2 Versions: "Mailing" & "Hand-Out Ad")

WOW!-Card® Résumé Tip:
The Logo Graphic can be used and scaled down from the main Résumé and thus achieve the unified "marketing look" including consistent fonts across all documents and presentation materials from any business cards to letters to potential future brochures. This *WOW!*-Card® Résumé functions as an expanded or enlarged business card (or very handy mini-brochure) that uses the Headings from the main Résumé with condensed but very detailed legible information.

WOW! RÉSUMÉS 2011-2012: Great Jobs...Extra Income...Happiness...

WOW!-Card® Résumé #5
Based on Résumé #54, **Massage Therapist / Physical Therapist / Life Coach**

ACTUAL SIZE of 4" x 6"

Back (Mailing or "Advertisement") Side of *WOW!*-Card® Résumé

Zara Saito

(808) 123-4567
zarasaitomassage@wowresumes.net

SKILLS

Swedish	Foot Reflexology	Deep Tissue
Polarity Therapy	Sports Massage	Acupressure
Neuromuscular	Shiatsu	Trigger Point
Aroma Therapy	Myofascial Release	Salt Glows
Paraffin for Hands & Feet	Cranial Sacral	Joint Mobilization
Hot & Cold Stone Therapy	Range of Motion	Body Clay Masks

PRICING/PROTOCOL

$80.00 Per Hour of Massage

$25 Per Hour Infrared Sauna

Nutrition/Life Coaching by Appointment

Professionally Draped
during Massage

(2011 U.S. Retail $199 for 100 2-Sided *WOW!*-Card® Résumés, 2 Versions: "Mailing" & "Hand-Out Ad")

Note:
This 2-sided *WOW!*-Card® Résumé can be handed out at Job-Fairs, Networking Meetings, with Employment Applications, and at Interviews upon entering or exiting, or used as inserts / enclosures with mailed out "thank you" notes or cover letters (or Unique Story Résumés) or used as ready creative substitutes for business cards and full Résumés. (See *WOW!*-Card® Résumé #1, page 180, for mail-out example.)

WOW! RÉSUMÉS 2011-2012: Great Jobs...Extra Income...Happiness...

WOW!-Card® Résumé #6
Based on Résumé #38, **Studio Technician / Audio Engineer / Music Business Developer**

ACTUAL SIZE of 4" x 6"

<u>Front</u> ("Main") <u>Side</u> of *WOW!*-Card® Résumé

DEMETRIUS JACKSON

1234 South Blvd. #123; Pontiac, MI 45195
(313) 123-4567
djacksonsounds@wowresumes.net

STUDIO & AUDIO ENGINEER

Technical Post-Production   ◨   Talent Management   ◨   Music Marketing & Promotions

Studio Business Development   ◨   Agency & Representation

PROFILE

- ◨ 15+ Years' Experience in Music Industry
- ◨ Wide range of musical tastes and cultures
- ◨ Personable with outstanding networking savvy
- ◨ Knack to discover, nurture and refine talent
- ◨ Proficient in studio/audio arts and technologies

EDUCATION

Detroit University, Detroit, MI
Multimedia Studies Program, 1999

Expression College for Digital Arts, Berkeley, CA
Bachelor of Applied Science, Sound Arts, 2002

(2011 U.S. Retail $199 for <u>100</u> 2-Sided *WOW!*-Card® Résumés, 2 Versions: "Mailing" & "Hand-Out Ad")

WOW!-Card® Résumé Tip:
With condensed but detailed information from the Main Résumé, a unified "marketing look" and message can be accomplished by using the same fonts, headings as well as unique bullets which in this case is a "Compact Disc" bullet. The "Back Side" of this *WOW!*-Card® Résumé combines different types of Experience under the one heading of "Professional Experience".

WOW! RÉSUMÉS 2011-2012: Great Jobs...Extra Income...Happiness...

WOW!-Card® Résumé #6
Based on Résumé #38, **Studio Technician / Audio Engineer / Music Business Developer**

ACTUAL SIZE of 4" x 6"

Back (Mailing or "Advertisement") Side of *WOW!*-Card® Résumé

DEMETRIUS JACKSON

djacksonsounds@wowresumes.net

PROFESSIONAL ABILITIES

◘ Quick and efficient with Pro Tools HD software

◘ Adept in music and post-productions workflow/techniques

◘ Expert with soldering cables and other electronics

◘ Experienced Disc Jockey with basic knowledge of music theory

◘ Great ability to follow guidelines and interpret creative requests

PROFESSIONAL EXPERIENCE

OWNER/HEAD ENGINEER, 2007 to Present	Eastwood Studios, Pontiac, MI
SOUND ENGINEER, 2007	Anton Film Works, Detroit, MI
VOICE OVER RECORDING ARTIST, 2006	Alta Image Group, Detroit, MI
DIGITAL EDITOR / SOUND ENGINEER, 2005 & 2006	Luxam Motowners, Detroit, MI
CONSULTANT/OFFICE MANAGER, 2003 to 2005	Tactics Uptown, Oakland, CA

BUSINESS APTITUDE

◘ Knowledgeable in the practical aspects of Intellectual Property

◘ Office management skills include accounting and receivables

◘ Experienced in telemarketing and email promotional campaigns

◘ Ability to raise appropriate capital and community grants for local talent

---

(2011 U.S. Retail $199 for 100 2-Sided *WOW!*-Card® Résumés, 2 Versions: "Mailing" & "Hand-Out Ad")

Note:
This 2-sided *WOW!*-Card® Résumé can be handed out at Job-Fairs, Networking Meetings, with Employment Applications, and at Interviews upon entering or exiting, or used as inserts / enclosures with mailed out "thank you" notes or cover letters (or Unique Story Résumés) or used as ready creative substitutes for business cards and full Résumés. (See *WOW!*-Card® Résumé #1, page 180, for mail-out example.)

WOW! RÉSUMÉS 2011-2012: Great Jobs...Extra Income...Happiness...

WOW!-Card[®] Résumé #7
Based on Résumé #46, **Web Master / Web Developer / Web Designer as Independent Contractor**

ACTUAL SIZE of 4" x 6"

Front ("Main") Side of *WOW!*-Card[®] Résumé

Manly Colombo
Web Master   Web Developer   Web Designer
(916) 123-4567

1234 Laguna Blvd. #123   Elk Grove, CA 95757

themanly@wowresumes.net

SUMMARY:

- ✓ Responsible, mature, client-focused goals & benefits
- ✓ Tremendous work ethic to meet budgets & deadlines
- ✓ Management includes projects, people & technology
- ✓ Experience with small businesses & start-up ventures
- ✓ Tech skills learned academically & at high tech cos.
- ✓ Track record of innovation, leadership & management
- ✓ Over 8 years in web design, development & marketing
- ✓ Flexible, good listener with abilities to adapt and act

- Varied knowledge of industries include: Fashion, Law, Construction, Real Estate, Restaurant, Dentistry, etc. -

TECH SKILLS:

PROGRAMMING:
⇨ ASP/PHP/SQL/MySQL, PERL/CGI, JavaScript
⇨ DHTML/HTML/CSS, UNIX, Linux, FileMaker   ⇨ ColdFusion, Oracle, Java, C/C++

PLATFORMS:
⇨ Irix/SGI, Solaris/SUN, OS/Mac, Blackberry   ⇨ Linux/DOS/WINDOWS/NT/XP

APPLICATIONS:
⇨ Photoshop, Dreamweaver, Flash, Illustrator   ⇨ QuarkXPress, MS Office Suite, QuickBooks

EDUCATION:

SAN JOSE STATE UNIVERSITY, San Jose, CA
B.S. in Computer Science, 2002

ORACLE UNIVERSITY, Palo Alto, CA
Training in Oracle Financials & CRM

LEARN IT, San Francisco, CA
Web Design & Web Programming

(2011 U.S. Retail $199 for 100 2-Sided *WOW!*-Card® Résumés, 2 Versions: "Mailing" & "Hand-Out Ad")

WOW!-Card[®] Résumé Tip:
The unified "marketing look" is achieved here with the use of the headings, technical info and unique font (for the Web Master's name). The "back of this *WOW!*-Card[®] Résumé will "advertise" what is available in the main Résumé: the "Top 10 Benefits for Hiring" that calls for more information and an interview!

WOW! RÉSUMÉS 2011-2012: Great Jobs...Extra Income...Happiness...

WOW!-Card® Résumé #7
Based on Résumé #46, **Web Master / Web Developer / Web Designer as Independent Contractor**

ACTUAL SIZE of 4" x 6"

<u>Back</u> (Mailing or "Advertisement") <u>Side</u> of *WOW!*-Card® Résumé

Manly Colombo
Web Master   Web Developer   Web Designer

themanly@wowresumes.net

CLIENTS & WEB SITES DEVELOPED:

☑ GreenTrikes.Com: Restaurant Delivery
☑ West Oakland Design, Inc: Architects
☑ Super Threads: Fashion Consignment
☑ Clinton L.T. Wong, CPA: Accounting

☑ Peter Huber, DDS: Family Dentistry
☑ O'Donnell Contractors: Construction
☑ Tantabaum & Associates, LLP: Law
☑ Laguna Lake Realty: Real Estate

TESTIMONIALS:

"Manly gave our practice the high-tech boost we were looking for." - Dr. Peter Huber, Sacramento, CA

"Mr. Colombo worked on our team for almost 9 months, creating a powerful and winning image for our operations." - John O'Donnell, Contractor-Owner

"Manly Colombo is meticulous, extremely competent and a consummate professional." - T.J. Lawson, Attorney, Tantabaum & Associates, San Francisco

FOR A DETAILED LIST
OF
THE <u>TOP TEN (10!) BENEFITS</u> FOR HIRING *Manly Colombo*
CALL/EMAIL OR GO TO: MANLYCOLOMBO.COM

(2011 U.S. Retail $199 for <u>100</u> 2-Sided *WOW!*-Card® Résumés, 2 Versions: "Mailing" & "Hand-Out Ad")

Note:
This <u>2-sided</u> *WOW!*-Card® Résumé can be handed out at Job-Fairs, Networking Meetings, with Employment Applications, and at Interviews upon entering or exiting, or used as inserts / enclosures with mailed out "thank you" notes or cover letters (or Unique Story Résumés) or used as ready creative substitutes for business cards and full Résumés. (See *WOW!*-Card® Résumé #1, page 180, for mail-out example.)

WOW! RÉSUMÉS 2011-2012: Great Jobs...Extra Income...Happiness...

<u>CHAPTER 10: *WOW!*-CARD® RÉSUMÉS</u>

WOW!-Card® Résumé #8
Based on Résumé #77, **Local Products Deliverer / Green Personal Shopper**

ACTUAL SIZE of 4" x 6"

<u>Front</u> ("Main") <u>Side</u> of *WOW!*-Card® Résumé

Alvin Jiles
1234 Cambie Street #123
Vancouver, BC, Canada V6T IL4
604-123-4567
alvinjiles@wowresumes.net

Low Carbon Deliveries of Groceries, Take-Out Food & Merchandise

GREEN STATEMENT:

The "greenest" food and consumer products are a function of how they are produced and the environmental impact of their journey from factory or farm to local market and ultimately to the consumer. The average produce from a supermarket in the U.S. can travel an average 1100 miles from farm to plate Locally sourced products are most often the "greenest" choice, so long as low or "zero" carbon delivery such as motorcycles or human-powered cargo-trailer bicycles are used.

EDUCATION:

University of Oregon, Eugene, Oregon   Bachelor of Arts, English Literature, 2003

WORK EXPERIENCE:

MASENGALE DOCUMENT DELIVERY   Portland, Oregon
Delivery Service founded by college associates and 2 Portland/Salem bike clubs
Bike Messenger   2003 to 2007

HUNGRY MIKE'S PIZZA   Portland, Oregon
Non-franchised pizza restaurant that practices local sourcing, full composting and green packaging
Co-Owner / Restaurant Manager / Pizza Delivery   2007-2009

GREEN TRIKES   Vancouver, BC, Canada
Local Delivery Service employing tricycles and mountain bicycles with cargo trailers
Co-Owner / Personal Shopper – Deliverer   2010 to Present

-SEE BACK FOR DETAILED DESCRIPTION OF THE GREEN TRIKES ENTERPRISE-

---

(2011 U.S. Retail $199 for <u>100</u> 2-Sided *WOW!*-Card® Résumés, 2 Versions: "Mailing" & "Hand-Out Ad")

WOW!-Card® Résumé Tip:

An example of a *WOW!*-Card® Résumé that combines Résumé information with marketing for a <u>green business</u>! An item in the main Résumé is expanded in the back of this *WOW!*-Card® Résumé. A full marketing package can thus be a Résumé, a *WOW!*-Card® Résumé, letters, brochures, signs, etc.

WOW! RÉSUMÉS 2011-2012: Great Jobs...Extra Income...Happiness...

WOW!-Card® Résumé #8
Based on Résumé #77, **Local Products Deliverer / Green Personal Shopper**

ACTUAL SIZE of 4" x 6"

Back (Mailing or "Advertisement") Side of *WOW!*-Card® Résumé

Alvin Jiles
604-123-4567
alvinjiles@wowresumes.net

www.GreenTrikes.com

Zero-Carbon LOCAL Tricycle DELIVERY CO.

DELIVERIES OF:
Groceries; Take-Out Food; Pizza; Starbucks/Café Drinks
Cases of Bottled Water; Liquor; Fresh Fruit; Fresh Vegetables
Just-Baked Bread/Pastries; Medicines; Laundry & Dry-Cleaning
Garage-Sale Items; Pet Food/Transport; Garden: Soil, Plants, Etc.
(Library) Books; Packages; EMERGENCY SUPPLIES!

"Rain or Shine, No Waiting in Line Nor Any Parking Fine."®

For More Info & Prices, Call 604-123-4567 or Go to: www.greentrikes.com

FACTOIDS & QUESTIONS
• 2 short car round-trips/week (within 3 miles) can release over 500 lbs/year of CO^2 into the atmosphere!
• If you avoid 2-3 hours per week of wasted time waiting, driving & parking, you could save 50+ gallons of gas & earn up to $10,000 extra/year
• How valuable is your time?

PERSONAL & BUSINESS GOALS:

To work for, venture with or start (and model or expand) a green local business that practices "low carbon" strategies while
promoting economic and employment sustainably in small communities in urban environments.

(2011 U.S. Retail $199 for <u>100</u> 2-Sided *WOW!*-Card® Résumés, 2 Versions: "Mailing" & "Hand-Out Ad")

Note:
This <u>2-sided</u> *WOW!*-Card® Résumé can be handed out at Job-Fairs, Networking Meetings, with Employment Applications, and at Interviews upon entering or exiting, or used as inserts / enclosures with mailed out "thank you" notes or cover letters (or Unique Story Résumés) or used as ready creative substitutes for business cards and full Résumés. (See *WOW!*-Card® Résumé #1, page 180, for mail-out example.)

WOW! RÉSUMÉS 2011-2012: Great Jobs...Extra Income...Happiness...

WOW!-Card® Résumé #9
Based on Résumé #90, **Network Marketing Representative / Independent Distributor, Pampered Chef**

ACTUAL SIZE of 4" x 6"

<u>Front</u> ("Main") <u>Side</u> of *WOW!*-Card® Résumé

Ashton C. Major
100 Featherstone Street
LONDON, EC1Y 8SY, UNITED KINGDOM
(44) 071-123-4567
ashtonmajor@wowresumes.net

Independent Distributor for Pampered Chef Kitchen & Food Products
Direct Selling of Kitchen Tool, Food Products and Cookbooks with the "Party Plan" System

PROPOSITION

Offer business and social opportunities for the cooking aficionado (the talented or enthusiastic cook or cook-to-be) and those who love food (who doesn't?) to sell desirable products and the concept of preparing delicious quality meals economically and quickly.

The Pampered Chef "Party Plan" is a time-tested direct selling approach (proven successful by Tupperware, etc.): using the products, a Pampered Chef Consultant (Independent Distributor) does a Cooking Show demonstration at a home. The Consultant cooks food and guests get to eat during the show!

PERSONAL PROFILE & BUSINESS BACKGROUND:
2 ½ Years as Pampered Chef Consultant
Weekly Cook/Volunteer at East London Homeless Center
Unemployed (since 2008) Barrister (Barclays Bank)
Education: LLD, 1998, King's College School of Law, London, U.K.
Married with 2 adopted children
Enjoy football, gardening and sailing

PERSONAL GOAL: 2011 Supplemental Income from Pampered Chef of 1,000 GBP (Pounds) = $1,550 U.S. Dollars/Month

-HONEST & REALISTIC "SHOW ME THE MONEY" INFO OF THIS BUSINESS OPPORTUNITY IN BACK-
Or Call or Email Me!

(2011 U.S. Retail $199 for <u>100</u> 2-Sided *WOW!*-Card® Résumés, 2 Versions: "Mailing" & "Hand-Out Ad")

WOW!-Card® Résumé Tip:
An example of a *WOW!*-Card® Résumé that promotes a network marketing opportunity! Specific product and pricing info are included and complements a main Résumé as well as company marketing materials. In competitive fields such as MLM, unique personal marketing can make a difference. (With company approval, personal marketing such as *WOW!*-Card® Résumés and main Résumés can include company logos and slogans.)

WOW! RÉSUMÉS 2011-2012: Great Jobs...Extra Income...Happiness...

WOW!-Card® Résumé #9
Based on Résumé #90, **Network Marketing Representative / Independent Distributor, Pampered Chef**

ACTUAL SIZE of 4" x 6"

Back (Mailing or "Advertisement") Side of *WOW!*-Card® Résumé

Ashton C. Major
(44) 071-123-4567
ashtonmajor@wowresumes.net

Independent Distributor for Pampered Chef Kitchen & Food Products

COMPANY & OPPORTUNITY INFO

PRODUCTS and SERVICES

Various quality kitchen and cooking tools, cookbooks and various food products such as kitchen utensils, cookware, pantry items and various innovative and useful products for kitchen and dining table. The gamut of items include Nylon tool sets, thermometers, roasting pans, skillets, sauté pans, griddles, stock pots, quality Stainless Steel, etc. etc.

PEOPLE (and Policies)

Founded in 1980 by Doris Christopher who implemented the Tupperware party plan system with kitchen and food products. Marla Gottschalk is the current CEO. Since 2002, Pampered Chef has been owned by Warren Buffet's Berkshire Hathaway.

PRICING (and Promotions)

Sample Retail Prices in U.S. Dollars:
Roasting Pan with Rack & Meat Lifters: $153.00
Reversible Bamboo Carving Board & Carving Set: $184.50
Stoneware Plates and Pans: $16 to $70

11" Square Grill Pan & Grill Press: $169.00
Large 18" x 15" Bamboo Platter: $31.95
Dining Table Pieces: $12 to $160 (16-piece set)

PROFIT (and Compensation Plans in U.S. Dollars)

To sign up as Consultant: Mini Starter Kit ($65) or Full Consultant ($155: ½ refunded if $1,250 in sales in 30 days)
8 Consultant Career levels from Consultant to National Executive Director: Commissions of group sales up to 31%
Targeted Retail Sales Scenario based on average (2009) Cooking Show Sales Average of $450 per Show:
2 Cooking Shows/Week = $850/month; 3 Cooking Shows/Week = $1,300/Month; 4 Cooking Shows/Week = $1,800/Month

FAIR WARNING:
"IF YOU TRULY LOVE COOKING, FOOD AND PEOPLE PLUS WORK PRETTY DARN HARD
YOU WILL BE A SUCCESSFUL 'PAMPERED CHEF' IN EVERY WAY"

(2011 U.S. Retail $199 for 100 2-Sided *WOW!*-Card® Résumés, 2 Versions: "Mailing" & "Hand-Out Ad")

Note:
This 2-sided *WOW!*-Card® Résumé can be handed out at Job-Fairs, Networking Meetings, with Employment Applications, and at Interviews upon entering or exiting, or used as inserts / enclosures with mailed out "thank you" notes or cover letters (or Unique Story Résumés) or used as ready creative substitutes for business cards and full Résumés. (See *WOW!*-Card® Résumé #1, page 180, for mail-out example.)

WOW! RÉSUMÉS 2011-2012: Great Jobs...Extra Income...Happiness...

CHAPTER 10: *WOW!*-CARD® RÉSUMÉS

WOW!-Card® Résumé #10 **with Photo**
Based on Résumé of Author of **WOW! RÉSUMÉS 2011-2012:** Great Jobs...Extra Income...Happiness...

ACTUAL SIZE of 4" x 6"

Front ("Main") Side of *WOW!*-Card® Résumé

NELSON ABAYA
LEED AP (Legacy Certified by U.S. Green Building Council)
(Leadership in Energy and Environmental Design Accredited Professional)

PUBLISHED AUTHOR / FOUNDER, *WOW!* Résumé SERVICE

PROFILE:
- 20 Years of Résumé Writing Experience in U.S./Asia: Previous Owner/Manager of Résumés Plus, USA
- Published Author including the Environmental Textbook: The 5 Factors of Green Wealth (amazon.com)
- Social Entrepreneur including the founding of Green Trikes Zero Carbon Delivery & Shopping Services
- Multiple Careers in Administration, Consulting, Real Estate Development and & Life/Health Insurance
- Member of the California Academy of Sciences and Ombudsman/Volunteer in California/Nevada RCFEs

EDUCATION:

SAINT MARY'S COLLEGE OF CALIFORNIA, Moraga, CA
Master of Science Degree in International Business

UNIVERSITY OF CALIFORNIA AT BERKELEY, Berkeley, CA
Bachelor's Degrees in English and Psychology

EXPERIENCE:

WOW! RÉSUMÉS, San Francisco, CA; Singapore, Singapore; Vancouver, BC, Canada
Owner / Manager / Editor / Writer, 2008 to Present

TEAM PACIFIC REAL ESTATE DEVELOPMENT, Sacramento, CA; Fernley, NV
Land Broker & Project Developer in Energy and Environmental Design, 2005 to 2008 and 2009 to Present

RÉSUMÉS PLUS, Ventura, CA; Las Vegas, NV
Résumé Writer / Editor, 1991 to 1997 and 1999 to 2005

(2011 U.S. Retail $199 for <u>100</u> 2-Sided *WOW!*-Card® Résumés, 2 Versions: "Mailing" & "Hand-Out Ad")

WOW!-Card® Résumé Tip:
This final example of a *WOW!*-Card® Résumé includes a small photo in addition to any graphics. The pluses and minuses of an included photo were discussed in the Introduction to this Chapter. Photo Résumés would be appropriate for Careers in Entertainment or in niche occupations such as modeling or perhaps Athletics or in the above case a bold intrepid Author who is looking to market a product and service.

WOW! RÉSUMÉS 2011-2012: Great Jobs...Extra Income...Happiness...

CHAPTER 10: *WOW!*-CARD® RÉSUMÉS

WOW!-Card® Résumé #10 **with Photo**
Based on Résumé of Author of ***WOW!* RÉSUMÉS 2011-2012:** Great Jobs...Extra Income...Happiness...

ACTUAL SIZE of 4" x 6"

Back (Mailing or "Advertisement") Side of *WOW!*-Card® Résumé

NELSON ABAYA

Founder, *WOW!* Résumé Service

888-503-3133 ✿ in U.S. & Major World Cities ✿ wowresumes.net

SERVICES:
- ➲ Individual Writer/Consultants from various fields/ backgrounds with proven excellence for winning results!
- ➲ Customized Résumés modeled from the *WOW!* Résumés Book and offered at discount to Members of wowresumes.net, Book Purchasers and Customers of affiliated Print Shops and Retail Outlets

PRODUCTS:
- ➲ Book: WOW! RÉSUMÉS 2011 – 2012 Edition: Get Great Jobs, Extra Income and Happiness!
- ➲ *WOW!*-Card® Résumés and other Printed and Marketing Products such as Cover Letters, Thank-You Notes, etc.

MEMBERSHIP & BENEFITS:
- ➲ FREE 1 year Membership @ wowresumes.net for Book Purchasers of WOW! Résumés 2011 – 2012 Edition or with any *WOW!* Résumé Service order or the purchase of any *WOW!* Marketing Products (including *WOW!*-Card® Résumés)
- ➲ Get 1-year Membership @ wowresumes.net for $9.99 that is a credit toward the purchase of any future Résumé or *WOW!* Product
- ➲ Get FREE non-restricted downloads of up to 5 *WOW!* Résumés from *WOW!* Résumés Book (can give to Friends/Family)
- ➲ FREE Résumé Posting on growing wowresumes.net Website and FREE Linking to Twitter, Facebook, LinkedIn & Google
- ➲ FREE 25 Copies on special Résumé Paper at Affiliated Print Shops/Copy Centers with any *WOW!* Résumé order
- ➲ 30% Instant Discount (occasional 50% to 90% Discounts!!) on purchases of *WOW!* Products or *WOW!* Résumé Services

DELIVERY:
- ➲ FREE Hard-Copy Shipping by U.S. Mail (in USA) or FREE Delivery in 24 Hours of Completed Résumés to Affiliated Outlets
- ➲ Extra Charges apply for Express 24-Hour Résumé Service (Consultation to Completion to Delivery) & for International Shipping

CONSULTATION:
- ➲ Connect by Phone (U.S. Toll Free: 888-503-3133) with your own individual Consultant Résumé Writer
- ➲ Appointments also available at Affiliated Print Shops/Copy Center/Retail Outlets

Ask your Retail Outlet to contact *WOW!* Résumés for Retail Registration to BENEFIT your local Store!

(2011 U.S. Retail $199 for 100 2-Sided *WOW!*-Card® Résumés, 2 Versions: "Mailing" & "Hand-Out Ad")

Note:
This 2-sided *WOW!*-Card® Résumé has personal and individual information on the "Front Side" while the "Back Side" displayed above is as detailed as a brochure but is more handy and versatile. A business owner or Manager of a business can market products and services and also present his or her own background/career info. Whatever desired marketing or advertising message can be the "Front Side" of a mail-out that can either be for an individual's or a company's "sales"/marketing info. (See *WOW!*-Card® Résumé #1, page 180, for mail-out example.)

APPENDICES

1 TO 4

Complete the 4 Guides in the following Appendices to fully customize and efficiently create a unique and powerful *WOW!* Résumé on your own or with assistance.

You can follow the formatting, fonts, headings, wording and aesthetics of Model Résumés in the previous 10 Chapters to fit your Job Title and your target industry or career/opportunity to create a main *WOW!* Résumé, as well as other personal marketing tools such as your own *WOW!*-Card® Résumés, "Unique Story Résumés", or if you desire to pursue any business or entrepreneurial ventures (big or small) you can model the featured Network Marketing Résumés. The Appendices are the Guides that will help create the final product of the *WOW!* Résumé.

Appendix 1 will contain basic data gathered from scratch or old Résumés or source documents that are factual material such as names, contact information, dates, titles, companies/organizations, schools, etc. Facts and specifics such as duties, responsibilities and other details are to be included in Appendix 1.

The rest of the Appendices (2 to 4) are the special information and well-thought out answers to the questions and topics in the appropriate sections that will create a truly *WOW!* Résumé! You can use this entire Book to create a great (*WOW!)* Résumé quickly and confidently or work with a trusted friend/mentor or use the (*WOW!)* Résumé Service mentioned in each Chapter Introduction and in the back of this Book.

After the Appendices a compilation of Keywords for a specific job search serves as a great resource to make sure that a customized *WOW!* Résumé contains the right terms and searchable keywords for the acceptance and approval of digital and human scrutiny.

The Model Résumés along with all the Guides will help you find your best attributes, skills, accomplishments and unique qualities that will lead to great jobs, extra income and overall happiness!

WOW! RÉSUMÉS 2011-2012: Great Jobs...Extra Income...Happiness...

BLANK PAGE

-FOR NOTES-

WOW! RÉSUMÉS 2011-2012: Great Jobs...Extra Income...Happiness...

APPENDIX 1

FILL-IN GUIDE FOR <u>STANDARD</u> *WOW!* RÉSUMÉ INFORMATION

To Create a *WOW!* Résumé on your own or with a *WOW!* Résumé Service Consultant/Writer, gather paper documents including current or old Résumés or fill in standard info below.

(You will get a chance to expand and make your background, achievements, skills, strengths and past history into a *WOW!* Résumé by doing the next 3 Appendices (2, 3 & 4) on your own or with a *WOW!* Résumé Service Consultant/Writer.)

(NAMES/TITLES/DATES/PLACES/DUTIES/FACTS/ETC.)

Your Name: _____

Street #: _____ Street Name: _____

City: _____ State/Province: _____

Country: _____

Telephone(s): _____ Email: _____

Your Current Occupation/Title/Status: _____

Your Objective: _____

Skills (include Technical, Computer, Industry or Specialized):

_____

_____

_____

_____

_____

_____

WOW! RÉSUMÉS 2011-2012: Great Jobs...Extra Income...Happiness...

APPENDIX 1
FILL-IN GUIDE FOR <u>STANDARD</u> *WOW!* RÉSUMÉ INFORMATION
(Continued)

<u>Employment History/Professional Experience:</u>

Company/Organization **1**: _____

City: _____   State/Province: _____

Country: _____

Job Title/Role: _____

Dates Worked: From _____ to _____

Duties/Responsibilities: _____

_____

_____

_____

_____

_____

Achievements / Accomplishments Projects / Challenges Faced / Goals Met
(Appendix 2 can expand on this section. Here just list factually information related to this company):

_____

_____

_____

_____

_____

_____

WOW! RÉSUMÉS 2011-2012: Great Jobs...Extra Income...Happiness...

APPENDIX 1
FILL-IN GUIDE FOR <u>STANDARD</u> *WOW!* RÉSUMÉ INFORMATION
(Continued)

<u>Employment History/Professional Experience:</u>

Company/Organization **2**: _____

City: _____   State/Province: _____

Country: _____

Job Title/Role: _____

Dates Worked: From _____ to _____

Duties/Responsibilities: _____

_____

_____

_____

_____

_____

Achievements / Accomplishments Projects / Challenges Faced / Goals Met
(Appendix 2 can expand on this section. Here just list factually information related to this company):

_____

_____

_____

_____

_____

_____

WOW! RÉSUMÉS 2011-2012: Great Jobs...Extra Income...Happiness...

APPENDIX 1
FILL-IN GUIDE FOR <u>STANDARD</u> *WOW!* RÉSUMÉ INFORMATION
(Continued)

Employment History/Professional Experience:

Company/Organization **3**: _____

City: _____   State/Province: _____

Country: _____

Job Title/Role: _____

Dates Worked: From _____ to _____

Duties/Responsibilities: _____
_____
_____
_____
_____
_____

Achievements / Accomplishments Projects / Challenges Faced / Goals Met
(Appendix 2 can expand on this section. Here just list factually information related to this company):

_____
_____
_____
_____
_____
_____

WOW! RÉSUMÉS 2011-2012: Great Jobs...Extra Income...Happiness...

APPENDIX 1
FILL-IN GUIDE FOR <u>STANDARD</u> *WOW!* RÉSUMÉ INFORMATION
(Continued)

School/Educational/Training
(Appendix 4 can expand on this section. Here just list factually information related to your Education):

Institution or Training Organization **1**: _____

City: _____   State/Province: _____

Country: _____

Dates Attended :   From _____ to _____

Major(s)/Degree/Certificate:

_____

Institution or Training Organization **2**: _____

City: _____   State/Province: _____

Country: _____

Dates Attended :   From _____ to _____

Major(s)/Degree/Certificate:

_____

Institution or Training Organization **3**: _____

City: _____   State/Province: _____

Country: _____

Dates Attended :   From _____ to _____

Major(s)/Degree/Certificate:

_____

WOW! RÉSUMÉS 2011-2012: Great Jobs...Extra Income...Happiness...

APPENDIX 1
FILL-IN GUIDE FOR <u>STANDARD</u> *WOW!* RÉSUMÉ INFORMATION
(Continued)

NOTES:
(Include Here Information or Research About Target Companies or Industries as well as Job/Career Objectives)

_____

_____

_____

_____

_____

_____

_____

_____

_____

_____

_____

_____

_____

_____

_____

_____

_____

WOW! RÉSUMÉS 2011-2012: Great Jobs...Extra Income...Happiness...

APPENDIX 2
FILL-IN GUIDE FOR <u>SPECIAL</u> *WOW!* RÉSUMÉ INFORMATION

BUSINESS, ORGANIZATIONAL & CAREER MATERIAL
(Relate information in this Appendix with the information in Appendix 1, <u>Employment History/Professional Experience</u> to make your *WOW!* Résumé accurate, logical and complete.)

THE "5 Ps"
(If you are using the services of a *WOW!* Résumé Consultant/Writer, he or she will assist you with these topics; or you can get the assistance of a friend or colleague if doing your own Résumé.)

Problem(s) Solved:

_____

_____

_____

_____

_____

_____

_____

People Helped (Inspired/Motivated/Assisted/RescuedTouched/Saved):

_____

_____

_____

_____

_____

_____

_____

_____

_____

WOW! RÉSUMÉS 2011-2012: Great Jobs...Extra Income...Happiness...

APPENDIX 2
FILL-IN GUIDE FOR <u>SPECIAL</u> *WOW!* RÉSUMÉ INFORMATION

BUSINESS, ORGANIZATIONAL & CAREER MATERIAL

<u>THE "5 **P**s"</u>
(Continued)

<u>**P**rofits Gained for Company or Organization / **P**roductivity Increased / **P**revented Losses</u>:

_____

_____

_____

_____

_____

_____

_____

<u>**P**rogress (in Career/Organization) Made</u>:

_____

_____

_____

_____

_____

_____

_____

_____

WOW! RÉSUMÉS 2011-2012: Great Jobs...Extra Income...Happiness...

APPENDIX 2
FILL-IN GUIDE FOR <u>SPECIAL</u> *WOW!* RÉSUMÉ INFORMATION

BUSINESS, ORGANIZATIONAL & CAREER MATERIAL

THE "5 **P**s"
(Continued)

<u>**P**roducts / Services / Ideas Developed or Sold (if applicable)</u>:

_____

_____

_____

_____

_____

_____

_____

<u>Miscellaneous Special or Unique Info on Business, Organization or Career</u>:

_____

_____

_____

_____

_____

_____

_____

_____

_____

***WOW!* RÉSUMÉS 2011-2012:** Great Jobs...Extra Income...Happiness...

APPENDIX 2
FILL-IN GUIDE FOR <u>SPECIAL</u> *WOW!* RÉSUMÉ INFORMATION

BUSINESS, ORGANIZATIONAL & CAREER MATERIAL
(Continued)

NOTES:

_____

_____

_____

_____

_____

_____

_____

_____

_____

_____

_____

_____

_____

_____

_____

_____

_____

_____

WOW! RÉSUMÉS 2011-2012: Great Jobs...Extra Income...Happiness...

APPENDIX 3
FILL-IN GUIDE FOR SPECIAL *WOW!* RÉSUMÉ INFORMATION

PERSONAL AND BACKGROUND MATERIAL
(Relate information in this Appendix with the information in Appendix 1 including Dates, Places, Events
and Facts to make your *WOW!* Résumé accurate, logical and complete.)

THE "5 **C**s"
(If you are using the services of a *WOW!* Résumé Consultant/Writer, he or she will assist you with these
topics; or you can get the assistance of a friend or trusted family member if doing your own Résumé.)

Character (Values/Attitudes/Family Background as appropriate):

_____

_____

_____

_____

_____

_____

_____

Competence (Skills/Knowledge/Abilities, as well as Personal Talents such as Time Management, etc.):

_____

_____

_____

_____

_____

_____

_____

WOW! RÉSUMÉS 2011-2012: Great Jobs...Extra Income...Happiness...

APPENDIX 3
FILL-IN GUIDE FOR <u>SPECIAL</u> *WOW!* RÉSUMÉ INFORMATION

PERSONAL AND BACKGROUND MATERIAL

<u>THE "5 Cs"</u>
(Continued)

<u>**C**harisma (Colorful Personality or Uniqueness as appropriate)</u>:

_____

_____

_____

_____

_____

_____

_____

<u>**C**ontribution (your Team Player/Human Factor attributes that make the work place better or great!)</u>:

_____

_____

_____

_____

_____

_____

_____

_____

WOW! RÉSUMÉS 2011-2012: Great Jobs...Extra Income...Happiness...

APPENDIX 3
FILL-IN GUIDE FOR <u>SPECIAL</u> *WOW!* RÉSUMÉ INFORMATION

PERSONAL AND BACKGROUND MATERIAL

<u>THE "5 Cs"</u>
(Continued)

<u>Change of Positive Nature (Self-Improvement especially due to Adversity, Conflict or Maturity)</u>:

_____

_____

_____

_____

_____

_____

_____

_____

<u>Miscellaneous Special or Unique Info on Personal Background</u>:

_____

_____

_____

_____

_____

_____

_____

_____

_____

_____

WOW! RÉSUMÉS 2011-2012: Great Jobs...Extra Income...Happiness...

APPENDIX 3
FILL-IN GUIDE FOR <u>SPECIAL</u> *WOW!* RÉSUMÉ INFORMATION

(PERSONAL AND BACKGROUND MATERIAL)
-Continued-

NOTES:

_____

_____

_____

_____

_____

_____

_____

_____

_____

_____

_____

_____

_____

_____

_____

_____

_____

WOW! RÉSUMÉS 2011-2012: Great Jobs...Extra Income...Happiness...

APPENDIX 4
FILL-IN GUIDE FOR <u>SPECIAL</u> *WOW!* RÉSUMÉ INFORMATION

SCHOOL/EDUCATIONAL/TRAINING MATERIAL
(Relate information in this Appendix with the information in Appendix 1 including Dates, Schools, Training Organizations, in addition to Transcripts, etc. to make your *WOW!* Résumé accurate, logical and complete.)

THE "5 As"
(If you are using the services of a *WOW!* Résumé Consultant/Writer, he or she will assist you with these topics; or you can get the assistance of a school colleague or academic mentor if doing your own Résumé.)

<u>**A**ccreditation (Degrees, Certificates or any Licenses)</u>:

_____

_____

_____

_____

_____

_____

_____

<u>**A**wards (Academic and any Athletic or Extracurricular)</u>:

_____

_____

_____

_____

_____

_____

_____

_____

WOW! RÉSUMÉS 2011-2012: Great Jobs...Extra Income...Happiness...

APPENDIX 4
FILL-IN GUIDE FOR <u>SPECIAL</u> *WOW!* RÉSUMÉ INFORMATION

SCHOOL/EDUCATIONAL/TRAINING MATERIAL

<u>THE "5 As"</u>
(Continued)

<u>A</u>ccolades (Recommendations, Commendations or References):

_____

_____

_____

_____

_____

_____

_____

<u>A</u>pplication (Examples of Academic Knowledge/Background applied to Work, Community or Life!):

_____

_____

_____

_____

_____

_____

_____

_____

WOW! RÉSUMÉS 2011-2012: Great Jobs...Extra Income...Happiness...

APPENDIX 4
FILL-IN GUIDE FOR <u>SPECIAL</u> *WOW!* RÉSUMÉ INFORMATION

SCHOOL/EDUCATIONAL/TRAINING MATERIAL

<u>THE "5 As"</u>
(Continued)

<u>**A**lways Learning (Continuing Education and Self-Improvement required or on own initiative)</u>:

_____

_____

_____

_____

_____

_____

_____

<u>Miscellaneous Special or Unique Info on Academic/Educational Background</u>:

_____

_____

_____

_____

_____

_____

_____

_____

_____

WOW! RÉSUMÉS 2011-2012: Great Jobs...Extra Income...Happiness...

APPENDIX 4
FILL-IN GUIDE FOR <u>SPECIAL</u> *WOW!* RÉSUMÉ INFORMATION

SCHOOL/EDUCATIONAL/TRAINING MATERIAL
(Continued)

NOTES:

_____

_____

_____

_____

_____

_____

_____

_____

_____

_____

_____

_____

_____

_____

_____

_____

_____

WOW! RÉSUMÉS 2011-2012: Great Jobs...Extra Income...Happiness...

ALPHABETICAL LIST OF *WOW!* ACTION VERBS AS KEYWORDS

A:

Abetted, Absorbed, Accelerated, Acclimated, Accompanied, Accomplished, Achieved, Acquainted, Acquired, Acted, Activated, Actuated, Adapted, Added, Addressed, Adhered, Adjusted, Administered, Admitted, Adopted, Advanced, Advertised, Advised, Advocated, Aided, Aired, Affected, Allocated, Altered, Amassed, Amended, Amplified, Analyzed, Answered, Anticipated, Appointed, Appraised, Approached, Approved, Arbitraged, Arbitrated, Arranged, Ascertained, Asked, Assayed, Assembled, Assessed, Assigned, Assisted, Assumed, Attained, Attracted, Attuned, Audited, Augmented, Authored, Authorized, Automated, Awarded, Availed, Averted, Avoided, Awed

B:

Backed, Balanced, Bargained, Bested, Bettered, Blasted, Blew-by, Bonded, Borrowed, Bought, Briefed, Bracketed, Branded, Broadened, Braved, Brokered, Budgeted, Built, Bylined

C:

Calculated, Calendared, Canvassed, Capitalized, Captured, Carried-out, Casted, Catalogued, Catapulted, Centralized, Challenged, Chaired, Changed, Channeled, Charted, Checked, Chose, Circulated, Clarified, Classified, Cleared, Closed, Co-authored, Co-chaired, Coded, Co-managed, Cold-called, Collaborated, Collected, Combined, Commissioned, Communicated, Compared, Compiled, Complied with, Completed, Composed, Computed, Conceived, Conceptualized, Concluded, Condensed, Conducted, Conferred, Consolidated, Constructed, Consulted, Contracted, Contrasted, Contributed, Controlled, Converted, Convinced, Cooperated with, Coordinated, Corrected, Corresponded, Counseled, Counted, Created, Critiqued, Crowd-Sourced, Curbed, Customized

D:

Dazzled, Debugged, Decoded, Decentralized, Decreased, Deferred, Defined, Delegated, Delivered, Demonstrated, Depreciated, Described, Designated, Designed, Determined, Developed, Devised, Devoted, Diagrammed, Directed, Disclosed, Discounted, Discovered, Dispatched, Displayed, Distinguished, Distributed, Diversified, Divested, Documented, Doubled, Downloaded, Drafted, Drove-up, Duplicated

E:

Earmarked, Earned, Eased, Encoded, Edited, Effected, elected, Eliminated, E-mailed, Embodied, Employed, Enabled, Encouraged, Endorsed, Enforced, Engaged, Engineered, Enhanced, Enlarged, Enlivened, Enriched, Entered, Entertained, Established, Estimated, Evaluated, Examined, Exceeded, Exchanged, Executed, Exempted, Exercised, Expanded, Expedited, Explained, Exposed, Expressed, Extended, Extracted, Extrapolated

F:

Facilitated, Familiarized, Fashioned, Fielded, Figured, Finalized, Financed, Fit, Fixed, Focused, Forecasted, Formalized, Formed, Formulated, Fortified, Founded, Framed, Freed, Friended, Froze, Fulfilled, Functioned as, Furnished, Furthered

G:

Gaged, Gained, Gathered, Gauged, Gave, Generated, Gleamed, Glistened, Googled, Governed, Graded, Granted, Grasped, Greened, Greeted, Grouped, Guided, Gulfed

WOW! RÉSUMÉS 2011-2012: Great Jobs...Extra Income...Happiness...

ALPHABETICAL LIST OF *WOW!* ACTION VERBS AS KEYWORDS
(Continued)

H:

Hailed, Hammered, Hovered, Headed, Heralded, Hired, Honored, Hosted, Humanized

I:

Iconized, Identified, Illustrated, Illuminated, Immersed in, Implemented, Improved, Improvised, Inaugurated, Indoctrinated, Increased, Incurred, Induced, Influenced, Informed, Initiated, Innovated, Inquired, Inspected, Inspired, Installed, Instigated, Instilled, Instituted, Instructed, Insured, Interceded, Intentioned, Interfaced, Interpreted, Interviewed, Introduced, Invented, Inventoried, Invested, Investigated, Invited, Involved, Ironed-out, Isolated, Issued, Iterated

J:

Jazzed-up, Jettisoned, Joined, Jimmied, Journaled, Jumped-in, Judged, Junked

K:

Keyed, Kicked-off, Knocked-out

L:

Launched, Lectured, Learned, Led, Legitimized, Leveraged, Lighted, Lightened, Liquidated, Lined-up, Linked, Litigated, Lobbied, Localized, Located, Lubricated

M:

Maintained, Managed, Manned-up, Magnified, Mapped, Marketed, Mastered, Maximized, Measured, Mediated, Merchandised, Merged, Met, Metered, Minimized, Mobilized, Modeled, Moderated, Modernized, Modified, Monitored, Motivated, Moved, Multiplied

N:

Named, Narrated, Navigated, Negotiated, Networked, Neutralized, Notched, Noticed, Nurtured

O:

Objectified, Observed, Obviated, Offered, Offset, Opened, Operated, Orchestrated, Ordered, Organized, Oriented, Originated, Overcame, Overhauled, Oversaw, Owned

P:

Paced, Packaged, Paid, Participated, Passed, Patterned, Perceived, Performed, Permitted, Persuaded, Phased-out, Pinned down, Pinpointed, Pioneered, Placed, Planned, Plumbed, Polled, Portrayed, Positioned, Prepared, Presaged, Presented, Preserved, Presided, Prevented, Priced, Primed, Printed, Prioritized, Probed, Problem-solved, Processed, Procured, Produced, Profiled, Programmed, Projected, Promoted, Prompted, Propelled, Proposed, Proved, Provided, Provisioned, Publicized, Pulled off, Pumped up, Purchased, Pursued, Pushed

WOW! RÉSUMÉS 2011-2012: Great Jobs...Extra Income...Happiness...

ALPHABETICAL LIST OF *WOW!* ACTION VERBS AS KEYWORDS
(Continued)

Q:

Quadrupled, Quantified, Qualified, Quantum-leaped, Quorumed, Quoted

R:

Racked-up, Raised, Ranked, Rated, Reacted, Read, Received, Recommended, Reconciled, Recorded, Recovered, Recruited, Rectified, Redesigned, Redid, Reduced, Referred, Refined, Refreshed, Refurbished, Regained, Regulated, Rehabilitated, Rehearsed, Reinforced, Reinstated, Rejected, Rejuvenated, Related, Remedied, Remodeled, Renegotiated, Reorganized, Replaced, Repaired, Reported, Represented, Requested, Researched, Resolved, Responded, Restored, Restructured, Resulted, Resurrected, Resuscitated, Retained, Retrieved, Revamped, Revealed, Reversed, Reviewed, Revivified, Revived, Rewarded, Righted, Role-played, Rung up

S:

Safeguarded, Salvaged, Sanctioned, Saved, Scheduled, Screened, Secured, Segmented, Selected, Sent, Separated, Served, Serviced, Settled, Shaped, Shared, Sharpened, Shaved, Shortened, Showed, Shrank, Signed, Simplified, Solved, Spearheaded, Specified, Specialized, Speculated, Spoke, Spread, Stabilized, Staffed, Staged, Standardized, Steadied, Steered, Stimulated, Strategized, Streamlined, Strengthened, Strove, Stressed, Structured, Studied, Stylized, Submitted, Substantiated, Substituted, Succeeded, Suggested, Summarized, Superseded, Super-sized, Supervised, Supplied, Supported, Surpassed, Surveyed, Synchronized, Synthesized, Systematized

T:

Tabled, Tabulated, Tailored, Targeted, Taught, Terminated, Tested, Testified, Texted, Thought-out, Thrived, Tightened, Took, Torqued, Totaled, Traced, Traded, Trained, Transacted, Transferred, Transformed, Translated, Transported, Traveled, Treated, Tripled, Trumped, Tweeted

U:

Unburdened, Uncovered, Undertook, Unified, United, Unlocked, Untied, Updated, Uploaded, Uplinked, Upgraded, Used, Ushered-in, Utilized

V:

Validated, Valued, Vended, Verified, Vested, Vied, Viewed, Vindicated, Volunteered, Voiced

W:

Warmed, Wedded, Weighed, Welcomed, Widened, Wikied, Wired, Withstood, Witnessed, Won, Worded, Worked, WOWed, Wrote

Y:

Yahooed, Yelped, Yielded

Z:

Zapped, Zeroed- in, Zeroed-out, Zipped, Zoned-in, Zoomed

WOW! RÉSUMÉS 2011-2012: Great Jobs...Extra Income...Happiness...

KEYWORDS:

FILL-IN GUIDE FROM JOB DESCRIPTIONS / SPECIFICATIONS

GET FROM COMPANY SOURCES OR POSTINGS OR CAN GOOGLE "JOB DESCRIPTION (JOB TITLE)"
(THE KEYWORDS CAN BE INCORPORATED INTO RÉSUMÉS, PROFILES AND APPLICATIONS AS WELL AS FOR INTERVIEWS)

_____

_____

_____

_____

_____

_____

_____

_____

_____

_____

_____

_____

_____

_____

_____

_____

_____

_____

_____

WOW! RÉSUMÉS 2011-2012: Great Jobs...Extra Income...Happiness...

KEYWORDS:

FILL-IN GUIDE FROM INDUSTRY INFO

GET FROM INDUSTRY INFO AND COMPANY DATA INCLUDING ANNUAL REPORTS, NEWS & ARTICLES
(THE KEYWORDS CAN BE INCORPORATED INTO RÉSUMÉS, PROFILES AND APPLICATIONS AS WELL AS FOR INTERVIEWS)

_____

_____

_____

_____

_____

_____

_____

_____

_____

_____

_____

_____

_____

_____

_____

_____

_____

_____

_____

WOW! RÉSUMÉS 2011-2012: Great Jobs...Extra Income...Happiness...

KEYWORDS:

FILL-IN GUIDE FROM JOB (HELP-WANTED) ADVERTISEMENTS / POSTINGS

GET SPECIFIC REQUIREMENTS FROM PRINT SOURCES OR WEB POSTINGS OR INTERNET JOB BOARDS
(THE KEYWORDS CAN BE INCORPORATED INTO RÉSUMÉS, PROFILES AND APPLICATIONS AS WELL AS FOR INTERVIEWS)

_____

_____

_____

_____

_____

_____

_____

_____

_____

_____

_____

_____

_____

_____

_____

_____

WOW! RÉSUMÉS 2011-2012: Great Jobs...Extra Income...Happiness...

INDEX

of

WOW! RÉSUMÉS

by

JOB TITLE / CAREER

TO FOLLOW

INDEX OF *WOW! RÉSUMÉS* BY JOB TITLE/CAREER

INDEX OF **WOW! RÉSUMÉS** BY JOB TITLE/CAREER

C

INDEX OF **WOW! RÉSUMÉS** BY JOB TITLE/CAREER

D

E

INDEX OF **WOW! RÉSUMÉS** *BY JOB TITLE/CAREER*

INDEX OF **WOW! RÉSUMÉS** BY JOB TITLE/CAREER

H

I

INDEX OF **WOW! RÉSUMÉS** BY JOB TITLE/CAREER

INDEX OF *WOW! RÉSUMÉS* BY JOB TITLE/CAREER

M

INDEX OF **WOW! RÉSUMÉS** *BY JOB TITLE/CAREER*

INDEX OF **WOW! RÉSUMÉS** BY JOB TITLE/CAREER

Q

R

INDEX OF *WOW! RÉSUMÉS* BY JOB TITLE/CAREER

INDEX OF **WOW! RÉSUMÉS** *BY JOB TITLE/CAREER*

Made in the USA
Charleston, SC
07 July 2011